THE CHATHAM DOCKYARD STORY

Revised and Expanded Edition

A general view of the Medway, together with the Dockyard, as they appeared in the nineteenth century.

A mid nineteenth century view of shipping in the Medway, with the Dockyard Ropery in the background.

The Chatham Dockyard Story

Revised and Expanded Edition

Philip MacDougall

MERESBOROUGH BOOKS
1987

First edition published by Rochester Press in 1981.

This edition published by Meresborough Books, 17 Station Road, Rainham, Kent. ME8 7RS.

Meresborough Books is a specialist publisher of books about Kent with about eighty books currently in print. Full list sent on request.

Front cover: the launch of *Cressy* on 21st July 1853. Originally designed for sail she was converted to sail and steam whilst under construction. This view of the launch also allows for a full appreciation of the dockyard slipways and their early timbered roofs.

Back cover, top: A dramatic and highly stylised engraving of *Waterloo*, 120 gun first rate. She is here seen leaving the old No.1 slip on 10th June 1833. At the time she was one of the largest warships launched at Chatham.

Back cover, foot: The *Royal Oak*, a timber hulled vessel that was converted to an iron clad design whilst under construction, is launched into the Medway on 10th September 1862.

ISBN 0948193 301

Printed by Whitstable Litho Ltd, Whitstable, Kent.

CONTENTS

INTRODUCTION TO 1981 EDITION

Chatham dockyard has a history which spans some five centuries. It is one of the nation's earliest industrial enterprises having been responsible for both the construction and repair of numerous historic warships. Established during the reign of Queen Elizabeth, Chatham was in its formative years, the nation's premier yard. Having, therefore, both local and national implications, it is surprising that only a few attempts have been made to produce a history of the dockyard. Edwin Harris, writing in 1911, produced a short guide whilst, more recently James Presnail, in his 'Story of Chatham' outlined major developments within the yard. Both, however, leave gaps. Edwin Harris restricted himself to but a few short pages, whilst Presnail manages to include a number of disturbing inaccuracies.

This particular book attempts to correct earlier shortcomings, adding to known facts through the use of previously untapped source material. Archives held at the British Library, National Maritime Museum and Public Record Office have been used, whilst interviews were conducted with former employees and others associated with the yard. Clearly though, in common with the previous writers, I have also omitted much detail. Perhaps this might offend the purists but, quite simply, I feel nobody could write a total history of the yard — especially if that history is to be restricted to one book. Both the Public Record Office and National Maritime Museum hold several thousand record and minute books relating to the yard, whilst each individual worker could record a great many tragic or amusing incidents.

My own history of the yard concentrates only upon certain aspects, being designed as a popular rather than an academic study. Social background, pay and working conditions feature prominently, whilst a building history of the yard is also traced. A brief summary of all listed buildings is included as an appendix, together with a list of ships built in the yard. This latter, the most complete ever published, was compiled by J.J. Colledge, author of 'Ships of the Royal Navy'.

PHILIP MACDOUGALL
Gillingham, 1981

INTRODUCTION TO SECOND EDITION

When 'The Chatham Dockyard Story' was first published towards the end of 1981 the Medway Towns was still in the midst of a campaign to keep the dockyard in naval hands. Indeed, the original book had actually been completed when, on Thursday 25th June 1981, the Secretary of State for Defence announced Chatham's closure.

It was only possible, at that stage, to note this dramatic turn in events, whilst hoping that the Medway Towns would continue to prosper from that expansive riverside area which had once been responsible for building and repairing a vast number of naval warships.

The present book, whilst remaining substantially unchanged, continues where the other left off. Instead of ending with the closure announcement, consideration is given to the three separate organisations that are now responsible for the former dockyard area.

Of equal importance is the inclusion of several new photographs and two updated appendices. The first appendix dwells upon buildings of interest, noting a number of structures that, in themselves, have only recently been given protected status by the Department of the Environment. A second appendix, being a list of ships built at Chatham, has also seen a number of amendments. For the most part, these are ships known to have been built or rebuilt at Chatham and not previously recorded. Whilst still not claiming the list to be totally accurate it is, as far as I am aware, the most complete list ever published.

PHILIP MACDOUGALL
September 1987

ACKNOWLEDGEMENTS

A large number of people were responsible for giving substance to this book, and it is difficult to fully acknowledge all of the help given. I would, however, like to thank, in particular, those listed below.

For granting interviews: Mrs D.A. Balcombe, Mr W.L. Bennett, Miss Mary Blackmore, Mrs M. Brenchley, Mr F.P. Cooper, Mr J.D. Crawshaw, Mrs M.E. Goodwin, Miss F. Follett, Mr W. Humphreys, Mr T.V. Jones, Mr D.C. Jordan, Mr E. Savage, Mr F.R. Scott, Mr S.R. Stears.

For providing help with illustrations: Mrs Wendy Hannah, Mr and Mrs A. Morris and the staff of Chatham and Rochester libraries.

For advice and information: Dr R.J.B. Knight of the National Maritime Museum and Mr Michael Moad, curator of Rochester Museum.

Others who, either wittingly or unwittingly, provided help were Miss L.A. Harries, Mr Harry Hewson and Mr A. Milne.

However, I must reserve a special thanks to Mr J.J. Colledge, author of 'Ships of the Royal Navy' who compiled a comprehensive list of Chatham built ships and which appears as appendix two.

Chapter One

TUDOR BEGINNINGS

'Ordre was given to the Lord Admyrall that the Kinges shippes shulde be harborowed in Jillyngham Water.'

(Order in Council dated 8th June, 1550)

Perhaps the one thing that King Henry VIII accumulated in greater abundance than wives was ships. More than any other British monarch, he can be considered the founder of the Royal Navy. In 1509, when Henry VIII came to the throne he inherited from his father a small royal fleet of little more than six merchantmen. By 1547, the year of his death, after reigning for thirty-seven years, seven months and seven days, Henry bequested to his own successor, for the defence of the country, a grand collection of over eighty seagoing vessels. Many of these were purpose built warships, whilst most of the others were heavily armed merchantmen. Unlike any preceding English king, Henry Tudor had seen the importance of sea power to an island nation.

During the closing years of Henry's reign, it had become the king's policy to winter a number of his ships in the River Medway. The Medway provided a safe anchorage with the added advantage of being close to the capital. Furthermore, the river's extensive mud banks, regularly washed by a not inconsiderable tidal flow, allowed ships to beach, so that the undersides could be cleaned. This was a process known as graving, and consisted of burning off the various accretions (such as barnacles) which, over the months, attached themselves to the bottom of a ship's hull, undermining the vessel's sailing abilities. Once this process was complete the ship would be tarred and caulked before it was floated away on a convenient tide.

Exactly when the Medway was first used as an anchorage for royal ships, one cannot be absolutely certain. Cleariy the policy must have been well in hand by the end of King Henry's reign for, in his final year, a storehouse was acquired alongside the banks of the Medway. This building would have been used for the winter storage of ropes, spars, masts and other pieces of equipment taken from the anchored warships. The storehouse was rented, and in a series of financial documents relating to the year 1547, a payment of 13/4d is recorded for this storehouse which is described as being close to 'Jillyngham Water'. Other than this rather vague indication of the building's position, we have no other geographical reference to exactly where it was sited. It would, however, seem reasonable to surmise that the storehouse was somewhere close to St Mary's church. The area of land situated between St Mary's and the river, later known as the gun wharf, was the original location of the Tudor dockyard as set up by Elizabeth I.

9

The reference to the rented storehouse in 1547 can be found in the Pipe Rolls held at the Public Record Office, Kew. Pipe Rolls are part of the nation's original accounting system, in which all receipts and payments are recorded. Under the naval section for 1547 there is a further interesting reference made to the Medway anchorage when it is recorded that, for certain work done in this area, a wage bill amounting to £4,167 was paid. Again, the reference is extremely bland and gives no indication of work actually carried out.

The appearance of the Royal Navy in the Medway was destined to bring a great many changes. For one thing, the Medway area, with the exception of Rochester, was not particularly rich, with Gillingham and Chatham no more than small villages. At the time Gillingham probably had a population numbering just on three hundred, whilst Chatham's was even smaller. Of these, few would have been anything other than peasant farmers and part time fishermen. A number would have lived in the small huts which were known to have existed along the river's edge, whilst others would have occupied the higher ground which is the present site of these two Medway towns. Neither village was outstanding in any way, possessing few buildings of interest beyond the church, mill and a manor house. As villages go, they were fairly typical of their time. But, of course, all this was to change. Providing for the needs of the navy would mean vast local employment and considerable prosperity. No more would the simple villager have to rely entirely upon what he could eke out from his small plot of land. In future, this would simply subsidise the wages obtained from government service.

Much of this, though, was in the future. The early graving and cleaning of ships which first took place along the banks of the Medway during the reign of Henry VIII involved no more than the crew of the respective ships. Of that first wage bill mentioned in the Pipe Rolls some, however, must have found its way into the pockets of one or two local inhabitants. For such families visits could be made, perhaps for the first time, to Rochester market where previously undreamt of luxuries could be purchased.

Further references to the navy's use of the Medway are to be found in the accounts for succeeding years. Between 1548 and 1550 further storehouses were rented. Some were in the Chatham/Gillingham area, whilst one was in Rochester. Also, money was used to rent areas of land immediately adjoining the River Medway. As an indication of the growing importance of the anchorage it is only necessary to turn to the victualling accounts which, for ships in the Medway, show a total expenditure of £3,729 for this same two year period.

On 8th June 1550, an even more important milestone was reached when an order made in council declared that all royal ships should be 'herborowed' in the Medway. The order, in full, stated:

'That all the Kinges shippes shuld be herborowed in Jillyngham Water save those that be at Portsmouth, to remain there till the yere be further spent for avoiding all inconveniences and that all the masters of shippes, gonners and pursers be discharged, except a convenient nombre, till the daunger of the yere be past, and afterwards to be ordered, as has been accustomed in tyme of peace.'

10

On 14th August 1550, it was further ordered that ships anchored off Portsmouth should be brought into the Medway. To see that these instructions were properly carried out, William Wynter, the Surveyor of Ships, was sent down to Portsmouth and supervised the removal of six ships to Chatham, at a total cost of £394.5s.2d.

With the removal of all de-commissioned ships to the Medway, Chatham, or what was always referred to as 'Jillyngham' at this point in time, was firmly on the maritime map.

Before continuing the story of Chatham Dockyard, however, it would seem appropriate to first examine the development of British sea power prior to the establishment of the naval anchorage on the Medway. As previously stated, Henry VIII was clearly at the centre of British maritime activities though the ship, as a weapon of war, was far from new. The Greeks, Romans and Vikings had all used it for their various warlike activities, as had earlier English monarchs. However, English kings before Henry VIII had been content with either acquiring or converting their own merchant ships as temporary wartime expediencies. Henry VIII had not done this, instead he took, for an English king, the unheard of step of having ships specifically built for war. His flag ship, the 800 ton *Mary Rose*, laid down at Portsmouth during the first year of his reign, was the first English battle ship ever built.

Prior to the sixteenth century, it was normal for British monarchs to rely upon merchants to supply them with any ships they might need. Few British kings had their own fleet; it being much simpler to order merchants to hand over their ships in time of war. That merchant vessels could be used for such purposes was not as difficult as it might seem to the modern day mind. The main use that ships were put to in time of war was that of troop carrying and the provision of military supplies. For this, a merchantman was perfectly adequate.

The medieval trading vessel, known as a 'cog', was strictly a fair weather ship, being both slow and cumbersome, single masted and distinctly round in appearance, it was double-ended, flat bottomed with a length hardly more than twice its beam. If acquired by the crown, these 'cogs' were fitted with temporary wooden platforms, known as castles, at both the fore and aft. Upon these numerous archers would gather, and any approaching enemy quickly fended off.

Sometimes huge sea fights would occur between opposing fleets. On such occasions the tactics employed were little different from those of land warfare. The fight would open with a barrage of arrows in which the English, using the long bow, invariably had superiority over the French — and other enemies — who favoured the crossbow. Eventually, one side would feel that its archers had done the maximum damage possible and the battle would move into the next stage when ships grappled and hand to hand fighting ensued. One of the earliest of successful British naval engagements occurred at Sluys in 1340 when a British fleet of 'cogs', using these tactics, virtually annihilated a French fleet. According to the contemporary chronicler, Froissart, the English fleet was well ordered,

11

A royal dockyard was first established at Chatham towards the end of the sixteenth century. This original yard was further to the south than the present day site, being where Lloyd's now have their administrative block. (Lloyd's)

'the greatest before, well furnished with archers, and even between two ships of archers he had one ship with men-at-arms'. In this particular battle the English opened the attack when they sailed directly into Sluys harbour, crashed into the French ships and then boarded them.

The inconvenience of keeping crews constantly ready, and the need for costly docking facilities, deterred English monarchs from building up fleets of their own. The much maligned King John, however, was an exception to this rule. In fact, he built up three royal fleets, which were given the major task of keeping the English Channel free, and enforcing the rule that any foreign vessel using the Channel should dip its colours. It was King John who was also responsible for building the country's first royal dock. This was sited at Portsmouth and was supposed to keep the royal fleet safe from storms during the winter months. Unfortunately, it was in a much exposed position and ships using it were frequently battered by winter gales. During the reign of Henry III the dock, itself, was much damaged by a particularly severe storm and it was consequently filled-in.

Henry V also had a royal fleet. Its task was that of supplying the English troops involved in the wars with France. This particular fleet, however, had only a very short life, being quickly sold off by Henry's successor.

It was not until the first Tudor monarch, Henry VII, that an English king once again determined upon maintaining a small royal fleet. Henry VII was very much a king who believed in a strong exchequer, and the main purpose of his

12

fleet was that of trading. Henry VII hoped that, by building up the royal fleet, and having some particularly fine vessels constructed in the process, it would encourage a similar move on the part of English merchants. For this reason, Henry's fleet of ships included the *Regent* and *Sovereign*, vessels considered particularly large in their day. With their construction, of course, came the need for various ancillary services such as docks and storehouses. In fact, the *Regent* was so large that there was no dock in her native country that she could freely enter. Moreover, ships of such size could not simply be graved on the nearest mud bank during the period of spring tides, something far more sophisticated was needed. For this reason a dry dock, the first ever in England, was constructed at Portsmouth.

During this period, the design of ships was undergoing a great deal of change. In the years preceding the Battle of Bosworth, the traditional 'cog' was being replaced by a style of ship far less rounded. In these ships, hulls were lengthened and the number of masts increased so that the 'cogs' of the latter middle ages had two, or even three, masts. Eventually the 'cog' was replaced by the three or four masted 'carrack'. The *Regent* was one step further on from the 'carrack'. From contemporary sources it would appear that she was basically square sailed and four masted, the main mast being replete with a top mast and a main top gallant. Although a merchantman she was heavily armed for her own protection and the fact that she had over two hundred guns on board — albeit somewhat small by later standards — is a further indication of her considerable size.

Obviously guns were now a further factor in the design of ships. It was the *Christopher of the Tower*, in 1410, that has the honour of being the first English ship known to have been fitted with guns, but as the guns were somewhat un-reliable, and few in number, they were merely subsidiary weapons to the long bow. These earliest guns were small breech loaders consisting of little more than a tube. Slowly, of course, guns improved in design and became far bigger and consequently more important. Merchant vessels were so designed to accommodate these new weapons. Usually this consisted of strengthening the fore and aft castles that they might withstand the recoil. The type of guns fitted to the *Regent* were known as serpentines. These fired shot, approximately a pound in weight, used as anti-personnel devices. Situated along the top deck they would be mounted on swivels which would provide the weapon with a wide field of fire.

For the nascent English navy, the year 1509 was to be a further turning point in its history. In that year Henry VIII succeeded to the throne and soon made his feelings clear as regards the need for a strong navy. As a king he was interested in continental adventures and was soon entering into a period of considerable naval expansion. Amongst the ships Henry VIII inherited from his father were the merchant ships *Regent* and *Sovereign*. As fine as these large ships were, he considered them quite inadequate for the purposes he had in mind. As a result, he embarked upon a maritime building programme of which the *Mary Rose* was an early product. Designed from the outset as a warship, the *Mary Rose* not only had a great number of the small serpentine guns, but also much larger muzzle loaders. These were placed on the lower decks, and poked out through specially designed gun ports. Because these muzzle loaders were cast in one piece they could take a much more powerful charge and consequently had a higher muzzle velocity.

Following the *Mary Rose* into service came a large number of smaller vessels, some designed as merchant ships whilst others, also, were purpose built warships. However, the show piece of Henry's navy came in the years 1536 to 1539, when the *Henry Grace à Dieu* was constructed at Woolwich (not at Chatham as an earlier writer has suggested). Her main features included two complete rows of gun ports, whilst her main and foremast had large grappling hooks designed to destroy the rigging of any enemy ship closely engaged. When fully armed she had twenty-one heavy bronze guns, one hundred and thirty iron guns and about one hundred hand guns. In addition, her stores would have contained sufficient bows for all the troops who sailed in her. Weapons might have changed, but fighting tactics had not. The object of Henry VIII's various warships was still to grapple and allow her crew to board the enemy's own ships.

Whilst building warships, Henry VIII did not ignore the need for dockyards, with sums of money being spent on creating adequate cleaning, repairing and victualling facilities. At the outset of King Henry's reign, Portsmouth was the country's major royal dock playing a highly important role in the building and repairing of the king's ships. The first Portsmouth built ship was constructed in 1497 and, since that date, the *Mary Rose* had been constructed there. On a number of occasions, following the succession of Henry VIII, this dockyard had also been enlarged. Despite this expenditure though, the importance of Portsmouth tended to decline in favour of the Thames side yards, and it is no mere coincidence that the *Henry Grace à Dieu* was built at Woolwich. Here the major yards were Woolwich, Deptford and Erith. Of these, Woolwich was clearly the most important, having been responsible for the construction of the *Henry Grace à Dieu* during the latter years of the reign. Deptford was the next in importance having steadily grown in size since 1517 when six hundred marks was paid for the building of a mast pond. The final yard, Erith, probably dates to 1514 when a certain John Hopton was appointed 'keeper of the new storehouses at Deptford and Erith for supplying the king's ships'. On 18th February, in that same year, £32 was paid to Robert Page for the purchase of land at Erith, on which a storehouse for ships' ordnance was built. In 1521 it is further recorded that the fittings, guns and ground tackle of some ships was kept there.

All four of these dockyards pre-date Chatham by a number of years. Indeed, it was not until the very final years of Henry's reign that the navy chose to make use of the Medway. Having considered Portsmouth's vulnerability to French attack it was, at first, decided to anchor warships in the Thames, with them being moved to the Medway at a later stage. Subsequently the decision, already mentioned, was taken in 1547 to hire a storehouse close to 'Jillyngham Water'.

Chapter Two

THE ELIZABETHAN DOCKYARD

'Under this bridge the Medway foams and rolls with great violence and rapidity, and presently abating both, forms a dock furnished for the finest fleet the sun ever beheld, and ready on a minute's warning, built lately by our most gracious sovereign Elizabeth at great expense for the security of her subjects and the terror of her enemies with a fort on the shore for its defence.'

(Camden)

The Medway's importance to the navy rapidly increased throughout the reign of Queen Elizabeth. As it did so, the surrounding locality began to attract the numerous persons so necessary in maintaining a timber built sailing fleet. Shipwrights, caulkers, carpenters, sailmakers, riggers and other artisans all found employment along the expansive mud banks of the Medway river. The area between Rochester Bridge and Upnor became a veritable forest of masts and spars, as the greatest ships of the day found space in the river anchorage. Close in-shore were the old hulks, the semi-retired vessels which were to become so much a part of the waterside scene during the following three hundred years. Further out stood the grand warships which were the very pride of the Elizabethan navy, whilst on the mud banks were the upturned boats, with their numerous workmen in attendance. Of this scene, and a few years later, William Lambarde was to write:

'No Towne, nor Citie, is there in this whole Shire, comparable in right value with this one Fleete.'

Most of those attracted to the area had to be given accommodation. Shipwrights, together with the other skilled artisans, were allocated rent money additional to their wages. Senior administrators were frequently given some kind of superior residence, whilst others were simply housed in the old hulks. These hulks were, in fact, former naval vessels that had come to the end of their useful life. Totally dismasted, they were kept for any sudden emergency that might occur. Each had a watchman whose task was both to secure the vessel and to undertake a minimal amount of maintenance work. Some of these hulks, though, did serve an additional purpose in that they were given simple lifting devices for the purpose of loading some of the warships. In later years, the Medway hulks were to become notorious when they were used to house prisoners of war in the most overcrowded and unhygienic conditions imaginable.

Amongst those known to have been accommodated in one of these hulks was Francis Drake. Later to become a household name, as a result of his many seafaring adventures, Francis spent his early youth on the Medway. The Drakes were

West Country people, and Francis, himself, was born near Tavistock. His father, Edmund, was a committed and highly outspoken Protestant who cared little for the preachings of Roman Catholicism. All this was fine, until the West Country folk, in 1549, demonstrated their distaste for the newly introduced prayer book. They turned their fury on anything and everything connected with the Protestant faith. Edmund, with a large family to look after, decided to flee his native home, and was next heard of in the Medway area. Here, he was given accommodation in one of the old hulks, and charged with the duty of preaching to seamen posted to Chatham.

When Edmund acquired this official post, Francis was no more than a boy of five. A boy full of adventure, the young Francis must have found life on the Medway very exciting. From this makeshift home, Francis would have been able to view the comings and goings of some of the finest ships afloat. From the watch-men on board the other hulks, men who were, after all, retired seamen, he would have heard tales of romance and adventure which would have set the hardest hearts a-flutter. So, it was hardly surprising that, when Francis was older, he expressed interest in a future at sea. Sometime around his twelfth birthday he was apprenticed to the master of a small boat which traded between the various Channel ports. Having been recruited into one of the hardest schools going, Francis learnt much that was to be of use to him in later life. Indeed, so well did Francis get on, and so much did he learn, that the master of the vessel bequeathed it to Francis upon his death.

It was while the young Francis Drake was still living on the Medway hulk that the Wyatt rebellion occurred. Its leader, Sir Thomas Wyatt, then resident of Allington Castle, was opposed to the planned marriage of Queen Mary Tudor to the Spanish King Philip. Part of a much more organised affair, of which Wyatt's was the only one that resulted in any real action, the men of Kent flocked, in considerable numbers, to the cause. The Medway was very much a centre of this revolt. From Gillingham, some actually joined the rebellion, whilst the dockyard supplied the rebels with guns. These guns probably came from ships anchored in the Medway and were brought to Sir Thomas Wyatt by men, such as Edmund Drake, who were in basic sympathy with the rebel cause. It was weapons, such as these, which enabled Wyatt to capture Rochester Castle, confront loyalist troops at Strood and undertake the siege of Cooling Castle. As a further memento to the dockyard administrators, the anti-marriage rebels also despoiled many of the warlike stores on board some of the Royal ships at anchor in the Medway.

For its part, the Medway anchorage continued to expand. Apart from supply-ing a safe and convenient harbour, the Medway was also of importance in the victualling of royal ships. In 1551, the accounts record the purchasing of a victual-ling storehouse in Rochester whilst, in the two year period starting in mid-1550, the total victualling bill for ships taking on supplies at Rochester was £6,137. For the same period, Woolwich and Deptford combined had a victualling bill amounting to £8,382, whilst that at Portsmouth (a dockyard then in temporary decline) was £2,407 and at Dover £646.

16

Total expenses for the Medway anchorage continued to rise as each year followed the next. In 1563 the combined wages and victualling bill had reached £3,700, and was to top the £4,000 a year mark within a short time. It should, perhaps, be noted at this point that although storage, victualling and other naval operations were carried out at Rochester, Gillingham and Chatham, the accounts refer to the entire undertaking as being at Gillingham. This did not change until 1567, when the name Chatham was introduced. A move made necessary due to a tendency to centre naval affairs upon this one small village with its highly convenient water front.

From 1570 onwards occurs the actual birth of the royal dockyard at Chatham. Its original site, before renewed expansion during the seventeenth century, was the area subsequently called the gun wharf. Here, in 1570, a mast pond was dug, in which there was room for seventy-seven masts. In 1571, further land was rented in the same area, and upon this further storehouses and a forge were erected. Clearly, then, this was the forerunner of the future dockyard. A fact made even clearer when it is recalled that officials, at about this time, purchased a flag bearing the cross of St George and used it to summon the one hundred and twenty shipwrights then employed at the yard.

Further buildings were added during the two years 1577 to 1578, when it is noted in the accounts that a good number of additional workmen were temporarily engaged. These workmen probably added sawpits and numerous other items which were essential for the maintenance of capital ships. Shortly after, in 1580, a new wharf, together with a crane, were added. The purpose of the wharf was to off-load ship's guns, and other movable equipment, before the vessel either wintered in the Medway or had essential repair work carried out. The crane, which was capable of carrying loads of up to three tons, would have had a treadmill drive located inside a protective house structure, from which a swing jib projected. The unloading wharf itself, was some three hundred and seventy-eight feet in length and forty feet wide. It is recorded that construction of the wharf was undertaken at a cost of five shillings a foot.

An important landmark for Chatham was reached in 1581, when a special dry dock was completed, the purpose of which was to grave the various galleys belonging to the Elizabethan navy. The galley (simply an oared sailing vessel) is, of course, more normally associated with the Mediterranean, being somewhat cumbrous for the unpredictable northern climes. Nevertheless, such ships were not unknown in the waters of Northern Europe and served the useful purpose of charting waterways and towing otherwise helpless vessels. As regards the navy of Queen Elizabeth, the number of galleys employed, during any one period of time, never exceeded five. Some were built in England, but it seems more normal for such vessels to have been captured in battle. The Medway anchorage was considered particularly suited to galleys as it fulfilled the essential deep water requirements that such vessels needed. The first galley to use the dry dock at Chatham was the *Eleanor*. Described by contemporaries as large, the *Eleanor*, later re-named *Bonavolia*, had a total crew of three hundred, and was originally captured from the French during the 1560s. With twenty-five rowlocks each side, and one hundred and fifty rowers, she must have been impressive. It was, perhaps, for this reason, that one role allocated to the *Eleanor*, whilst at Chatham, was the entertainment of foreign dignitaries whom the Queen wished to impress. Other than this, the main use to which the royal galleys were put, was that of towing dismasted vessels (though the *Eleanor* was responsible for carrying out a survey of the Thames in 1588).

The graving dock built at Chatham was originally constructed with an earthen entrance. This entrance had to be laboriously broken-up, and then repaired, every time a ship moved in or out of the dock. Although this was the normal design for such docks at the time, this system, obviously, had its drawbacks. Thus, about a year after the dock first came into use, it was fitted with a pair of flood gates.

The use of Chatham for the anchorage and graving of the royal galley fleet continued into the following century. In the year 1602, four new galleys were built, the *Superlativia*, *Advantagia*, *Gallarita* and *Volatillia*, and, as with their predecessors, this new fleet of galleys was also wintered in the Medway. However, these particular galleys suffered much from the vicissitudes of the weather and far greater consideration had to be given to the repair and upkeep of these vessels. For this reason, it was decided that the sum of £1,800 should be expended on the erection of special workshops for the repair of galleys at Chatham. Work on these buildings started in 1605.

For the newly emergent dockyard, and naval base, at Chatham, the 1580s could not be anything else but a time of considerable activity. For these particular years were, after all, the years in which England's enmity with Spain at last reached its peak. Elizabeth I's relationship with Spain had never, to say the least, been good. Religious differences had created a long and protracted quarrel which eventually erupted into full scale war together with the launching, in 1588, of the Great Armada.

Fear that Spain would launch just such an enterprise as the Armada had, over the years, been responsible for a great deal of attention being given to the nation's defences. Throughout the south-east, in particular, fortress garrisons were strengthened, new castles established and possible landing areas surveyed. The Medway, of course, was considered a particularly sensitive area, and its defences were the subject of more than one detailed examination.

Particular attention was given to the lower reaches of the river and, especially to where it joins the sea. In the days of Henry VIII, this area had been defended by a blockhouse built at Sheerness in 1540 whilst he had also been responsible for strengthening the medieval castle at Queenborough. Built during the fourteenth century, the castle at Queenborough had been designed to combat the raids of French pirates. Well situated, it served the dual purpose of preventing the capture of Sheppey and hindering any maritime raid upon the Medway.

A document dating to 1532 also shows that at this time the entire mouth of the Medway was subject to a permanent plan for its defence. At that time, the vulnerable area of Queenborough, Sheerness and the Isle of Grain were commanded by one Nicholas Arnolde who, in that year, took delivery of artillery pieces, together with seventy-two bows, eighty morris pikes and fifty 'handgunnes'. Amongst the artillery pieces were three brass demi-cannons and thirty culverins. The culverin was a particularly massive gun and weighed over two tons, firing shot of eighteen pounds. The demi-cannon, which was nearer three tons in weight, fired a shot of thirty-two pounds.

The first moves to strengthen the Medway's defences under Elizabeth came at the very beginning of her reign. A tangled web of political intrigue and religious allegiances had resulted in a threatened French invasion and a civil war in Scotland. The French, had every intention of invading English shores, but had to give their immediate attention to the civil war in Scotland. All eyes turned to the north where the French made an all out effort to quell the fighting in Scotland and maintain a government which was sympathetic to a Franco-Scottish alliance. Elizabeth, in turn, found it advantageous to encourage the rebels who were, for the most part, Protestants in sympathy with England. Initially, Admiral Winter was despatched to the Medway where he was given instructions to ready the fleet for the defence of the coast. Shortly after he was given the more inspiring task of sailing all available vessels north. So, on 27th December 1560, the royal fleet left the Medway, having been ordered to rendezvous in the Firth of Forth where it was to give succour to the Protestant cause, and so spike any immediate plans for a French invasion.

For Chatham, the departure of the fleet, on this occasion, may have been rather fortunate, for it appears that the French may have backed an attempted raid on the Medway, and one not too dissimilar to a Dutch endeavour carried out just over one hundred years later. The object of the attack, if it had been carried out, was to pen the English fleet in the Medway, and so burn and destroy as many ships as possible. Certainly such plans were brought to the attention of the French ambassador in England, who passed them onto his superiors. It appears that the ambassador was approached by a French naval captain, Trefforest, who had been spying on the fleet which, at that time, was anchored in the Medway. During his expeditions to the Chatham area, Trefforest had also witnessed the departure of the fleet and was forced to terminate these plans. Further, if the French had any thoughts about using such plans at a later date, this also had to be cast aside. For, in 1560, the French cause in Scotland was soundly defeated and a peace treaty was drawn up between England and France.

Nevertheless, it was clear that the Medway needed to have a considerable sum of money spent on it, so that ships anchored there could be adequately defended. If such money was not found, then an enemy strike upon the Medway could easily be rewarded by the destruction of numerous ships, most of which would be dismasted and without guns. Clearly a strong, and permanent defence structure was needed. For this reason the Privy Council, in 1560, ordered that 'a certain bulwark be made at Upnoar'. The exact site was an area of land measuring some five acres, and owned by one Thomas Devenyshe of Frindsbury. At first the land was only rented, but in 1568 it was purchased by the government at a cost of £25. Work upon the new fort was started in 1560, but progress in its construction was noticeably slow for, during the following year, the Queen felt it necessary to write to the Lord Admiral requesting the castle's completion. The bulk of the structure was subsequently completed in 1564, but it was not totally finished for another three years. As completed in 1567, the castle at Upnor consisted of the main building and the water bastion. This main building, two storeys in height, with a third floor dropping below the level of the river bank, gives access to a bastion which projects into the river. From this projecting platform, the castle's garrison could defend the anchorage from attack. The additional flanking towers, castle moat, and enclosing courtyard that are such familiar features of the castle today, were not added until the close of the century when, once again, the Medway's defences were under review.

Hardly had the castle at Upnor been completed when fears began to be expressed that the Spanish might well be planning a raid upon the Medway. Relations with Spain had deteriorated over past years, and with Spain firmly in control of the Netherlands, such an attack was a very real possibility. In order to help defeat any such Spanish plan, the call went out for all able-bodied men to be ready to guard the Queen's ships in the Medway. In addition, the number of guard ships in the river were increased with four vessels detailed to lie off Sheerness, and examine all passing vessels. As a further precaution, the garrison at Upnor was strengthened.

It was this fear of Spanish aggression which again prompted the need for a further review of the defences. Sir William Winter returned to the area with instructions to find the best site for a new fort, the object of which would be to defend the mouth of the Medway. The Admiral carried out an exhaustive survey, in which he rejected both Grain and Sheerness and determined, instead, that the best position for a fort would be Swaleness. Here, it would effectively prevent enemy incursions along the Swale, which, it was considered, could provide a relatively easy access into the Medway itself. Work on this new fort started in 1574, and was completed the following year. As it was constructed of no more than timber and earth, perhaps the term fort is a little grand, for its earthen walls were of no more than eight feet in height. It was probably intended as an emergency measure and the walls, of closely beaten earth, designed to give no more than shelter for musketeers — musketeers who had the added protection of a wide ditch in front of the walls. As such, the fort would not be permanently occupied.

Over the next four years, the main area of concentration within the Medway was that of locating and removing weaknesses in the river's defences. In 1575, for instance, the precaution was taken of blocking up St Mary's Creek with stakes. Lying opposite Upnor Castle, this particular part of the river could, without any great effort, be used by an enemy wishing to avoid the guns of Upnor. Further, in 1579, the rapidly decaying blockhouse at Sheerness was put into some sort of order when the Privy Council commanded Sir John Hawkins to impress men for the reconstruction of this building.

In 1580, Sir John Thomas, Assistant to the Queen's Household, visited Upnor Castle as part of a wider review regarding precautions taken in the event of an invasion. He ensured that a regular watch was being kept at the castle and that warning beacons were in full readiness. These beacons, which were situated throughout the country, were to be lit in the event of any invasion armada being sighted. In the North Kent area there were beacons situated at Gravesend, on the Hoo Peninsula and near Chatham. They were subject to regular inspection, a job carried out by Nicholas Gilbourne, who had been appointed scout master for Kent. Once the beacons were fired, it was the job of all men between the ages of sixteen to sixty to assemble at certain strategic points in order to help repel any landing. Such a system dated into antiquity and was certainly in existence at the time of Edward I. Of these beacons, the early Kentish topographer, William Lambarde states:

'I find that before the time of King Edward the third they were made of great stacks of wood (of which sort I myself have seen some in Wiltshire) but about the eleventh yeer of his reign it was ordeined that in our Shire they should be high standards with their pitch pots.'

At regular intervals along the coastline watchmen were appointed whose duty was to alert the neighbourhood in the event of an enemy fleet being sighted. As a support to these watchmen a further precaution was taken with the adoption of a series of vessels whose task was to sail along the coastline and so gain advance notice of enemy activity. Carrying out this task in the Medway area were the small pinnaces *Scout* and *Acates,* both of which kept station in the mouth of the Thames estuary. If they should see any ships trying to force entry into the Medway they were to fire their guns in warning.

By the 1580s it was clear that the much feared Spanish invasion could not be long in coming. Again, a review of the Medway's defences was undertaken when a new committee was established, and given the joint task of organising the defences of both Portsmouth and Chatham dockyards. A leading member of the committee was Sir John Hawkins who gave the whole matter of Chatham's defence much detailed thought. In a letter written to Lord Burghley, the Queen's principal secretary, and dated March 1585, he strongly recommended that a chain be placed across the Medway and that it should be lowered in order to allow movement in and out of the Medway. Hawkins further recommended that the chain be guarded by two or four armed pinnaces stationed on both sides.

Such a scheme was readily adopted by the government, and an area just opposite Upnor Castle was selected for the chain. At the far end it was firmly secured to a base on St Mary's Island, whilst on the Upnor side it was connected to a wheelhouse which raised and lowered the chain as the need arose. The chain was supported in mid-river by a series of moored lighters which helped maintain it at a suitable height.

All this was completed by October 1585 at a cost of £250 for the chain, and a further £360 for the wheels, timber work and lighters which were needed to

The drawing office of a Tudor shipwright with a young apprentice writing down a series of figures as they are read off by the master. The 'sweeps' or compass were usually of this size, being used for acquiring the shape of lengthwise curves. It is not impossible that this, in fact, is Matthew Baker, the man usually credited with designing, or strongly influencing the design of, the *Sunne*, Chatham dockyard's first launched ship.   (Science Museum)

operate the chain effectively. The erection of the chain was 'tedyous and cumbersome but now stretched over the river in good order yt dothe requyre many lyghters for the bearynge of it'. Two pinnaces were stationed at each shore end.

Further orders were adopted in January 1586. These mainly concerned the stationing of additional ships along the Medway, and whose task was to carry invasion warnings to Upnor and Rochester. A further order, however, stated that ships anchored between Upnor and Rochester were to be lit up at night 'for the better suertie and preservacion of the flete'.

Towards the end of 1587 it was absolutely clear that Spain had not only gathered a massive armada of ships, but that in the spring of the new year it would sail with England as its ultimate destination. Nothing was now clearer.

On 21st December 1587, Charles, Lord Howard of Effingham, was appointed commander-in-chief of the royal fleet. Immediately he made his way to the Medway where the grand fleet for the defence of the kingdom had assembled. A great number of these vessels had been maintained and readied by the shipwrights of Chatham. Certainly these shipwrights had done their job well. Shortly after Lord Howard's arrival in the Medway, the new commander-in-chief carried out a rigorous inspection of every ship in the anchorage. Look, as he might, for both rotting timbers and shoddy workmanship, all he could find were ships of the finest quality. 'There is not one', he wrote, 'but I durst go to the Rio de la Plata in her.'

On 29th April 1588, this fleet sailed out of the Medway and then westward to Plymouth where it joined a smaller fleet commanded by Sir Francis Drake. Amongst the vessels sailed from the Medway on that day in April was the *Sunne*. What makes this fact worthy of note is that this vessel was the first ever to be constructed in the dockyard at Chatham. A pinnace, the *Sunne* was said to be of about forty tons in weight, and carried a crew of some twenty-six mariners and four gunners. The pinnace, of course, was one of the smaller ships of the Tudor navy being designed to carry messages and to keep watch in advance of the fleet. As such, the *Sunne* played its role in the defeat of the Armada. Under the captaincy of Richard Buckley she was placed at the disposal of the Channel squadron under Lord Henry Seymour. With the Channel squadron the *Sunne* participated in the decisive Battle of Gravelines. This was a final engagement, in which the Armada was forced to sail into the North Sea and away from the South coast where the planned landing of 60,000 Spanish troops was to have taken place.

At this point in time, Chatham was not a major builder of ships and, in fact, the *Sunne* is the only vessel which can definitely be associated with Chatham yard during the sixteenth century. But Chatham had, nevertheless, made its own very special contribution to the Armada's defeat. It was at Chatham that most of the Queen's ships were maintained to the high standards that so pleased Lord Howard; and it was at Chatham that most of the ships damaged in battle returned for repair.

The events in that year of 1588 were also responsible for a further land mark in the history of Chatham and its dockyard. Following upon the defeat of the Armada, Sir John Hawkins felt sufficiently moved to establish two charitable institutions for the support of destitute seamen. As treasurer of the navy, Hawkins had been responsible for raising seamen's wages, but he felt he could do more than this. Doubtless he was shocked by the somewhat shoddy treatment dished out to the heroic sailors once the armada had been soundly defeated. The nation's ingratitude is clearly illustrated by a letter written by Lord Howard of Effingham to Burghley during that summer of 1588:

'My good Lorde, Sickness and mortallitie begin wonderfullie to grow amongst us: and yt is a most pitifulle sighte to see here at Margate, how the men, haveing no place to receive them into here, dye in the streets. I am driven myselfe, of force, to come a-lande, to see them bestowed in some lodgeynge: and the best I can get is barnes and outhouses; and the reliefe is small that I can provyde for themme here. It would grieve anie man's harte so to see themme that have served so valiantlie to dye so miserabillie.'

It was, perhaps, the crew of the *Elizabeth Jonas* which suffered more than any other. The vessel seems to have been disease ridden for the shipwrights at Chatham described her as being 'pestered in the hold'. Anyway, during the summer of 1588 the *Elizabeth Jonas* had been involved in action against the armada, but any fatalities suffered then were as nothing when compared with the two hundred or more of her crew who died from disease in the ensuing weeks.

Events such as these clearly shocked both Sir John Hawkins and Sir Francis Drake. For this reason they determined that the nation's mariners should have some kind of pension scheme to aid them in such times of difficulty. The outcome was the Chatham Chest — a fund for the relief of elderly shipwrights and mariners. Quite simply it was an iron chest with five separate locks with each key in the hands of a different official. In the top of the chest was a small opening into which monies collected could be placed. The money from the chest came from those serving in the navy and who paid sixpence per month if their wages were ten shillings or more (those receiving less paid smaller amounts).

Intended 'for the perpetual relief of such mariners, shipwrights, and seafaring men, as, by reason of hurts and maims received in the service' the idea of the Chatham Chest was a bold attempt at removing a major iniquity. Unfortunately, it never worked as well as Hawkins had intended. Despite five keys, and five separate officials who were appointed as a means of preventing any embezzlement of the funds, the chest became, over the years, a standing joke. Although a great deal of money went into it, very little ever seemed to be paid out to those in real need. More frequently the administrators used it as their own personal money supply, whilst on one occasion Charles I used it to pay seamen's wages. Furthermore, by 1660 the chest had actually been brought into debt and had to cease making any payments at all. At this time there were over eight hundred pensioners relying on the chest. In 1658 it was stated that delays in payment had reduced these pensioners 'to such extreme misery that . . . many of them have perished of late'. A number of attempts were made to correct the situation, but the matter was not finally resolved until 1803 when management of the chest was transferred to the naval hospital at Greenwich.

The Sir John Hawkins' Hospital was given its charter of incorporation in 1594. Set up by Sir John Hawkins, it was endowed with lands and tithes which, at that time, amounted to an annual value of just over £66, in those days, of course, quite a tidy sum and sufficient to allow the hospital to house twelve elderly seamen, or shipwrights. Each was given a separate room and a weekly allowance of two shillings. The number admitted to the hospital was later reduced to ten but, on the whole, it endured far more successfully than the Chatham Chest.

Chapter Three

THE PREMIER NAVAL DOCKYARD

'Sir Robert Jackson Kt for the rent of certaine grounds called Lords Lands contaigning by estymation 71 acres . . . part whereof is used for the newe dockyard and rope waie part for a brycke and lyme kiln and part for waies to the Docks and kylns at £14 p.a. half a year ended at Christmas 1622 . . .£7'
Pipe Office Accounts (re-quoted from Archaeologia Cantiana Vol LXXIII)

During the first decades of the seventeenth century, Chatham became the country's premier naval base — a position made even more secure by a massive re-building programme during the 1620s. The accounts for this period amply demonstrate the point, as they show, for any one year, that something like ten times as much money was expended upon Chatham, than on the dockyards of Deptford, Woolwich and Portsmouth combined.

The dockyard at Chatham had a great number of advantages, not the least of these being its ideal geographic position. Close to London, it also gave access to the Channel, and thus allowed Chatham based ships to cruise the shoreline of those countries with which seventeenth century England was most frequently at war. Portsmouth, on the other hand, was some distance from London, with resultingly high transport charges leading to a continued decline in its importance. Deptford and Woolwich, though, were still highly valued, being mainly engaged in the construction of ships. However, for the laying up of ships, neither of these two yards proved suitable. The fresh waters of the Thames, at this point, only serving to rot the hulls of ships whilst the Medway, being salt water, was much more acceptable. The result was that both Woolwich and Deptford found themselves increasingly subservient to Chatham. Indeed, at one time, consideration was given to the transfer of all Deptford's work and equipment to Chatham.

Not that this naval reliance upon Chatham was without its critics, as William Lambarde noted:

'I have heard some wish, that for the better expedition in time of service, some part of this Navie might ride in some other haven, the rather bicause it is many times very long before a ship can be gotten out of this River into the Sea.'

Shortly after the turn of the century, Admiral Sir William Monson spent some time considering the virtues of Chatham, and went to the trouble of listing them. According to him:

'Chatham is so safe and secure a port for the ships to ride in that his Majesty's may better ride with a hawser at Chatham than with a cable at Portsmouth.

'The nearness from Chatham to London, from whence they may be supplied with all things they shall stand in need of, for that London is the storehouse of all England. It is necessary therefore that the navy should be kept at Chatham rather than Portsmouth . . .

'Our trade to the Eastland returns their commodities to London, which furnishes us with all materials belonging to shipping, as, namely, cables, cordage, pitch, tar, rosin, masts, yards &c., which cannot be done at Portsmouth, the place yielding nothing that creates a trade.

'The water at Chatham flows sufficiently every spring tide to grave the greatest ships. And it is a doubt whether it can be made to heighten so much in Portsmouth as do the like.

'No wind or weather can endanger the coming home of an anchor in Chatham, and the river affords sufficient space for every ship to ride without annoying one another. As to the contrary, a storm, with a wind from the north-east to the south-south-east, will stretch the cables in Portsmouth; and if any of their anchors come home they cannot avoid boarding one another, to their exceeding great damage and danger, the channel being so narrow.'

Not that Monson viewed Chatham to be without disadvantages, and amongst these he included the hazardous shoals to be found in the Medway. Overall, however, he strongly favoured the continued use and expansion of Chatham:

'If Holland or the Eastland become our enemies, then doth Chatham lie most with our advantage to annoy them, if they attempt any part of our North coast, or Norfolk, Suffolk, Essex, and Kent, which are places of most peril considering their nearness to the city of London.

'If we have wars with France there is little advantage gotten betwixt Chatham and Portsmouth. For being at the Downs at Dover, we shall be over against France, and nearer to the Isle of Wight than Brest is, or any part of Brittany, where I suppose the fleet of France will be made ready. And for the two navies, English and French, meeting at sea, no place or time can be assigned them, ships' being in continual action, and sailing one day on one coast and another day on another.'

Further on he states:

'To answer the objection of sands and shoals to endanger us in our coming about from Chatham, we see that by the care and skill of pilots no memory or record can tell of a ship of his Majesty's so lost, as out of Portsmouth it is fresh in old men's mouths, and the ribs of the ship I have often seen, called the Great Henry, a principal ship belonging to the Crown of England in the days of King Henry VIII, there perished. I likewise remember in the days of Queen Elizabeth, and in the year 1586, that the Revenge, after taken by the Spaniards, was near doing the like coming out of the harbour of Portsmouth.'

As a final note, Monson concludes:

' . . . in comparison betwixt Chatham and Portsmouth, Chatham is the best and safest place, and I wish that our whole navy may be kept at Chatham, and not make any continual residence but there only, considering the former reasons. Never hurt befell any of them that made their being there, either by weather or attempt of enemy. And yet, I must confess, they are not altogether so safe and secure from the assault of a fleet that shall be brought with an easterly wind; and therefore it behoves us to be cautious and wary of it.'

One might, at this point, consider Monson to have slightly exaggerated the advantages of the Medway. It may have been a relatively safe anchorage, but there can be little doubt that the approaches were not without danger. There are a certain number of references to vessels running into submerged sand banks or receiving storm damage whilst at anchor in the river. Not the least of such tragedies occurred in April 1636 when the *Anne Royal* ran aground and was completely capsized. A great number of her crew were drowned.

It is also interesting to note that Admiral Sir William Monson was amongst those who considered the possibility of an enemy raid upon the Medway – a factor which, of course, was never taken seriously enough, other than by the Dutch. Monson felt that Upnor Castle should be the lynch pin of the Medway defences and that it should be strengthened on the landward side:

' . . . that it may be out of the power of an enemy suddenly to surprise it; with order that all the trained soldiers thereabouts upon evry alarm do repair to the defence of it, for if it can be made so strong as to hold out but ten days not five times the force of eight or ten thousand men can take it.'

Also:

'I advise and wish in case our ships shall be assailed that the ordnance, or greatest part of them, be continually kept aboard the ships, both mounted and fitted. The powder and shot to be likewise kept continually on board, with the powder to be double barrelled for fear of taking moisture for the nature of the water is to take away the strength, and that, as in the case of Upnor Castle, the trained soldiers of the country have order to repair on board the navy with their arms.'

Admiral Monson clearly attached some considerable importance to the dockyard at Chatham. Others also thought like him, and so in 1618, steps were taken to expand the naval dockyard. It was a decision that should have been taken a decade earlier. Failure to take such a decision was due to King James I and the all time low into which he had allowed the navy to fall. No longer was the Royal Navy the proud and enviable force it had been during the days of Queen Elizabeth. Profiteering, theft, looting, embezzlement and plain inefficiency were the main features of the Stuart navy.

The man nominally in control of the Royal Navy was one Sir Robert Mansel, Treasurer. He was totally unsuited for such office. As a favourite of the king he used his position to line his own pockets – he was one of those who frequently

Phineas Pett, first of Chatham's resident commissioners, and the leading shipwright of his day.
(National Portrait Gallery)

'dipped' into the Chatham Chest. But, as if this was not enough, he maintained a system of privately purchasing naval commodities, and then re-selling them to the navy at greatly inflated prices. A further feature of his administration was a habit of allocating large amounts of money to vessels which were no longer in naval use, with the money actually going to Mansel.

With such a man in control of the Navy, it is hardly surprising to learn that little, or no check was kept by the administration on the navy's rapidly deteriorating situation. The dockyards, themselves, were in a truly piteous condition. An enquiry set up in 1618, found that most of the wood kept in stock was rotten, the cordage bad and dockyard material knowingly sold off for private gain. On the Medway, Upnor Castle was cited by the commission as being a 'den of thieves' whilst guns stored in the dockyard at Chatham were being frequently sold to the king's enemies abroad.

The man most responsible for this state of affairs at Chatham was the Master Shipwright, Phineas Pett. As early as 1608 a Commission of Inquiry had been set up to examine his activities. Amongst the facts unearthed was that, in 1604, Pett had privately built a ship of 160 tons using timber originally purchased 'for the king's use at Chatham'. Further, her sails and rigging were either 'borrowed out of the store' or purchased at knock down prices and with the connivance of other dockyard officers. Not content with just building the ship, Pett then appears to have had the audacity to load the ship with guns, ammunition and general stores belonging to the fleet, and sailed the ship to Spain where he sold most of this material for £300. The Commission of Inquiry also considered a number of other charges made against Pett, and these ranged from private gain made on the repair of ships 'when they were not worth the labour nor the charges', to accepting the stores of less value than paid for. On this latter point, the commission report stated:

> 'When timber and other materials came to be received into the stores, of the Clerk of the Check combining closely with the deliverers to increase the quantity of that which is delivered some time to a third part above true measere, which increase is shared between both . . . '

A further charge against Pett concerned the considerable expense, which was described as 'wasteful and lavish', incurred when he carried out repair work on the *Anne Royal*. Apparently he charged £800 for a task which should have cost but half.

The overwhelming weight of evidence against Pett clearly indicates his guilt in these matters. That he was not removed from office in 1608, or in 1618 for that matter, relates partly to his considerable skills as a shipwright, and also his ability to worm his way into favour with King James. The result of the Inquiry was a severe reprimand.

Between 1619 and 1626 work went ahead on a completely new dockyard at Chatham, the task of supervision being given to Phineas Pett in his capacity of Master Shipwright. The Old Yard, that area in front of St Mary's church, was considered inadequate for the new buildings, docks and slipways which were now planned. An area of eighty acres was acquired to the north of the old yard (land which, for the most part, is now managed by the Chatham Historic Dockyard Trust). Some seventy-one acres of this was land originally leased from Sir Robert Jackson, with the remainder being acquired from the Dean and Chapter of Rochester and the Manor of Westcourt.

Perhaps the most important feature of the new yard was the addition of a dry dock. The building of a new dry dock at Chatham had been canvassed as early as 1611. From that particular year there dates a document, to be found in the British Library, containing a carefully reasoned argument for such a structure at Chatham. A number of advantages were mentioned, not the least of which was the fact that so many shipwrights were, by then, employed at Chatham, that the building of the dock anywhere else would be economically undesirable. The estimated cost of building the new dock was put at £4,000. The dry dock was subsequently built in 1619 replete with wharves and two cranes. Following the completion of the dry dock there followed a mast dock (1619), sail loft (1620), a rope house (1621), officers' residences (1622) and two further dry docks (1623 and 1624).

All this re-building brought a totally new character to the dockyard at Chatham. Before the 1618-26 period, the yard had been mainly engaged in the repair and improving of vessels, with only the occasional ship actually being built there; these being of the smaller pinnace type. In his autobiography Phineas Pett mentions one such vessel which was completed at Chatham in 1612. It was a pinnace designed to sail with the *Prince*, a first rate ship built at Woolwich. Of the pinnace, Pett gives the following specifications:

' . . . being in length 72 foot, in breadth 24 foot, and to draw 11 foot water, of the burden 250 tons and tonnage, or thereabouts.'

The expansion of Chatham, naturally enough, necessitated an increase in the work force employed there. Over the years the number of dockyard workers had risen from an average of a hundred and twenty during the 1570s, to a figure approaching two hundred and fifty in the late 1620s. By 1660 this figure had actually reached some eight hundred. But these men were not employed all the year round. During the spring and summer months the numbers employed reached their maximum levels, but during the winter these numbers were substantially curtailed. The unskilled labourers would be drawn from the local villages, such as Chatham and Gillingham. For such individuals the dockyard proved a useful but not essential means of employment as most would either have their own small holdings or easily acquired farm labouring jobs. Attracting the skilled shipwright to Chatham was a little more difficult. The area did not have a tradition of boat building, and there was no ready core of shipwrights to call upon. Instead, shipwrights had to be impressed from further afield — sometimes from the other royal dockyards. Not that these shipwrights would have objected. They all would have received a lodging allowance 'as shall suffice them', together with travelling money.

The wage of the skilled shipwright was also good, or at least compared favourably with other trades. Under Queen Elizabeth the daily wage was about 1/3d, with board and lodging allowances added. By 1618 this had increased to 2/-. A further benefit bestowed upon shipwrights was the rather controversial one of allowing them to take bundles of chips (small pieces of waste wood) out of the yard each evening. These bundles were supposed to be no more than the amount which can be carried under the arm and no piece of wood was to exceed three feet in length. The right of chips, though, was frequently abused. Often the bundles would be used to conceal other more valuable objects, whilst it was not unknown for larger pieces of wood to be sawn down to the required length for removal from the yard. For the shipwright, there can be little doubt that chips were a much valued addition to their wage as it could be used for both building purposes and heating fuel. Finally, usually in the summer only, shipwrights were given the opportunity to work 'extra' or overtime. Measured in units of tides (1½ hours) and nights (5 hours), such work was paid at a higher rate than day work.

The shipwright was the most important of the dockyard workers. They were responsible for the entire construction, or repair, of any ships in the yard. Their work started with the laying of the blocks on the slipway, through the assembling of the frame to the final laying of the planks. Other dockyard workers, such as mastmakers, caulkers, joiners, sailmakers and scavelmen, simply fitted themselves into the routine set by the shipwright. The joiners undertook the lighter form of woodwork, whilst the caulkers ensured the hull of the ship under construction was water tight. The caulkers trade was, in itself, a considerable skill. Taking oakum, which would be picked from old rope by the young 'oakum boyes', they would roll it into strips to fit the seams in the hull. Sufficient oakum had to be used otherwise leaking would occur, but too much and the seams would spring. Having filled the seams, pitch would be applied with a pitch mop. Heating, and attending to the pitch was not one of their particular tasks, as unskilled labourers — known as pitch heaters — would be employed.

Amongst the unskilled workers were the scavelmen. They worked closely with the shipwright, undertaking many of his non-specialised tasks. They also fully maintained the dockyard and would have been responsible for pumping out the new dry docks. The ordinary labourer held a lower status than that of the scavelmen, being responsible for shifting the timbers, keeping the yard clean and acting as general messengers and domestic servants.

Another group of workers, and administered separately from the actual dockyard, were those attached to the rope yard. The rope yard stood to the south of the new dockyard, between this and the old yard. Its main feature was the extremely long and narrow rope house in which the spinning and laying of rope was undertaken. The peculiarities of rope making meant that the building concerned with this process had to be as long as the longest length of rope. Hence the rope house was over a thousand feet long. This building, together with a number of store houses were all added during the 1618-1626 period. The main group of workers employed in the rope yard, other than labourers, were the spinners and hatchellors. After the hemp was sorted it was combed out by the 'hatchellor' and bundled. Following this, the rope was sent to the rope house, for spinning into strands, before being twisted into rope.

Dockyard employees, by modern day standards, worked extremely long and arduous hours. The standard day was ten hours in length — but this was not uncommon as no thought was then given to the workingman's leisure time. Normally work would start at 6 a.m. and finish at 6 p.m., with an hour's lunch break. Perhaps the hours were long, but the intensity of work was not as great. Strict time schedules were rarely adhered to, with employees being able to set their own pace of work; wives and children were not banned from the dockyard and, as such, there was no total separation of the family; furthermore, the lower standards of living accepted at the time meant that employees felt less inclined to appear for work every day. All in all, a far more relaxed atmosphere prevailed.

Perhaps the major grievance felt by the Chatham artisans was the length of time that often elapsed before payment was made. To start with, workmen were paid quarterly, but in addition to this, the government's method of raising and accounting money was so peculiar that it was often years before the dockyard workmen were paid. Furthermore, payment initially consisted of the distribution of tickets which could only be turned into money at the Navy Office in London. The result was that shipwrights and other workers had to seek additional employment for more immediate cash remuneration or make extensive loans from 'buyers'. Frequently there was trouble at Chatham resulting from this system of payment. In 1627, for instance, the shipwrights at Chatham were owed money dating back eighteen months. To remedy this, they determined to march on London to seek immediate settlement. For nearly three weeks they besieged the Navy Office, but even then only received promises of payment in the near future. The following year they were still without pay, and it was recorded that the men were so desperate that most resorted to theft from the naval yard as the only means of staying alive. In 1631, when Charles I visited the yard, £6,717 was owed in wages.

This particular visit by Charles I was, by all accounts, a fairly magnificent affair. During that year Charles had determined upon visiting all the royal dockyards and, in June, it was the turn of Chatham. Phineas Pett, in his autobiography states:

'Wednesday, being the 15th day of June, all the ships in the Navy at Chatham being completely trimmed in all points, rigged, and all their sails at yards, and ordnance on board, his Majesty, attended with divers lords, came to Strowde about 2 o'clock afternoon, where the Officers of the Navy attended his Highness with barges and boats, and being embarked rew down the river . . . At his Majesty's embarking the ships did orderly discharge their ordnance.'

Overnight the king stayed at the Crown, Rochester. The following day he visited all the ships assembled in the Medway and observed 'the course and order of the discharging of their ordnance'. Later in the day he entered the original Tudor dockyard before walking to the new yard which, of course, was situated nearby. On the way he also viewed the recently built ropery together with a number of adjacent storehouses. Finally, upon completing his visit to the dockyard, the king:

'went to the top of the hill on the back side, where his Majesty stood to see the ordnance fired from the ships.'

At this point in time, Phineas Pett makes a fairly good witness to events at the dockyard as, in 1630, he was appointed resident commissioner at Chatham, and was the first man to hold such office. As commissioner, Pett was totally responsible for the running of the dockyard and, in addition, automatically acquired a position on the all powerful Navy Board — the body responsible for dockyards. During his tenure of office, which lasted until his death in 1647, Pett still got up to some of his old tricks, not the least of which was the sale of a large quantity of naval stores. Pett claimed that there was nothing of value, and that he had merely been disposing 'of old ends and decayed junk'. Whatever might have been the truth as regards this matter, there was certainly much evidence to suggest that some of the money from the sale was deliberately kept back. On 22nd February 1634, Pett was removed from office for having sold the material without authority, but on 1st March, King Charles came to the rescue and granted him a full pardon.

Pett tells us that during these years, Chatham was very much a centre of naval activity, with considerable numbers of ships either anchoring in the Medway, or being repaired at Chatham. He only mentions, however, two vessels actually being built there during his years as commissioner. Both were pinnaces of 70 tons burden, and were named the *Henrietta* and *Maria*, being named after the Queen. It does not seem unlikely, however, that other ships were built at Chatham and that Pett simply neglects to mention them.

It was Phineas Pett who was commissioner of the dockyard during the early years of the civil war. Thus it was he who was responsible, on 24th August, for placing the dockyard into parliamentary hands. As a sympathiser with parliament he would not have found this a distasteful task. Nevertheless, he would have had little option as the dockyard stood in an area much opposed to the actions of the king. The dockyard, together with a considerable amount of ordnance, was surrendered to Colonel Edwin Sandys who had been dispatched from London, with a troop of soldiers, specifically for this purpose. Those ships anchored in the Medway, together with Upnor Castle and its two sconces were, likewise, taken over.

In April 1647 Phineas was succeeded in his office as commissioner by his son Peter. Born in 1610, Peter Pett had served his apprenticeship at Woolwich where, for many years, he had been Assistant Master Shipwright. Within a short space of time, Peter Pett was confronted by a serious royalist uprising. Many of those living in Kent had become dissatisfied with the uncompromising rule of parliament, and in 1648 a royalist uprising was hatched. Taking the government completely

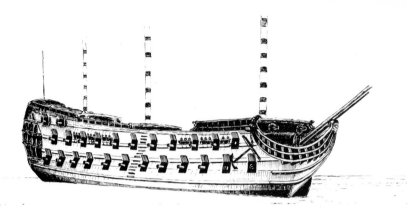

Fairfax, a 'Speaker' class frigate that was launched at Chatham during the year 1653.

(J.S. Morris)

by surprise, it quickly spread throughout the entire county. A great number of the inhabitants of both Rochester and Chatham were sympathetic to the rebel cause, and it was not long before both were in royalist hands. On this occasion Peter Pett did not surrender the dockyard despite the fact that it was surrounded and besieged. Furthermore, the rebels were also able to capture the castle at Upnor, together with the three guardships on the Medway. In fact the situation was only saved when parliament dispatched a good number of troops into the county, whilst offering to consider a number of grievances said to be the cause of the rising.

Peter Pett was very much a follower in his father's footsteps. Apart from being a truly brilliant shipwright, he was not beyond defrauding the government out of anything going. As early as 1651, only four years after taking up his new post, numerous accusations were being made that he, and numerous other members of the Pett family, were involved in 'grand abuses'. During these years a great number of the Pett family were found employment at Chatham, with brothers, cousins and nephews of Peter Pett occupying various important positions. For instance, Phineas Pett, Peter's brother, was clerk of the cheque and responsible for wages; Joseph Pett, a cousin, was Assistant Master Shipwright and a nephew Richard Holbourne was Master Mast Maker. All of these, at one time or another, were accused of being involved in schemes of fraud. Indeed, those making the accusations against the Petts stated that they were 'so knit together that the devil himself could not discover them, except one impeached the other'.

The initial accusations against the Pett family were made by two dockyard officers in a letter to the Navy Commission. In addition, William Adderley, the dockyard preacher confirmed the accusations and specifically accused Peter Pett and Joseph Pett of embezzlement, whilst Richard Holbourne was said to be using government timber for his own purposes. The Petts not only denied all this, but accused Adderley of such misdemeanours as swearing and failing to carry out his duties. The final upshot of it all was that there appears to have been insufficient evidence and it was decided to drop the various charges.

Chapter Four

DUTCH WARS

'An English Pilot too (O Shame, O sin!)
Cheated of Pay, was he that show'd them in.'
Andrew Marvell (The Last Instructions to a Painter)

The mid-seventeenth century brought renewed importance both to Chatham dockyard and the naval anchorage on the Medway. This was because England now had a new enemy, and one whose geographical situation placed the Medway in a position of strategic importance. The new enemy was that of the Nether-lands, a country whose trading ambitions together with maritime pretensions could only lead to eventual enmity with England.

It is easy to follow the course of events that eventually led to the first clashes between these two northern European states. During the years of Spanish occu-pation English troops had actually fought alongside the Dutch, but when peace was agreed in 1648, the former friendship between England and Holland rapidly turned sour as each realised that the other was a threat. A slow drift towards war ensued. A war made even more certain by the Navigation Act of 1651, in which an English parliament declared that only English ships could carry English imports, whilst exports could only be carried by English ships, or those of the country to which these goods were destined. The Act was clearly aimed at the Dutch and the successful maritime trade they had managed to build up over the years. The two countries also began to bicker over a number of other points, but it was not until May 1652 that the first real clash took place. On that occasion a Dutch fleet in the Channel refused to salute an English squadron, and thus recognise English sovereignty over 'the narrow seas'. The war that started in that year was to continue, with a number of lengthy breaks, until the year 1674.

The Medway, providing the nearest naval anchorage to the Dutch coast, found itself in an absolutely key position. Ships at anchor in the Medway could, with a minimum of delay, not only take offensive action against the Dutch nation but could also be quickly used to defend the areas most likely to come under attack. Moreover, the dockyard at Chatham provided the most obvious destination for any ships damaged whilst patrolling the North Sea or Channel areas.

From what has been said so far, it is obvious that the Dutch wars were, essentially, maritime affairs. Yet, at their outset, the English navy was a much neglected organisation. The early part of the century had seen it in the hands of either corrupt officials or parsimonious tax payers. The result was that few new ships had been built, and a great deal fewer were fit for sea. Thus, at the very hint of war with the Dutch it was necessary to inaugurate an extensive ship-building programme. As a result, Cromwell was responsible for seeing that large sums of money were diverted into shipbuilding, with the numerous small private yards, and the larger government yards all working to the maximum of their capacity in building and repairing ships. During the years of the Commonwealth (1649 to 1660) something approaching half the government's total revenue was expended on the navy, with one hundred and ninety ships added to the fleet. In 1654, for instance, a year in which £1,117,000 was used for naval purposes, no fewer than twenty-two men-of-war were launched. Of the various dockyards, Chatham clearly dominated. The accounts indicate that at Chatham, during the Commonwealth years, an expenditure of £413,301 was incurred, a sum far in excess of the £260,641 allocated to Woolwich, Deptford and Portsmouth combined. Among the ships built at Chatham at this time were the 52-gun *Fairfax* (launched 1653) and the 64-gun *London* (1656) together with a whole host of smaller vessels.

The restored monarchy of 1660 found, at its disposal, a fleet of two hundred and twenty-nine vessels. Sadly, however, this huge fleet also came replete with a million pound debt. Moreover, the dockyard workers at the various government yards, including Chatham, had not been paid for a good many months and were on the point of mutiny. Thus, Charles II was forced to reverse the entire naval programme in a desperate effort to curtail expenditure — a decision made even more necessary by the paltry amount of money granted to him for the running of the country. True, at this time the war with the Dutch had temporarily abated but, on the other hand, it was more than a little clear that the earlier conflict was bound to be renewed within a short time.

With little or no money for naval purposes it was, perhaps, fortunate that the administration of the navy was placed in somewhat better hands than those which had dominated it during the years in which the previous Stuart kings had ruled. The Navy Board, the body responsible for administering the dockyards, consisting of four principal officers and two commissioners, was much more competent than when Sir Robert Mansel was one of its members. Of the various Navy Board officers none is, perhaps, more well-known than the then clerk of the acts. The holder of this most junior post was the diarist Samuel Pepys. Responsible for all of the Navy Board's paperwork and administration, Pepys, in his diaries has handed down to us a highly enlightening account of how the Navy Board operated during those years immediately following the Restoration.

Samuel Pepys, in his capacity of clerk of the acts during these years made a number of visits to Chatham dockyard. Once again, everything is recorded in his diary. His first visit to Chatham was on 8th April 1661, where he was to supervise a number of goods to be sold by auction. He travelled to Gravesend by barge and then took a coach to Rochester. It was customary for Navy Board officials to be accommodated, whilst visiting the dockyard, at Hill House. Originally acquired sometime around the turn of the century this was a spacious brick building situated close to St Mary's Church. It was, in fact, the official residence of the commissioner at Chatham. Of this house, Pepys confided to his diary:

'And I find a pretty pleasant house — and am pleased with the armes that hang up there.'

On the 9th Pepys was conducted on a tour of the yard and 'viewed all the storehouses and the old goods that are this day to be sold'. The particular items to be placed under the hammer were goods associated with the former commonwealth, and consisted of such items as books and coats-of-arms. The method of sale is particularly intriguing as an inch candle was used. While the candle was burning anyone could place a bid for the goods in question with the person making the last bid before the candle burnt itself out, actually acquiring the goods.

'The sale being done, the ladies and I and Capt. Pett (Phineas Pett, clerk of the cheque) and Mr Castle (William Castle a shipbuilder of Deptford) took barge; and down we went to see the *Sovereigne*; which we did, taking great pleasure therein singing all the way; and among other pleasures, I put my lady, Mrs Turner, Mrs Hempson, and the two other Mrs Allens into the lantern and I went into them and kissed them, demanding it as a fee due to a Principall officer.'

Needless to say, Mrs Pepys rarely accompanied her husband on these 'business trips'.

The *Sovereign*, incidentally, was one of the greatest ships of the day. Originally built at Woolwich, and launched in 1637, she was the first three decker ever constructed. Towards the end of the Commonwealth period she was brought to Chatham for what is now termed a major re-fit. In fact the vessel underwent a total re-building being launched in 1660. The Navy Board took considerable pride in this vessel, as she was not only the nation's premier flagship but the world's most richly decorated warship. Known as the 'Golden Devil', her heavily ornamented sides were almost completely covered by gold leaf. The lantern, to which Pepys refers, was but one small part of the ship's decor. Located on the poop deck, it too was covered in gold leaf. The *Sovereign* was eventually to finish her days at Chatham as well. Again re-built in 1685, ships had a long life in those days, she was eventually destroyed by accident in 1696. On this occasion the ship had been brought to Chatham for a further re-build when a careless cook left a candle burning in his cabin. A fire was quickly created which soon engulfed the entire vessel.

In August 1662, Pepys made a further visit to the dockyard at Chatham. On this occasion, the diarist leaves a picture of a dockyard obviously short of money, and somewhat inefficiently run. Government cuts in naval expenditure were having their effects. Again, he stayed at the Hill House.

'Up by 4 a'clock in the morning and walked to the Docke, where Commissioner Pett and I took barge and went to the Guardshippes and mustered them, finding them but badly manned. Thence to the *Souveraigne*, which we find keeped in good order and very clean, which pleased us well; but few of the officers on board. Thence to the *Charles*, and were troubled to see her kept so neglectedly by the boatswain Clements, who I always took for a good officer. It is a very brave ship. Thence to Upner Castle; and there went to the top; where there is a fine prospect, but of very small force. So to the yard and there mustered the whole ordinary; where great disorder by multitude of servants and old decrepit men, which must be remedyed; so to all the storehouses and viewed the stores of all sort and the hempe; where we find Captain Cockes very bad, and some others.'

Pepys, it would appear, was becoming increasingly unhappy with the way that Peter Pett was running the dockyard. During a visit to the yard made in July 1663 Pepys declares in his diary:

'. . . being myself much dissatisfied, and more than I thought I should have been, with Commissioner Pett, being by what I saw since I came hither, convinced that he is not able to exercise that command in the yard over the officers that he ought to do.'

That this inefficiency was not restricted just to the dockyard but to the entire anchorage was verified when Pepys together with a clerk determined upon visiting the various warships laid up. The visit was made close to midnight and Pepys hoped to discover an alert guard upon each of the ships:

'Thence to the *Souveraigne,* where I find no officers aboard, no armes fixed, nor any powder to prime their few guns which were charged, without bullet though.

'So to *London,* where neither officer nor anybody awake; I boarded her and might have done what I would, and at last could find but three little boys.

'And so I spent the whole night in visiting all of the ships, in which I find, for the most part, ne'er an officer aboard nor any men so much as awake . . . '

During that year, another visit was made to Chatham in which, again, Pepys was most dissatisfied with the level of discipline prevailing. A conversation took place with Commissioner Pett in which Pett was asked to make more effort at correcting his officers. On this occasion Pepys was accompanied by Sir William Coventry, one of the commissioners to the Navy Board. It was clear that neither was impressed by Pett's promises to make a greater effort in his management of dockyard affairs:

'But being gone thence, Mr Coventry and I did discourse about him (Pett) and conclude that he is not able to do the good in the yard that he might and can and may be will do in another — what with his old faults and the relations that he doth to most people that act there.'

On 2nd August 1663, a further comment concerning Pett appears in the diary:

' . . . troubled to see how backward Commissioner Pett is to tell any faults of the officers and to see nothing in better condition here for his being here then they are in other yards where there is none.'

This last is a reference to the fact that Chatham yard was the only royal dockyard to have a resident commissioner.

It was in March 1665, that the Second Dutch War was declared. As such, the Medway could no longer remain neglected. Consideration was therefore given to both strengthening the river's defences and laying the foundations for a new and smaller royal dockyard at Sheerness. It was for this reason that on 18th August 1665, Pepys was again in the area of the Medway. This time the purpose of the visit was to find a suitable site for the dockyard, as well as a site for a fort whose purpose would be to defend both the mouth of the Medway and the new dock-yard. Included in the party on this occasion were such august bodies as the king himself, together with the Duke of York, then Lord High Admiral, and Sir Bernard de Gomme, Chief Engineer and Surveyor of the Ordnance. Once again the diary of Samuel Pepys tells all:

'To Sheerness, where we walked up and down laying out the ground to be taken in for the yard to lay provisions for cleaning and repairing the King's ships and a most proper place it is for this purpose.'

Nevertheless, despite such grand ideas there was still insufficient monies to pay the dockyard workers. In November 1665 Pett was reporting that the men were on the verge of mutiny and there was absolutely no way of disciplining them. Most of the men at Chatham were under-employed for the lack of money also meant a lack of stores. In November all the workmen in the yard laid down their tools and attended a mass meeting in which they demanded their wages. Further trouble was only averted when a number of the leaders were put into the dockyard stocks before being transferred to prison. With something like £18,000 owing in wages to the men at Chatham this could hardly be a solution and there were a number of incidents in which the men stopped working com-pletely. For the yard itself, however, more serious was that these unpaid workers turned to theft in order to keep themselves alive, and many of them were cutting up supplies of much needed timber stocks for firewood. The Navy Board was certainly aware of the situation and requested the king for an additional £50,000 which would help alleviate the situation by paying the men's wages and acquiring new stores. The king, instead, offered to advance a sum of no more than £6,000.

Throughout 1666 the chronic shortage of money meant that England was only just able to keep a fleet at sea. Nevertheless, it was still a fleet able to win the occasional victory. Using successes gained in that year, Charles II was advised to negotiate peace terms whilst he still held the upper hand. Thus, the year 1667 opened with sound prospects for peace. Indeed, the Admiralty was so sure of this outcome that it was decided against a fleet being fitted out. The Dutch, on the other hand, fully aware of the situation, determined upon one outstanding action designed entirely to strengthen their position in any future bargaining.

The plan adopted by the Dutch was a raid upon the Medway in which their ships would do as much damage as possible to the many anchored vessels in that river. They did not see it as an easy plan to carry out but, aware of the ill-coordinated and badly manned defences along the Medway, they knew that if skilfully conducted it could reap them a harvest for any planned peace talks. Throughout the early part of 1667 the various components of the plan were assembled. English seamen, with a knowledge of the Medway, were recruited from Dutch gaols (many of them unpaid for years were only too willing to serve the Dutch); a force of over 3,000 soldiers was assembled, whilst a fleet of well over eighty vessels (including fifty-one men-of-war) was made ready. To confuse the English as to the purpose of these preparations a small squadron of ships began a series of raids on the Firth of Forth.

Along the Medway the English were not unaware that the Dutch might attempt such a bold stroke. Indeed, Admiral Sir William Monson had warned of just such a possibility many years earlier. At the outset of 1667 orders were given to speed up completion of the newly planned fort at Sheerness. However, little more than the foundations had been laid and there was absolutely no possibility that it would be ready before the summer. The rest of the defences were little better. Swaleness fort had fallen into decay and it was not even considered worth fortifying. In fact, it was only at Upnor that a building stood which was capable of putting up any kind of resistance. But at the outset of 1667 even this building was of limited use as it was partly used for storage and most of its garrison had been paid off. Moreover, the two small sconces designed to work in cooperation with the castle had also fallen into disrepair and were of absolutely no use during that summer of 1667.

One final line of defence remained. This was the chain stretching across the river from Gillingham to Hoo Ness. The chain erected on the instructions of John Hawkins in 1585 had long disappeared and, at the outset of 1667 no chain existed. But with the possibility of a Dutch raid in the air it was decided to commission a new chain. Although it was supposed to have been completed by April, this chain was not ready until May. Constructed by John Ruffhead, anchorsmith of Chatham dockyard, at a cost of £573.8s.11d, it was a massive affair weighing in excess of fourteen tons. Each link was nearly two inches thick, and to ensure it would remain above water, it was attached to four floating stages. Once complete the chain was installed across the river. At both Gillingham and Hoo, simple cranes were installed to draw the chain tight in time of need. Finally, the chain was strengthened by a number of ship's cables.

It was on Monday, 10th June 1667, that the first shots were fired in the most embarrassing maritime defeat that England has ever suffered. During the previous few days a squadron of Dutch ships, under the command of Vice Admiral Willem van Ghent, had sailed into the Thames, burnt and ransacked Canvey Island, whilst preventing the movement of shipping in the area. Not content with this, however, the Dutch squadron then proceeded to Sheerness where, at 5 p.m. on that Monday in June, they began to lay siege to the still unfinished Sheerness fort. The defenders, heavily outnumbered, put up as stout a resistance as they were able. Hampered by incomplete walls, and guns so badly mounted that when fired the recoil sunk them deep into the earth, they found themselves in a hopeless situation.

Because of the small amount of return fire, the Dutch had little difficulty in maintaining a constant and accurate fire which was soon to take its toll. The outcome of the battle was a foregone conclusion, made even more certain by a landing of Dutch soldiers further along the island. Not wishing to be outflanked, the defenders at Sheerness left their guns and wisely retreated.

When news of the Dutch attack on Sheerness reached Chatham panic broke out. Orders given by one were countermanded by another. Ships that should have been moved to safety were left on the far side of the chain, whilst all but a few ships remained unarmed. Worse still was the decision, taken on the Tuesday, for a number of perfectly good ships to be sunk in a quite hopeless attempt at preventing the Dutch reaching Upnor. Indeed, more English ships were sunk during that week by the English than by the enemy. Peter Pett, the man who should have been in charge of the whole situation, was later to come under particular criticism. He used a number of useful men, not for protecting the dockyard, but for carrying away to safety many of his valuable ship models. The Duke of Albemarle, reporting to the House of Commons upon the events that took place on Tuesday 11th June was one who criticised Pett:

'I found scarce twelve of eight hundred men which were then in the king's pay, in his Majesty's yards; and these so distracted with fear that I could have little or no service from them. I had heard of thirty boats, which were provided by the direction of His Royal Highness; but they were all, except five or six, taken away by those of the yards, who went themselves with them, and sent and took them away by the example of the Commissioner Pett, who had the chief command there, and sent away his own goods in some of them.'

The only positive move that seems to have been made during this day of respite, prior to the Dutch drive down the Medway, was the strengthening of the chain. With the first news of the Dutch entry into the Medway it was duly raised and three large ships were placed close to the chain to prevent the Dutch lowering it. These ships were the *Unity, Mathias* and *Charles V*. A battery of guns was also placed near the chain, whilst a number of gunships were placed along the river bank to further hinder the Dutch.

On the morning of 12th June van Ghent's squadron was once more under way. Supported by an exceptional high tide together with a favourable breeze, they soon came within sight of the nearby laid chain. Aware that further progress depended upon neutralising the various ships brought to its defence, the Dutch determined upon an attack upon the *Unity*, the only large vessel to be moored forward of the chain. In the event, she was boarded and captured without a great deal of difficulty, so allowing fire ships to approach and then ride over the chain. Their targets were *Mathias* and *Charles V*, with both vessels being reduced to blazing hulks that could provide no further defence.

For the Dutch the day was not, as yet, over. They still had the greatest prize of all to capture. This was the one hundred gun *Royal Charles*, flagship of the English fleet. Yet, quite amazingly, this particular vessel was captured without a single shot being fired. Anchored just below Upnor, it was totally unguarded, and all that was required of van Ghent was an order to dispatch nine men, nine men who simply clambered aboard the *Royal Charles* and proceeded to strike the English flag.

Once again the Dutch anchored for the night and made plans. They now had only five fire ships left, and were approaching a narrower part of the river. The thing they feared was a second fleet penning them in from behind. Nevertheless, before departing, they agreed that they ought to create as much damage as possible. Therefore, it was decided that on the following day they should send all the remaining fire ships up river with an escort of men-of-war.

It was this plan which was subsequently put into operation. On the Thursday, despite the Dutch ships receiving a good deal of battering from the guns of Upnor Castle, three more English ships were successfully fired. These were the *Royal Oak*, *Royal James* and *Loyal London*.

As successful as the operation had been so far, the Dutch decided to go no further. For one thing, the guns of Upnor Castle were proving to be a considerable hazard and, for another, the Dutch had expended all of their fire ships. As a result, van Ghent's squadron carefully picked its way back down river on the fourteenth where, in the Thames estuary, it rendezvoused with the main Dutch fleet, commanded by Admiral de Ruyter.

Once the Dutch had withdrawn, the nation showed itself to be incensed. No one could understand how an enemy fleet had penetrated the Medway and wreaked such considerable damage, whilst suffering the loss of fewer than a hundred lives. Immediately the search for a scapegoat began, with the country's wrath falling almost entirely upon the shoulders of one man — Peter Pett. He was blamed for every conceivable error imaginable and quickly thrown into the Tower of London. In October 1667, he was brought before a committee of the House of Commons in order to answer various charges laid against him. These charges ranged from negligence in his capacity of dockyard commissioner, to refusing to obey orders given to him. Of all these charges, however, the most serious related to the loss of the *Royal Charles*. According to the Duke of Albemarle, Pett had been given orders in March to move this vessel up river, but had totally failed to do so. In addition, on the day following the Dutch capture of Sheerness Albemarle himself, had ordered Pett to move the *Royal Charles*, but that Pett had once again refused to do so. According to Pepys:

'Commissioner Pett of all men living did make the weakest defence of himself: nothing to the purpose, not to satisfaction, not certain; but sometimes one thing, and sometimes another, sometimes for himself, and sometimes against him ... '

Orders were, in fact, given to impeach Pett on these various charges, but as Pett would undoubtedly improve his defence and, doubtless, implicate a good many other persons, his impeachment was carefully forgotten. Dismissed from office in February 1668, this remained the only punishment meted out to him. Retiring into the country he died, in 1672, a broken man.

Peter Pett who, in 1647, succeeded his father as Chatham dockyard's resident commissioner. This particular painting, which is in the style of Sir Peter Lely, also depicts the 100-gun warship, *Sovereign of the Seas*. Although this particular vessel was originally launched at Woolwich, she has a number of links with the Chatham yard. In the year 1660, and once more in 1685, she was totally rebuilt at Chatham being re-launched first as the *Sovereign* and later as the *Royal Sovereign*. Furthermore, her career was also to end at Chatham, being accidentally burnt at this port during the year 1697.   (National Portrait Gallery)

More positively, plans were made for the strengthening of the Medway's defences. It was very much in the style of 'bolting the stable door', but at least it showed that such things would never happen again.

Prince Rupert was dispatched to the Medway, in his capacity of senior naval admiral, to give directions for improving the defences of the river. During this period, long term plans were made for the construction of forts at Sheerness, Gillingham and Cockham Wood. As well as these, plans were also made for a number of batteries to be placed along the river. More immediately, the existing defences were strengthened, with a new boom placed across the river at Gillingham, and consisting of a chain strengthened by a cable.

The three new forts were the backbone of the redesigned defences. All three were similar in principle, being designed to protect both the Medway and the immediate hinterland. Work on the forts started as soon as was practicable, and all were under construction by 1669. In September of that year Major Manley, who was in charge of construction work, wrote to the Duke of Lennox concerning progress:

'this summer there hath beene made a goode progress in ye works att Sheerness and the forts att Gillingham and Cockham Wood side, both these are like to have towers in them which besides the keeping of stores are to be a retreat to the soldiers in case of necessity; they are to have fifty pieces of cannon in each of them, the least of which is to carry twenty-four pound ball.'

It is this tower which is the most uncommon feature for such defences. Not only did they carry out the functions described by Major Manley but, because of their height (some thirty feet), they were also used for observation and the mounting of light weight cannons.

The fort at Gillingham has now completely disappeared. It was situated on a small island at the mouth of St Mary's creek, which has long since been incorporated into the docks at Chatham. It had fifty-four guns of various calibres and most of which were directed towards the river. A description of the fort appears in the book 'Summer Excursions Along the Thames and Medway', published in 1847:

'By the brink of the river, some distance to our right, is a red brick building, dignified by the name Gillingham fort . . . It stands upon a small piece of ground usually surrounded by water, and is no longer applied to any warlike purpose, being converted into a station for the coast guard.'

Although construction of the fort at Cockham Wood was started as early as 1669, it was not completed until 1700. Designed by the eminent seventeenth century military engineer Sir Bernard de Gomme, it had, in all, forty-eight guns. A number of these guns were taken from nearby Cooling Castle, which had long been a ruin. Nowadays, though, little remains of the fort at Cockham Wood, apart from a few stones which mark the site. The most urgent construction work went into the partially dismantled fort at Sheerness. The Dutch, during their occupation had removed much of the stonework, and rebuilding had to be started more or less from scratch. A sum of £10,000 was voted for this purpose, and this allowed the fort to be completed by 1669. An additional reason for the urgency in rebuilding Sheerness was that the fort here was now recognised as London's first line of defence.

On completion Sheerness fort had two hundred and fifty cannon, each firing twenty-four pound projectiles. Some of these guns were in the main citadel, but most of them were situated in the surrounding wall which was on the very banks of the Medway. To stop the fort being outflanked, as happened during the Dutch raid, two batteries were also placed on Sheppey, and not far from the new fort.

As well as the two-gun batteries at Sheerness, there were numerous other batteries built between 1669 and 1700. One of these was placed on Hoo Ness, a small island in the middle of the Medway, with the purpose of giving added protection to the boom. Three batteries, Buda, Middle and Quaker, were all sited on the Isle of Grain, at the mouth of the Medway, whilst two others were built at Upnor, with further batteries at Gillingham and Hoo.

The castle at Upnor, which had been of such a hindrance to the Dutch, now declined in importance. In 1668 it became 'a place of Stores and Magazine' and continued in this role until the nineteenth century. As a gunpowder store it became, in importance, second only to the Tower of London.

In the years immediately following the Dutch raid, a great deal of time and effort went into the repair of the Medway defences. Yet, surprising as it may seem, it was a comparatively short period before complacency set in. During the eighteenth century long periods of peace prevailed and the spending of huge sums of money on defence was frequently seen as a nonsense. Instead, economy became the order of the day, with a considerable number of the Medway's forts and batteries being allowed to fall into decay.

By the end of the nineteenth century, the situation was quite unbelievable. The Medway's defences, far from being ready to repel such dangerous foes as post-revolutionary France, were in such a poor state that even the weakest of enemies would have had little difficulty in duplicating the Dutch success of 1667. It was during this period that a certain Major McCrae, who produced a survey of existing defence structures, showed that of the gun batteries sited along the Medway, only Hoo Ness still remained — and even this battery had no guns mounted. Of the various forts, Gillingham was in ruins, Cockham Wood had no guns mounted and Sheerness had too small a garrison to adequately repel a surprise attack. The Medway, once again, was undefended.

Chapter Five

PERIOD OF EXPANSION

'That you forthwith enter unto contract with said John Rogers for the building of the said dock, outwharves and Peer heads in manner, time, Price, Tearmes of Payment, and all other circumstances answerable to the conditions before referred to in your said papers.'
Letter written by Samuel Pepys and referring to the new dry dock of 1685.

The Anglo-Dutch wars, which first began in 1652, did not reach a final conclusion until 1674. Throughout these years Chatham dockyard continued in its pre-eminent role, taking responsibility for maintaining virtually the entire royal fleet. Not only were war damaged vessels repaired, or totally reconstructed but, in addition, a large number of new and even greater war ships left the Chatham building slips, ready to confront the Dutch in a baptism of fire.

One such vessel, the *Prince*, a first rate[1] of one hundred guns, was launched in 1670. Having a length of one hundred and sixty-seven feet and a beam of just over forty-five feet, she was, for her day, a very large warship. In fact, she was designed as a symbol of national prestige and flagship for the fleet. Her considerable dimensions produced at least one problem for, of all the royal shipyards only one, that of Chatham, had a dry dock large enough to receive this vessel.

Undoubtedly the *Prince* was amongst the finest of ships ever to be constructed at Chatham. She was designed by Phineas Pett who, at that time, was Master Shipwright at Chatham. This particular Pett was also the son of Peter Pett, the dishonoured Commissioner at Chatham and, like many of the Petts, seems to have been engaged in a number of shady business deals. Leastways, eighteen months before the launching of the *Prince* he was temporarily dismissed from government service when it was discovered he was dishonestly handling dockyard timber.

That the *Prince* might receive the nation's accolade, large sums of money were lavished upon her exterior ornamentation. A contemporary model, now on display at the Science Museum in London, shows her to have had carefully detailed carved wreaths around each of the gun ports, faces and figurines decorating the cathead, with a stern bearing a massive coat-of-arms finished in gold leaf. One can only hope that the ordinary seaman serving aboard, living in the stench emitted from the bilges, surviving on rancid butter, slimy water and weevil-infested biscuits, appreciated these finer points of artistry.

With such an elaborate external appearance, it would be easy to forget the true purpose for which the *Prince* was constructed. She was a warship and, as such, mounted a great variety of guns distributed along three of her decks. The largest of these were the huge forty-two pounders mounted on the lowest broad-side tier. Their extreme weight, which restricted such guns to this level, meant they were only of use at the closest possible range — usually less than 250 yards. Naturally, when brought into use, they could inflict very real damage upon an opponent. A complete broadside would shatter even the strongest of hulls, reducing good oak to matchwood. Gun crews, themselves, would be faced with a terrible and painful death as flying metal and clouds of jagged timber tore into flesh and bone. Such men must have been brave indeed. Submitting themselves to such a hideous onslaught they, nevertheless, continued to prepare their own guns for just such a return fire.

On the middle gun deck were the lighter eighteen pounders, and these did have a slightly increased range. But they, too, were rarely used at a distance of more than four hundred yards. Finally, along the upper gun deck were a collection of nine, six and three pounders. With their added height, and a much greater range, they could be used for raking enemy ships during the period in which opposing vessels closed upon one another.

As a warship, the *Prince* was no real advance upon a number of vessels which had gone before. She was merely bigger and more expensive than most. Further, she was a continuation of a prevailing policy which entailed building large ships and loading them with as many guns as deemed feasible. The result, however, was that the *Prince* was over-gunned. In 1692 it was considered necessary that she re-enter Chatham dockyard for lengthening — a process which consisted of adding a new central section. Certainly there was no finesse in the way that ships, such as the *Prince*, were employed during times of war. Little consideration was given to the possibility of out-ranging an enemy ship, as the sole tactic employed was that of closing to point blank range and firing the entire comple-ment of guns in one solid salvo. The larger the ship, and the greater number of guns, the better its chance of survival. As the Duke of York's flagship at Solebay, a sea fight fought against the Dutch in May 1672, the *Prince* found herself en-gaged in just one such 'flogging match'. Having become separated from the rest of the English fleet, she was surrounded by a Dutch squadron. This, most certainly, was her baptism of fire.

Although the *Prince* had been launched in 1670, she did not go to sea in that year. She was simply harbour rigged and allowed to ride in-ordinary[2] until the end of 1671. In December of that year, John Cox, who was then the commissioner at Chatham, was given the *Prince* to command. His first task was to enlist a suitable crew. As first lieutenant, John Narbrough was appointed, an intelligent young man who methodically kept a daily journal of events aboard the *Prince* during the succeeding months. One of his earliest entries in this journal was made on 5th January 1672:

'This day the Boatswain employed the seamen to take down the harbour rigging, the ship having nothing in her but ballast, which was about 200 tons.'

Rigging the ships was a process which went on for about two weeks, and this was not completed until the first week of February. Soon after, Narbrough was given instructions to take on a larger complement of seamen. The journal entry for 5th February states:

> 'I went and caused a drum to beat through Strood and Rochester and Chatham for all seamen to repair on board the *Prince*. I gave the drummer three shillings for his hire.'

Also on that same day:

> 'At high water the *Prince* was hauled into the dock . . . The builder heeled the ship to port and graved and tallowed all the starboard side over the graving down to the keel and made her clean on this side this afternoon.'

The 'larboard' side was graved on the following day, prior to her leaving dock and being moored to the *Victory*. It was necessary at this time to moor her to another ship as, so far, the *Prince* was without anchors. This *Victory*, incidentally, was the second of the name, having been launched at Deptford in 1620. Later she had been rebuilt at Chatham being enlarged from a 42-gun vessel to an 82-gun second rate.

By 23rd February the *Prince* had received a complete suit of sails and was ready to be moved further down river in order to complete her victualling and to receive guns. Most of these items were to be brought down the Thames from Deptford and Woolwich, thus it was more sensible for the *Prince* to be anchored off the Black Stakes, opposite the Isle of Sheppey, rather than to remain at Chatham.

> 'All things that was on board at her sailing was men and masts and yards and sails and rigging complete and two anchors and four cables and some hawsers and 206 tons of ballast and 42½ tons of round iron shot.'

Over the next few weeks the *Prince* was to receive several hundred butts of beer, numerous casks of water, biscuits, bread, beef, pork, anchors, hawsers together with the all essential guns. Most of this was completed by 1st April when Narbrough recorded:

> 'This day the *Prince* has all her provisions and stores aboard and all things in readiness for the sea. Men on board 578; men entered in the ship's book, which I do expect will go to sea in the ship, is 680. The ship now draweth 22ft abaft and 20ft 9in. afore; I judge that all the weight that is now on board her is 940 tons. The provisions which is on board is 14 weeks' fresh butter and cheese and fish and peas for 800 men, which is her complement complete. Beer on board, 180 tons, and bread on board 65,000 pounds. The ship can stow more provisions, both in the hold and bread-room, but she carries her guns too low; the lowest edge of the lowest port in the midships is but 3ft 6in. above water now; there must come yet more on board 50 tons in water, men and lumber. The ship sinks very much with little weight.'

On the following day James, Duke of York and Lord High Admiral boarded his new flagship prior to joining the main fleet assembling in the Channel. On Friday 5th the sails were finally set:

'This morning His Royal Highness commanded the fore topsail to be loosed and the ship to be unmoored, and get her undersail, which was done. At 11 oclock we sailed, the tide serving, it being half flood and the wind at WNW, a fine fresh gale and some small rain.'

The *Prince* was now on her way to that previously mentioned baptism of fire. She was a fine ship, despite riding low in the water, and Narbrough records few other criticisms. Certainly she steered well, and had all the qualities demanded of a seventeenth century man-of-war. Chatham dockyard had produced its masterpiece.

Only seven and a half weeks after leaving the River Medway the *Prince* was engaged in that bloody conflict. A superior Dutch fleet both out-manoeuvred and surprised its opponents when it attacked the assembled English fleet in Southwold Bay. Far from ready, the Duke of York had no prepared battle line. Many ships were becalmed in the lee of the bay and this allowed the Dutch to single out the *Prince* as a worthy target for a squadron of their ships. That the *Prince* was able to withstand the concerted bombardment must forever be credited to her crew and those shipwrights at Chatham who pieced together her mighty timbers. Narbrough's account of the action vividly portrays the events that followed:

'At 8 oclock (that morning) we in the *Prince* were warmly engaged with the Dutch Admiral, de Ruyter and his seconds and van Ghent and his seconds. There was seven Dutch ships at once firing at us very briskly and we at them, being about a musket shot distance from each other, and quite calm and the water as smooth as possible might —as the saying is, as smooth as a milk bowl. We being all alone made it the warmer with us; none of our Squadron could get up with us for their lives, they being so becalmed. The Dutch finding us to ply our guns so fast, dare not venture to board us, although they had so great odds. His Royal Highness went fore and aft in the ship and cheered up the men to fight, which did encourage them very much. The Duke thought himself never near enough to the enemy, for he was ever calling to the quarter master which cunded (sic) the ship to luff her nearer, giving me commands to forbear firing till we got close up to them. Between 9 and 10 oclock Sir John Cox was slain with a great shot, being close by the Duke on the poop. Several gentlemen and others were slain and wounded on the poop and quarter deck on both sides of the Duke . . .

'Between 11 and 12 oclock our ship was much disabled in the mast and rigging. A great shot from the enemy cut our main topmast clear asunder, that it fell down on the deck and put us past the use of our mainsail, so that we could not work the ship to keep the wind, nor use the guns on the upper deck for rigging; neither could any man work aloft about mending the rigging for shot flying so thick, we being got so near the enemy's great ships and fireships, that our ship was in more than ordinary danger. It being very little wind, we could not bear off from the enemy, to favour ourselves; nor could any relief come to our assistance . . . '

Clearly, then, the *Prince* was in a hopeless situation, and Narbrough resorted to the only possible solution:

> 'Seeing we were thus alone, I caused two boats which were manned, to take hold of a tow rope and tow the ship's head off from the enemy to the northward towards our ships, which they did in time, and we helping and assisting what we could with our headsails.'

Yet this was no easy task. They were still heavily engaged with:

> ' . . . our great guns plying all this time as fast as our seamen could load and fire at the enemy's men-of-war and fireships; the enemy shooting as fast at us, killing and wounding our men very briskly and slapping the ship's sides and rigging, and shot down the fore topsail, so as we then had but little help of our sails . . . '

Slowly, though, the *Prince* was drawn into the protecting fire of other English ships and was eventually in a position to withdraw from the action.

The cost of this engagement to the *Prince* was enormous. Her hull was shot through in a great number of places, whilst she was entirely dismasted. All this, however, could be repaired. Less fortunate were the fifty-one men (including John Cox, commissioner of Chatham dockyard) who were slain. But, perhaps, they were the lucky ones. Fifty-two others were hideously wounded. Many of them had lost limbs and, in this day and age, it meant that they would spend the rest of their lives in poverty. These pitiful, limbless creatures, many of them natives of Chatham, would return to that town with no other occupation than that of beggar. For them war had no glory, and the nation no rewards.

The *Prince* had a happier fate. Running repairs were carried out under the supervision of the ship's carpenter. Once a suitable mast had been erected, the ship made her way to Sheerness where, on 6th June dockyard

> 'carpenters went to work to mend the ship's side, and the other officers made good what was amiss.'

Later, on 12th June she entered into the recently completed dockyard at Sheerness:

> 'to have new masts and to mend the shot holes in her side.'

On 13th June the final major repair was complete:

> 'This day I had the hulk on board and took out our masts and set the foremast again and clapped rigging on it.'

The *Prince* was, once more, ready to confront the Dutch.

The eventual peace settlement, signed with the Dutch, brought with it the usual economies that led both the fleet, and the nation's dockyards, to be totally ignored. At the time this was hardly sound policy. A major reason for peace was not the sudden solution to all Anglo-Dutch problems, but rather the serious threat which France now presented to both of these warring nations. Over the years, the French king had carefully built up an extremely powerful navy. In terms of

The River Medway as viewed from Frindsbury Hill towards the end of the seventeenth century. In the foreground are various naval ships belonging to the Chatham ordinary. The dockyard, by this date, was the most important in the country, responsible for both constructing and repairing most of the navy's larger warships.

simple numbers, the French had now sufficient warships to equal the combined fleet available to both the Dutch and English. Moreover, the French showed every indication that they were prepared to use this fleet.

Despite the warning signs, and frequently expressed fears, the government of the day continued to impose economies upon both the Admiralty and Navy Board. The fleet, most of which was then lying in the Medway, did not seem to merit even sufficient expenditure for routine maintenance. Not surprisingly these ships began to rot. Fungus, the size of a man's fist, was soon a common sight on even the proudest of the king's ships. It was a dismal, but fortunately short-lived episode in the nation's maritime history. Eventually, the inherent dangers in this situation impressed themselves upon those in power. In 1684 Charles II initiated a spending programme designed to improve the sad state into which the Royal Navy had been allowed to fall. In 1685, this more enlightened attitude continued when the former Lord High Admiral (the Duke of York) ascended the throne as James II. He had a very real interest in maritime affairs and saw the need for a high level of expenditure upon the navy. During his four year reign, the much needed repairs to the fleet were completed, a number of new warships were constructed and a greater number of guardships were kept at sea. These guardships were of particular importance as they monitored enemy movements and were meant to give warning of any possible attack being mounted by a potential enemy. James II also gave some consideration to the dockyards. At Chatham twenty-one new storehouses were erected, together with two much-needed dry docks.

Of suggested improvements to Chatham dockyard during these years one, in 1682, was made by Phineas Pett. His proposal was for a wet dock large enough to contain twenty-five second rates closely anchored. Such a scheme would have considerably hastened the re-fitting of such vessels. The Navy Board, though, was not particular enamoured of the scheme, as they feared the possibility

51

of a fire rapidly spreading through so many ships in such close proximity. The knowledge that finances for such a scheme were unlikely to be granted during this period could hardly have encouraged the Board to give the scheme their support.

Although the suggested wet dock failed to materialise, reference has already been made to the new dry docks which were built only a few years later. Work upon their construction began during the final few months of Charles II's reign. Sited to the north of the main dockyard, they were built upon land most of which had been acquired in 1618. Further land was added in 1685, being obtained from the Dean and Chapter of Rochester, together with the Manor of West Court. Not all of this land was utilised immediately but, overall, it did represent a sizeable increase to the dockyard's river frontage.

New dry docks at Chatham were long overdue. The old single dock, together with the double dock, both built during the early years of the century, were clearly showing their age. Neither was really suited to repairing the nation's warships, for both were now of a totally inadequate size. In fact, the double dock was only forty-five feet in breadth, a size clearly sufficient when built, but no longer suited to the increasing size of warships. It was said of the docks at Chatham that there was scarcely enough room to swing a caulker's mallet when a first rate was under repair. Moreover, some first rates, such as the *Britannia*, launched at Chatham in 1682, had a breadth of 48½ feet and were quite unable to enter even the largest dock. At the time of the *Britannia*'s launching, in fact, there was no dry dock in the country able to accommodate her.

Of the two new dry docks (both of which were to measure 200 feet by 54 feet), one was to be built by the dockyard workforce, and the other by contract. The contractor was John Rogers, a housecarpenter, whose tender was for £5,310. The late James Presnail, in his 'Story of Chatham', reproduces a letter written by Samuel Pepys, and relating to this particular dock. It appears that Rogers was to complete the work within fifteen months, and that the tendered sum was to be paid in the following fashion:

At signing of contract	£1,000
the next month after	400
3, 4, 5, 6 and 7 months after, each	400
8, 9 and 10 months after, each	300
11, 12, 13 and 14 months after, each	200
after complete finishing	610
	£5,310

At this time, Chatham was still the largest of the government dockyards, employing a labour force nearly twice the size of that at Portsmouth and exceeding the combined totals for Woolwich and Deptford. Furthermore, additional importance was given to the Medway (though perhaps not Chatham) with the construction of a further dockyard at Sheerness. Although this particular yard was engaged in the construction of ships, its main purpose was that of providing minor repair and careening[3] facilities. This removed the necessity of ships always having to navigate the sometimes treacherous shoals of the River Medway.

The dockyard at Sheerness was governed by the Commissioner of Chatham yard and initially it drew its workforce from those employed at Chatham. Not that dockyard workers rated Sheerness a particularly popular yard. It was situated in the midst of the North Kent marshes and, subsequently, was subjected to a high incidence of 'marsh fever'. In reality, this was indigenous malaria which was a common feature of English marshlands during earlier centuries. In 1744, for instance, large numbers of illnesses at Sheerness resulted in an abnormally high rate of absenteeism. The Commissioner of Chatham was forced to request overtime be given to the housecarpenters, bricklayers and labourers to make up for lost time in the fitting out of ships. To help offset this unwholesome reputation, Sheerness was the only yard which provided free accommodation. Another problem suffered at Sheerness was that of having no natural water supply. A number of bore holes were sunk over the years, but none achieved success. Until the nineteenth century all fresh water supplies to Sheerness were barged there from Chatham.

For these two reasons, Sheerness always remained the smallest of the government dockyards. It was used fairly extensively during the final years of the Dutch wars, but at that time consisted of no more than a building slip and an area set aside for cleaning. In 1714, however, a small dry dock was added.

In some respects, of course, a dockyard at Sheerness led to a certain reduction in the amount of work being undertaken at Chatham. On the other hand, the yard at Chatham could now concentrate on the building of ships together with major items of repair. In fact, Chatham was not particularly suited to minor repair work due to the length of time it sometimes took to reach this dockyard. As a result of the various twists and turns in the Medway there were very few winds which were totally favourable to a large sailing ship journeying to Chatham. A report drawn up in 1774, but no less relevant to this earlier period, put this problem particularly well. It stated that there were:

' . . . only six points of the compass for a wind with which ships of the line can sail down, and ten to sail up and that only for a few days in the spring tides.'   (British Museum, Kings 44)

When such winds were not available then a great deal of time had to be spent tacking. The constant shoaling of the Medway was a further hindrance, and it was not unusual for a ship to run aground with further delays. The problem of shoaling was first noted in the seventeenth century, with a special dredging engine being acquired in 1680.

The reign of James II lasted but a few short years. In 1688 his throne was usurped by William of Orange. James was aware of the likely invasion and mobilised the fleet during mid-summer of that year. On 25th August, Pepys, who was now a member of the Admiralty Board, sent two members of the Navy Board to Chatham in order to hasten work there. Additionally, the workforce was increased, so that by November 1688 it had reached a record figure of 886. To this can be added a further eighty, made up of soldiers drafted into the dockyard as an emergency measure. All this, though, proved of little consequence. William's armada, made up of both warships and transports, sailed in early November. Managing to avoid the English fleet, it anchored off Torbay, and landed the fifteen hundred men, which was all that William needed to carry out his bloodless coup.

Although both James II, and his successor William III, had considerable religious differences, they were both aware of England's need for a strengthened navy. As a result, William continued much of the fine work which had been undertaken by his Stuart rival. Considerable sums of money continued to be ear-marked for naval expansion. In fact, during the first ten years of William's reign, a hundred and three completely new ships were added to the fleet. Additionally, the dockyards at Chatham and Portsmouth were now updated with a totally new yard being built at Plymouth.

James II, for his part, fled to France. This gave the French a much sought after opportunity, and they were quick in attempting to reinstate James. As a spearhead for their plans, an army was landed in Ireland. Their efforts would almost certainly have been crowned with success had they made better use of their navy. However, this was not to be. Their activities were marked by numerous strategic errors. By 1690, the Boyne had seen the defeat of their Irish venture, and whilst the war continued for another seven years, its outcome was obvious to all but the French king. England had now gained mastery of the sea, and she was not to lose this prized possession until our own century.

Even while the French were being engaged in battle, much needed reconstruction work was being undertaken at Chatham. These improvements included the addition of numerous stores, a mast pond constructed upon further land taken up from the 1685 lease, smitheries, forges and offices. In more detail, and taking the chronicle of changes to a few years prior to the reign of William III, these alterations were as follows. In 1686 work was completed on a brick storehouse measuring 660 feet. Situated in the ropery, it was completed at a cost of £5,324.1s.7d. In the same year ten new mast houses were completed and each measured 112 feet by 17 feet. Their total cost was £2,020. Another particularly expensive item was the new mast pond. Close to the river front, it was constructed upon reclaimed marshland. An interesting feature of this mast pond was that it had thirty-two brick arches which kept the masts permanently submerged. The total cost was £3,180.4s.4d. and this included the important excavation work, two pairs of gates, wharfing slips and the arches. Next to the mast pond, a new mast house was constructed, costing a further £872. As the mast pond represented an extension, it was soon enclosed by the dockyard wall, giving Chatham a total river frontage of 3,500 feet. In her visit to Chatham, in 1697, Celia Fiennes recorded her impressions of the dockyard and, more particularly, the new mast pond:

' . . . I saw severall large shipps building others re-fitting; there was in one place a sort of arches like a bridge of brick-work, they told me the use of it was to let in the water there and so they put their masts into season.'

(The Journeys of Celia Fiennes)

Other, less extensive alterations carried out between 1688 and 1698 were a number of additional buildings constructed of either brick or timber. Included amongst these was a store for cordage, an oarmakers' shop (timber, valued at £8), a smiths' shop (timber, valued at £133), a painters' shop (timber, valued at £43), a new anchorage forge (valued at £93) and wooden capstan cranes constructed along the waterfront. Two substantial brick residences were also built, one for the surgeon and one for his assistant. Each had wooden extensions which, in the case of the surgeon's house included two porches, a surgery and a privy. Both houses were valued at £388 each.

These important improvements which took place during the latter part of the seventeenth century naturally increased the capacity of Chatham dockyard. Not only that, but also allowed Chatham the opportunity of retaining its premier position amongst the royal dockyards. Whereas the other four established dockyards could only muster five dry docks between them, Chatham could boast four of her own. Whilst Chatham was able to build five major warships at the same time, Portsmouth, Deptford and Woolwich could build only eight between them. Furthermore, the new storehouses and workshops at Chatham were far superior to those of the other yards.

Unfortunately for Chatham, however, its superiority over the other yards was not to remain unchallenged. The new century was to bring a great number of wars, of which France was invariably the enemy. Battlegrounds changed, with the Atlantic, and eventually the Mediterranean, being the future theatres of war. Chatham, of course, was somewhat ill-placed when compared with the other royal dockyards. Portsmouth began to expand and, within a few years, was able to boast a greater workforce than that at Chatham. Plymouth, too, grew rapidly. Established in 1691 it had, by 1703, a workforce just under half that employed at Chatham. By mid-century this had expanded so that it was about equal to Chatham. However, it was the American wars which really gave Plymouth its importance so that by the 1770s it too was larger than Chatham.

Not that Chatham ceased to have an important role to perform. Increasingly it was seen as a dockyard most suited to constructing the nation's warships and less suited to fitting out fleets during times of mobilisation. The result was that many of the nation's greatest warships — including the *Victory* — were to be built there. The dockyard at Chatham had lost one task, but was to take on a new and equally important role.

1. In 1653 the British Admiralty had adopted the battle line, with each ship rated according to its fire power. A first rate, therefore, was a ship of ninety guns or more, whilst a second rate had over eighty.
2. Laid up.
3. Careening. A nautical term which refers to the cleaning of a ship's hull.

Chapter Six

THE AGE OF FIGHTING SAIL

'The buildings here are indeed like the ships themselves, surprisingly large, and in their several kinds beautiful: The warehouses, or rather streets of warehouses, and storehouses for laying up the naval treasures are the largest in dimension, and the most in number that are anywhere to be seen in the world. The ropewalk for making cables, and the forges for anchors and other iron work, bear a proportion to the rest; as also the wet dock for keeping masts, and yards of the greatest size, where they lye in the water to preserve them . . . '

Daniel Defoe, during a visit to Chatham dockyard c. 1720.

The eighteenth century was a period in which war became an increasingly frequent phenomenon. England always seemed to be in conflict with at least one of her European rivals and, as often as not, this was France. Unlike the previous century, naval warfare now ceased to be restricted only to that small area which existed between England and the continental mainland. Instead, fleet actions started to centre upon either the Mediterranean or to be far out in the Atlantic.

The first of these more distant naval conflicts resulted from a number of rival claims to the Spanish throne. Known, in history, as the War of the Spanish Succession, it lasted from 1702 until 1713. It was during this war that a British fleet first operated in the Mediterranean, successfully capturing Gibraltar as an advanced base for future activities in this area. In the War of Jenkins' Ear, 1739 to 1748, which was, in fact, the maritime side of the War of Austrian Succession, much of the fighting centred around the Caribbean. The peculiar title of this war, comes from Richard Jenkins who, as master of the Glasgow brig *Rebecca,* claimed that while trading in Central America, he had his left ear removed by Spanish officials. The ear, subsequently preserved in a jar of pickle, was eventually displayed to an aghast House of Commons. In this particular round of hostilities, such Admirals as Vernon, Anson and Hawke, all jostle with one another for their individual claims to fame. Perhaps Vernon can be considered the winner. His eccentric cloak, made of grogram, a kind of silken fabric, bestowed upon him the title of 'Old Grog'. And with this latter name he passed into posterity when he introduced the navy's rum ration.

The Seven Years War (1756-1763) was, for England, the most satisfying of the eighteenth century naval escapades. It was the war in which the Royal Navy gained absolute supremacy, whilst Canada was established as a British possession. The fleet found itself engaged in action off the American coastline, in the Bay of Biscay, the Mediterranean and in the Indian Ocean. As an active fighting force, it could do little wrong. The year 1759 saw such a complete series of victories that a first rate, then being built at Chatham, had its name given in honour of the year — she was called *Victory*. Following the Seven Years War came the War of American Independence, and a conflict mostly fought in the Atlantic. It resulted in the loss of the American colonies, and it was at least one war which did not reach a conclusion for which the British government strived.

During the eighteenth century the Royal Navy was always expected to achieve victory — no matter what the odds. That British warships did achieve quite considerable successes was, in no small way, a result of the men who sailed in them. But rarely was the ordinary seaman given a fitting reward. He was very badly paid, and what he did receive was usually much in arrears. Further, his living conditions rank as amongst the worst imaginable. The seamen's quarters, on board ship, were cramped and overcrowded. They were thrown together in tiny dark areas which did not even provide sufficient standing room. Even worse, the allocated sleeping area was only fourteen inches! Soap was not issued; drinking water always had scum floating on it; food was stale, underweight and usually quite inedible. Navy peas, for example, were most frequently likened to the lead shot issued for hand guns, and this only after they had been boiled for an entire day. No wonder the press gangs were becoming an increasingly common sight in Chatham!

During these numerous eighteenth century naval wars, the emphasis slowly moved away from the large first rate, which had been so much a product of the royal dockyards during the previous century. Instead, the Admiralty began to demand an increasing number of third rates and frigates. The third rates specified, were usually of seventy-four guns and showed themselves to be considerably more manoeuvrable than the larger three deckers. Even more important, though, a properly trained gun crew could quite easily match, shot for shot, the larger enemy warships, even those of 100 guns.

The frigate, which usually mounted 32 guns, was of course even smaller, but made up for this in terms of speed and ease of handling. As such, they were a much prized command. Usually acting as scout ships they permitted a free hand to anyone fortunate enough to captain such a vessel. The first of the 32-gun frigates to be constructed at Chatham was the *Pearl* which was launched in 1762. The term frigate, though, actually dates to the seventeenth century, with the *Constant Warwick*, launched at Chatham in 1646, being accorded the title of first English frigate. According to Pepys, she was a speedy and sleek little vessel, being built on the lines of a Dunkirk privateer. Later, the term frigate was applied to any fast ship of great strength.

For the dockyard at Chatham, it is possible to divide the eighteenth century into three distinct phases. The first lasted until 1720, when the on-going improvement programme, started during the previous century, was completed. A second phase, lasting until the end of the American war, saw little or no money being expended upon the dockyard at Chatham. This period of over sixty years meant that Chatham, by the end of it, was in a semi-derelict state. Most of the yard buildings had been allowed to decay, with docks and building slips considered

A nineteenth century engraving of the main gate. Built in 1720 its two wings once provided accommodation for the yard porter and boatswain. As well as the original gatehouse, part of the eighteenth century wall also survives, but can only be seen from within the yard itself.

to be more than a little unsafe. Whilst money was being found to improve both Plymouth and Portsmouth yards, Chatham was simply allowed to rot. It was still considered of importance, but was not in a position to compete with the inexhaustible demands made by these other dockyards.

The final phase into which the eighteenth century can be divided, consists of the last two decades of that century. This was a period in which much-needed rebuilding was carried out. Docks were improved, storehouses added, a completely new ropeyard built and numerous workshops renovated. The result of all this, was that Chatham was well situated to take on France in one final twenty-three year conflict.

The changes which came to the dockyard at the beginning of the century are of particular interest as many of these buildings still remain. In brief, the additional buildings of this period include Medway House (1703), the Anchor Wharf Store (1719), Main Gate (1720), the Clocktower Store (1722), the Hemp House (1729), the Sail Loft (1734) and the Officers' Terrace (1722-1731). Of these, the most familiar structure is, undoubtedly, the Main Gate. It was during the years 1718 to 1720 that the dockyard was given a new and much higher wall. To this, during the final year of building, was added the Main Gate, which is so dated upon its inner face. In appearance, it has an obvious Vanbrugh influence resulting from the massive arches, towers and otherwise military details.

Medway House, which also still remains, was formerly the residence of various dockyard commissioners. Constructed during the early years of Queen Anne's

The commissioner's house, which is the oldest surviving building in the dockyard, as it appeared during the latter days of naval occupancy.

reign, it is typical of this era both in style and general appearance. Built in plum brick, it is of three storeys and has a very fine internal staircase. Regarding this area of the house, there is a particularly impressive ceiling, located above the stairs, and painted by Sir James Thornhill, a master decorator of that time. It depicts Neptune crowning Mars. Perhaps a little over elaborate, it clearly demonstrates, however, the extremities of lifestyle then prevailing. While the commissioner lived a life of opulent luxury, both seamen and dockyard workers were deprived of all but the most basic essentials.

In 1731 the new officers' terrace was completed. It replaced a row of rather aged houses which dated back to the 1620s. In all, twelve houses were constructed, and they remain to this day. Set apart from the rest of the dockyard, they stand peacefully in their own tree-lined avenue. At one time the large porches to be found in front of these houses were used by the porters employed to carry sedan chairs. This was the means by which the yard officers were able to tour the dock-yard without suffering any undue strain. That the houses are so large results from the numerous servants that each officer was allowed.

The sail loft of 1734 still remains as does the hemp house of 1729. This later building, which can be found close to the ropehouse and was used for the storage of raw hemp, has also seen a number of later extensions. Another building to be altered in later years was the clocktower store, originally completed with a timber-built upper floor and ground level saw pits.

As already indicated the eighteenth century saw a considerable reverse in the fortunes of Chatham dockyard. A small amount of cash was injected into the yard after the Seven Years War, when two new building slips were erected. Additionally, in 1753, new mast houses and a mould loft were also constructed. The mast houses, of which there were originally eight, and linked to form one

A further view of the officers' terrace and this time showing the large porches that were supposedly used to accommodate waiting chairmen and linkboys for sedan chairs.

The officers' terrace as completed in 1731. They were originally built to accommodate the first* and second* master attendants, the master caulker, the master shipwright*, the clerk of the cheque*, yard surgeon, the first and second assistant master shipwrights, clerk of the ropeyard, master ropemaker, clerk of the survey* and storekeeper*. Those marked with an asterisk were given the slightly larger houses that are to be easily identified by the more decorative designs incorporated into their upper façades.

The mast houses of 1753. Adjacent to the South Mast Pond, a mould loft was added over the central bays.

complete structure, were used both for the dry storage of masts and the shaping of the huge timbers. For purposes of convenience these mast houses were sited close to the mast pond. It was here that the massive mast timbers were kept submerged that they might be properly seasoned before transfer to the mast house. The mould loft was actually constructed on top of the two central mast houses and was used for laying down the full-scale plan of any ship under construction. From this plan templates would be cut, and timbers accordingly shaped. Because the planned outline of a ship was scribed, or chalked, onto the floor of the mould loft, such a building had to be of a suitable length. As the dockyard had only limited space, then it was usual for such structures to be placed on other buildings (such as a mast house) in the form of a loft.

A map of the dockyard, dated 1746, gives the dockyard area as 61 acres and 1 rod; this map indicates a planned extension of the boathouse, but later maps show this work was never carried out. Shortly after the building of the two new slips, the yard was further extended on its northern boundary, bringing the total area of the yard to 68 acres. Within this area of reclaimed marshland, a small mast pond was constructed (there were now three) together with a reed house, whilst an area of open space was put over to the storage of timber.

Compared with the other yards, however, reconstruction work at Chatham, during this period, was negligible. At both Portsmouth and Plymouth improvements were made throughout the century, with the result that both soon exceeded Chatham in facilities and numbers employed. Whereas the Seven Years War, which

A more general view of Chatham dockyard as it appeared in 1755. Amongst buildings to be seen are three of the watch towers (b) in the dockyard wall together with a large group of boat houses (e). The fully rigged ships in the foreground (a) are guardships whilst the roofed hulk is a quarantine ship. Upon the slipway is a 20-gun ship under construction with two further vessels in dry dock.

The clocktower storehouse of 1723. Originally established at a time when additional storage space was required nearer the docks and slips, it replaced an earlier sail and rigging loft. A mould loft was included in the upper storey.

had brought with it the realisation that the various yards were unable to supply sufficient ships in an emergency, led to two new building slips at Chatham, it brought to Portsmouth and Plymouth far more. In 1764, orders were issued by the Admiralty, then under the Earl of Egmont, which were to transform totally both yards. At Portsmouth the proposed cost was £352,240.4s.3d. and it was to include further docks, building slips, various workshops and landing wharves. At Plymouth, the improvement plan included a new rigging house, sail loft, stores, mast ponds, a dry dock and wharves. During this same period large sums of money were also expended upon Deptford, Woolwich and Sheerness. Deptford, at this time, received a new mast house, mast pond and building slip and all constructed on new land recently added to the dockyard there.

The factor chiefly responsible for the long term neglect of Chatham dockyard was the constant shoaling of the river Medway. During the eighteenth century this became a very real problem. In 1702, for instance, nearly £2,000 was invested in a project for deepening the river, but all this proved quite ineffective. The problem was no better by 1724, when the commissioner at Chatham complained of the difficulties involved in the navigation of capital ships using the River Medway. In 1745 the Admiralty took a hand when they:

'Resolved that orders . . . be sent to the Navy Board, to appoint such persons as they shall judge most proper to take a careful and exact survey of the River Medway, and report their opinions for our information, what methods may be most effectually taken for rendering the navigation thereof convenient and most safe for the Great Ships . . . '

The problem, however, was more than simply that of navigation. In former years it had been customary to use the Medway for the laying-up of the nation's major warships. By the middle of the eighteenth century this was no longer practicable, unless the larger vessels were only lightly ballasted. The Admiralty, though, was reluctant to consider this solution owing to the fact that wooden ships, allowed to ride high in the water, simply rot.

In 1771 it was reported:

'It is found on enquiry that the depth of water in this port is scarcely adequate for the draught of the capital ships built according to the present estimates, as few of them can have the proper quantity of ballast on board, and remain constantly on float. The consequence of which is very apparent by their sheir which weakens them greatly and makes them sooner unfit for service.'

A survey of 1774 also made this same point when it considered a number of ships then lying in ordinary:

'The moorings for ships laid up there extend from a little below Rochester bridge, to the lower part of Gillingham Reach, and extend of about 4 miles, within that space there is only five moorings for ships of 74 guns and upwards where there is water sufficient for them to lay up and swing or float at low water in Spring tides if they are properly ballasted, but there is for 20 such

One of the few buildings to be completed in the mid-century period is the guardhouse which was originally designed to accommodate marines who, for a short period, were responsible for dockyard security.

ships if they are kept at light draught of water but this is very prejudiced to them.'

To all this must be added the general difficulties of navigating the Medway's somewhat crooked course. Ships might well take some three weeks to travel the eight short miles which separate Chatham from Sheerness. With such a situation prevailing, it meant that Chatham could no longer be regarded as the most convenient of dockyards for the cleaning, repairing and refitting of the nation's warships. Furthermore, the establishment of a dockyard at the mouth of the Medway also strengthened the Admiralty's reluctance to make full use of Chatham. Instead, the cruisers of the North Sea fleet were cleaned at Sheerness and only dispatched to Chatham if major repairs were found necessary.

Yet, despite all that has been said, Chatham was not a small dockyard. Nor was it thought of as such by the Admiralty. Certainly, when output is taken into consideration, it was still as important as ever, 'except for the speedy equipment of great ships'. Rarely was the dockyard under-employed. Invariably the building slips were bustling centres of activity, and always occupied by ships in their varying stages of construction. Likewise the dry docks. They, too, were in constant demand as ships were brought in to undergo their annual or triennial refits. As an example of its continuing importance one need only consider the very high proportion of naval ships constructed at Chatham. In 1774, for instance, of the twenty first and second rates in existence, exactly half were built at

Chatham. As further proof of the dockyard's not inconsiderable value, one should note that throughout the eighteenth century, Chatham witnessed, on average, one new launching every year. Now this might not sound much until it is realised that a warship of this era might take anything up to four years to complete, whilst the *Victory* remained in the stocks for nearer six years. Admittedly a war-time emergency would see ship construction hurried along, but even in years of peace Chatham readily found employment for a truly immense workforce.

Not surprisingly, Chatham was the largest employer of civilian labour through-out the entire south-east of England. At the beginning of the century, in 1701, Chatham dockyard employed just over a thousand workers. For a time this was a peak figure, and fell to around the seven hundred mark in 1718. After that it steadily began to rise again, so that by 1756 the dockyard was employing a work-force in excess of one thousand seven hundred. In 1770, a peacetime year, this figure had fallen back to 1,378 but, ten years later, it reached 1,632. During the final year of that century, 1799, there were over two thousand employed at the dockyard.

The workforce employed at Chatham varied considerably, but basically there were three different types of workers. White collar, skilled artisan and the unskilled. In 1774 a particularly accurate breakdown of the workforce indicates that there were twenty-one yard officers and twenty clerks employed. The skilled workers such as shipwrights, caulkers, smiths and housecarpenters formed the bulk of the yard, and there were about nine hundred of these. Also employed were a number of semi-skilled workers such as forty-six riggers and ninety-eight sawyers. Of unskilled labourers the yard employed about two hundred and fifty.

Naturally, with the dockyard employing such large numbers, a great many people were attracted into the Medway Towns. Sometimes they were employed directly by the dockyard, and at other times by one of the many secondary industries associated with shipbuilding. One such alternative employer was the victualling yard, which stood at the north end of Chatham High Street, and kept the fleet supplied with essential foodstuffs. It had a cooperage, pickling house, a bakery and numerous stores. Elsewhere, there were the merchant yards who frequently undertook repair for the navy, and found it advantageous to be near a government dockyard. One such, was the company of Greaves and Nicholson, based at Frindsbury. They were responsible for refitting a number of warships whilst they also constructed the 74-gun *Bellerophon*, of 1786, and the *Spy* of 1776. Another large firm based in the Medway Towns was owned by the Best family. They were concerned with the brewing of beer, often supplying it to the victualling yard, but also responsible for the supply of nearly fifty public houses in Chatham alone.

The eighteenth century placed a tremendous strain upon the town of Chatham. An investigation of baptismal records indicates a truly remarkable growth in its size. Between 1620 and 1720, for instance, the number of recorded baptisms, per year, multiplied five fold. Thus, in the 1620s, there were 42.2 baptisms per year, but in the 1720s the average had risen to about 201 per year. It is, of course, possible to go a little further than this. Referring to the poor rate returns, these indicate that in the year 1720 there were over eleven hundred houses in Chatham. Using this information, and assuming the level of occupancy to be of around five or six, it is possible to suggest that Chatham had a population of 6,500 at this time.

In terms of population, one is on slightly firmer ground with the national census of 1801. This gives the total population for Chatham as being 10,505. Yet even this is not strictly accurate. It is merely an assessment of the civilian population. In that year Chatham also had a large military presence. This particular census ignores the naval personnel lodged in the various hulks, it ignores the numerous prisoners of war also in these same hulks and it ignores all those soldiers billeted either in the town, or in the two military barracks. These were the marine barracks situated immediately to the south of the dockyard, and Chatham barracks. The marine barracks had accommodation for over six hundred men, with any additional number being billeted in the various public houses. The Chatham barracks had room for two infantry battalions, two companies of foot artillery together with two infirmary blocks. In all, it could house 2,632 men.

This huge military presence was not unconnected with the dockyard. Since the days of the Spanish Armada troops had been stationed along the Medway to defend the dockyard. Usually these troops were stationed at Upnor Castle or the various other forts and batteries built in the aftermath of the Dutch raid. In 1715, however, a much more ambitious scheme was proposed for the defence of the dockyard. The idea was that the entire yard should be enclosed by a series of forts and embankments later known as the Cumberland, or Chatham Lines. These defences, of which construction did not start until 1756, were to stretch from the Gun Wharf, out towards Gillingham, enclosing the community of Brompton, and then returning to the river at a point immediately to the north of the dockyard. As completed in 1758 they consisted of a line of earthwork bastions with ditches and ramparts. Before the end of the century the Amherst and Townsend redoubts had been added.

It was these improved defences that prompted the construction of Chatham barracks. With large numbers of troops permanently needed to man the Lines, it became necessary to institute a more permanent billeting arrangement.

The Chatham dockyard worker preferred, where possible, to live in close proximity to his place of work. As such, there was a great demand for building land, and accommodation, in that area which lay closest to the dockyard. Not surprisingly, this explains the rather sudden growth of Brompton. Situated behind the dockyard it was, at the beginning of the eighteenth century, one of the few areas relatively undeveloped. Indeed, a map of 1698 clearly indicates that there was no housing in this area at all. Yet, by 1719, according to a further map, extensive land development had occurred. One of the first buildings in the area was the 'Sunne in the Wood', a public house which dates to 1705. That the development of Brompton continued at a rapid pace is confirmed by the 1756 dockyard map which indicates considerable new building. In this map, six streets are named: High Street, Wood Street, Middle Street, West Court Street, Prospect Row and River Row. Of Brompton, Hasted, writing towards the end of the eighteenth century, states:

'. . . consisting of about 400 houses, most of which have been erected within the memory of persons now living, and from its pleasantness and near situation, to the dockyard is continually increasing.'

Brompton was also a more prosperous area than Chatham, and tended to be occupied by the dockyard officials and the better paid artisans. Number fifteen Prospect Row, for instance, was the home, for many years, of Thomas Hamond, master blacksmith in the dockyard.

Not all dockyard workers lived in Brompton by any means. The outskirts of Chatham were within easy walking distance of the dockyard, with Smithfield Banks being the nearest residential area. This was a very bleak and poor area. It consisted of King Street, Queen Street and Cross Street, and was undoubtedly the poorest area of Chatham. Insanitary conditions prevailed, whilst the streets were unlit and the houses in a very poor state of repair. During the seventeenth century the Banks had been the residential area occupied by dockyard officials, but Chatham's rapid development led such middle class individuals to vacate their more centrally located properties. These once palatial houses were sub-divided, tenemented and generally succumbed to the process of inner city decay. Of the various dockyard workers, only the very poorest chose to live there.

Slightly further away from the dockyard is the High Street. By the middle of the eighteenth century this formed one solid block of housing stretching some two miles. It, too, was occupied by a large number of dockyard workers. A cosmopolitan area of the town, it housed both affluent artisans and poorer labourers. Referring to the High Street, Hasted felt prompted to write:

'It is like most sea ports, a long, narrow, disagreeable, ill-built town, the houses in general occupied by those trade adapted to the commerce of the shipping and sea faring person, the Victualling Office, and the two breweries being the only tolerably built houses in it.'

Another area of recent development was the Brook. This stood between the High Street and Smithfield Banks. According to Hasted, once again:

'It consists of a long row of houses, which have of late been greatly increased with streets leading from them up the hill, about the middle of which, at some distance from all others, is a number of houses, built closely together, called Slicket's Hill, so as to form a little town of itself. It is exceeding populous, owing to its numerous connections with the several departments of government, and the shipping business carried on at it.'

The dockyard worker could also turn to the parish of Gillingham for accommodation. A solution which, incidentally, became increasingly common towards the end of the eighteenth century. Whilst the village of Gillingham was situated

some two miles from the dockyard, the outskirts of the actual parish were somewhat nearer. Hasted, in noting this, comments on that part of Gillingham nearest
the dockyard and declares it:

'. . . mostly inhabited by persons belonging to the dockyard and other departments of government belonging to it; or by those who have belonged to the
royal navy; and have retired from the service.'

This, then, was where the Chatham dockyard worker lived and worked.
Chatham became uniquely theirs. Probably thirty per cent of all families gained
their livelihood from the dockyard, with a great many more connected to the
secondary industries. Many of these workers originated from London. They
brought with them their harsh cockney accents, with the original Kentish burr
disappearing from the town of Chatham. The 'Chatham cockneys' had taken
over. Apart from accents, the design of houses was influenced by the dockyard.
Dockyard timber, either pilfered or removed legally, became the major building
material.

The dockyard also affected the morality of the town. Church attendance was
limited, whilst prostitution was rife. Chatham had a particularly high female
population, and many of them were country girls attracted by rich pickings.
When a warship drew into Chatham, boatloads of females would soon be in
attendance. The sailor, home from the sea might have three years wages to spend.
These 'virtuous' young ladies would soon help him spend it!

This was eighteenth century Chatham. It was not a place in which many would
choose to live. Those who did so, lived there because it provided them with a
livelihood. It was an ill-planned and unhealthy town. There was no town council,
and no central control. If one wanted to build a house, a tiny space was simply
found and the house accordingly erected. Thus, overcrowding occurred. Some of
those involved in the property market had no scruples. They built two roomed
houses, back to back, with communal toilets in the nearest courtyard. Perhaps a
hundred people might have to use these 'necessaries' as they were frequently
termed. The demand for housing meant that such property would soon be let at
some kind of extortionate rent.

The compensation for living in this dirty, ugly, town was the certainty of a
secure job. The dockyard, come peace or war, rarely laid off its established workforce. In peace time it was inclined to employ more than actually needed, but
this was a good policy. This inflated workforce would certainly be needed during
the next war . . . and the next . . .

So this was Chatham. It was a Chatham that few loved, but most accepted. It
was a fact of life. Further, in eighteenth century England there were many other
towns like it. Chatham was no worse, and because of the secure wages brought
by steady employment, it was a town a lot better than some.

Chapter Seven

VICTORY: A CHATHAM BUILT SHIP

'It will always be said of us with unabated reverence, "They built ships of the line". Take it all in all, a Ship of the line is the most honourable thing that man, as a gregarious animal, has ever produced.'

John Ruskin

To a great many people it comes as an undoubted surprise when told that the *Victory*, the nation's most famous warship, was a product of the dockyard at Chatham. Many people, of course, tend to associate this vessel with Portsmouth. Yet, this is one honour which cannot be claimed by that particular dockyard.

Launched at Chatham in 1765, the *Victory* was to remain in the Medway for a further twelve years. Unlike warships of today she was not given an immediate commission. There was no need. Her design was unlikely to become obsolete, whilst the country was not in the habit of maintaining a large peace time fleet. Instead, temporarily unwanted warships entered the ordinary. This was what happened to the *Victory*. Her services were simply not required at the time she was launched. Instead, she was allowed to ride at anchor in the Medway, and it was not until 1778 that her skills were eventually called upon.

Later still, in 1797, she was to return to the Medway, not as a warship, but in the guise of hospital ship. This, for the *Victory*, must have been a particularly sad era. Anchored off Gillingham, her decks were crammed with hundreds of French and Dutch prisoners. She was no ordinary hospital ship, as hers was the role of tending to the enemy sick and wounded. For these poor and dejected individuals, many miles from home, survival was only a very remote possibility. Weakened by their wounds, undernourished and prone to debilitating attacks of 'marsh fever', the death toll amongst these brave souls was enormous. As a fact, this can simply be borne out by reference to the numerous entries to be found in the parish burial register — for most of these pathetic individuals were buried in the churchyard at Gillingham.

As a hospital ship, the *Victory* served but a very short career. In 1799, orders were given for her conversion into a prison hulk. If these instructions had been fulfilled, then this would have been the last heard of Nelson's future flagship. Once converted to a hulk, there was no possibility of her ever returning to sea. Fortunately though, a reprieve was issued. Instead, new orders stated that she was to be re-built. Thus, in 1800, she re-entered the dockyard at Chatham and emerged, some several months later, a superb fighting ship and ready to take on the nation's enemies. Chatham had been the dockyard to build her, and Chatham was the dockyard that prepared her for Trafalgar. What further epitaph could be needed to extol the skills of all those who worked in this eighteenth century dockyard?

HMS *Victory*.

(Ministry of Defence)

It was in December 1758 that the commissioner at Chatham dockyard, then Thomas Cooper, a post captain, was first informed that a new first rate was to be built at Chatham. He was instructed:

'. . . to prepare to set up a new ship of 100 guns as soon as a dock shall be available for the purpose.'

At that time, of course, money had only just been voted by parliament for the construction of this, and eleven other vessels of lesser rates. It was, therefore, going to be some time before the actual work of building the ship could begin. At this moment there was still a great deal of preparatory work that had to be undertaken.

The building of a new first rate was a rare occurrence. Indeed, throughout the entire eighteenth century the Admiralty ordered only ten preferring, instead, smaller and more manoeuvrable warships. Nevertheless, such ships were the marvel of their age. Nothing afloat could compare. Such vessels were usually built as flagships, with no more than two being in commission at any one time. And, if one bears in mind that the complement of such ships was 850 men, then such a policy appears sound. It was for this reason that the first rates saw little service outside of European waters, and rarely strayed beyond the Baltic and Black Sea.

In their day, the first rate was a truly massive vessel, being constructed from the timber of over four thousand oak trees. In battle she was quite impregnable. The three extensive gun decks were able to carry the largest ordnance available for sea going ships. The lower deck carried 42-pounders, the middle deck 24-pounders and the upper deck 12-pounders. This resulted in a broadside of 1,176 pounds. No other ship could match such a tremendous fire power. Even second rates, which carried 90-guns, were simply no match. Severely limited in the size of ordnance available to them, they could produce only an 812 pound broadside. Not surprisingly, then, no English first rate was captured throughout that century. Moreover, the one French first rate to be captured, the 104-gun *Ville de Paris,* which struck at the Battle of Saintes (1780), only did so after six major warships had concentrated their combined fire power upon her. Even then she only lowered her colours once all her shot had been spent.

The new 100-gun warship ordered to be built at Chatham was to be constructed on the same lines as the *Royal George,* a first rate launched at Woolwich in 1756. It had been designed by Thomas Slade, senior surveyor of the navy, and was considered a highly satisfactory vessel. Nor was it unusual for one ship to be based on the draught of an earlier successful design. Perhaps more surprising, though, is the number of years over which one draught layout would be used. The essential design for the *Victory* dates to the establishment of 1746, and it was this same basic layout, if somewhat amended, which was used for two second rates ordered in 1801 and two first rates ordered in 1812 and 1813.

It was in early June 1760 that the plans, or sheer draught, for the, as yet un-named, first rate, were received at Chatham:

71

Victory as she appeared in the early years of the present century. Then one of the oldest ships still afloat, she had long since been commandeered as flagship of the Portsmouth command. By 1922, however, the state of her timbers had become a matter of some concern and, for this reason, she was brought into dry dock for eventual restoration.

The clocktower mould loft. Built during the 1720s it is thought, by some, that the lines of *Victory* were laid off within this building. However, it should be pointed out that it has also been suggested that her lines were actually laid upon the floor of the mast house mould loft.

'Sheer draught proposed for building a First Rate ship of 100 guns at H.M. Yard at Chatham pursuant to an order from the Rt. Hon. Lords Commissioner of the Admiralty of 13th December last and of the dimensions undermentioned viz.,

Length of the gun deck 186 ft
Length of the keel for tonnage 151 ft. 3 ⅝ in.
Breadth moulded 50 ft. 6 in.
Breadth extreme 51 ft. 10 in.
To carry on the lower deck 30 guns of 42 pounds
To carry on the middle deck 28 guns of 24 pounds
To carry on the upper deck 30 guns of 12 pounds
To carry on the after deck 10 guns of 6 pounds
To carry on the forecastle 2 guns of 6 pounds
Admiralty Office.'

Detailed preparations were now put in hand at Chatham. From the sheer draught, which was drawn to a one-forty-eighth scale, a full size plan of the ship had to be drawn up. This would be scribed into the floor of the mould loft and, from the evidence available, it appears that some of the lines of the *Victory* can still be seen located on the floor of the Clocktower mould loft. At least this is the feeling of the former dockyard authorities, as a plaque has been erected which declares that lines still visible are those of the self same *Victory*.

On 23rd July 1759, the keel of the *Victory* was laid in what is usually referred to as the Old Single Dock (present No. 2 dock). This was one of the original dry docks, being constructed in 1623. Usually, of course, ships were constructed on the various building slips, but first rates were too large for a normal slipway launch. Instead, it was far simpler for them to be built in dry dock and, when ready, the gates simply opened up and the ship gently floated out. But this part of the operation was far away. In this first year of construction, government estimates allowed £3,500 for the building of the *Victory*.

During the first few months of construction, progress was rapid. The war was still being fought, and there was an obvious need for such a ship. The building sequence went ahead in the time honoured fashion. After the laying of the first keel timber, others were added. In all, seven keel timbers were scarf jointed and measuring a total of 150 feet by 20 inches square. Then a stern post, which had to be a single piece of first class oak, was set into the keel. Following this, the stem, made up of several oak timbers, was placed into position. Other timbers were soon added, and the bare skeleton of the ship began to take shape. Many of these had names dating into the dim mists of time. There was the wing transom which was scarf jointed to the stern post; the deadwood, fitted to the top of the keel and so enabled the square frames to be attached to the keel; and the beak head, which was situated at the bow.

Once the basic core of the ship had been completed, work could begin on the frame. Shaped from the previously cut templates, these timbers formed a sort of ribbing throughout the entire ship and were the timbers to which the planking,

73

or skin, would later be attached. The first section of the frame that was laid, was the floor, and this ran at right angles to the keel. Following this, the 'futtocks' were bolted into the floor timbers. The 'futtocks' were the huge timbers which formed the sides of the ship. The lowest, or first 'futtock', was about level with the bilge and, as such, had to have a distinct upward curve. It was made from what was known as a 'compass' timber — an oak timber which had been naturally curved during growth.

With the frame complete, and locked into position, the entire entity was covered over and left to season. This was obviously a very important aspect of a ship's construction. The longer it was left to season, the stronger the finished product. For the *Victory*, this was quite an extensive period. Her original period of seasoning was extended, due to conclusion of hostilities which occurred during this time. The result was that the *Victory* stood in frame for nearly three years, and her extraordinarily long survival was undoubtedly due to this thorough period of seasoning. Certainly it can be pointed out that a number of other vessels, built at about the same time, but improperly seasoned, were recorded as being little more than rotting hulks after a lapse of no more than fifteen years. The *Victory*, on the other hand, was to last some while longer!

For the construction of the *Victory*, or any English man-of-war for that matter, four types of timber were needed: oak, elm, beech and fir. Of these, the most important was undoubtedly the oak, and more particularly that species which originated in England — *'Quercus Robur'*. The Navy Board felt that there was absolutely no substitute for English oak, with the counties of Kent, Hampshire and Surrey providing the best areas for its growth. Yet, by the middle of the eighteenth century there was a severe shortage of such timber.

Over the years, the oak growing areas of southern England had rarely been subjected to any far-sighted attempts at conservation. Chatham dockyard, alone, had been responsible for clearing many thousands of oak growing acres in Kent, and without a thought to their replacement. For constructing the *Victory*, however, dockyard officials had been just a little more fortunate. Her timbers had actually been set aside some years earlier, when plans had been put in hand for the construction of a first rate which had been subsequently cancelled. Much of this timber was too large for any other vessel, and had been stored until the dockyard was called upon to build another first rate. Nevertheless, for ships such as the *London* and *Ramillies*, which were also under construction at Chatham, the timber problem proved somewhat more serious. Finding suitable oak was becoming virtually impossible and delays, as a result, were considerable. Indeed, a number of Chatham built ships were completed with timber so recently cut, that it was still green in places. Naturally, such ships had a very short life span.

The timber purveyor at Chatham was constantly forced to search further and further afield. Normally oaks for the dockyard at Chatham were acquired from the Weald of Kent, but increasingly the search was taken to Essex and other areas not particularly noted for the quality of its oak. A further alternative was the increasing use of substitutes. Foreign oak was used for planking, whilst elm was frequently used below the water line where the exclusion of air allowed it to remain well preserved. Fir, on the other hand, was a little more versatile. It was possible to build an entire warship of fir, but it had a tendency to splinter in battle. More usually, this timber was preserved for the masts. Yet, even given these alternatives, they were no real replacement for the oak. It was not only the strongest of timbers, but in areas subjected to intermittent exposure to both moisture and air, only the oak was adequate.

Reliance on the English oak was considerable. Keel, frame and much of the planking was made from *'Quercus Robur'*. However, of all the various timbers in demand, the most difficult to acquire were the 'great' and 'compass' timbers. For the construction of a 100-gun ship, single oaks of forty feet, and with a twenty-eight inch diameter, were required. These were the 'great' timbers which went into the frame. As such, they were virtually impossible to obtain as most oaks were felled long before they reached such a size. To allow a tree to grow beyond eighteen inches in diameter was a considerable gamble. Well beyond their maturity, such trees were prone to decay. Landowners rarely wished to take such a risk. The compass timbers were equally difficult to obtain. Shaped by the weather, they were usually found only in the hedgerows, but could be shaped if a young tree was pinned down. Scarcest of all, though, were wing-transom knees, consisting of two long arms set almost at right angles. Such a tree had not only to be allowed growth beyond maturity, but its shape was very much a matter of chance.

Towards the end of 1762, work upon the *Victory* was due to be re-started, but progress within the dockyard was now at a much reduced pace. In November of that year, the Treaty of Paris was signed, it resulted in the following letter from the Navy Board:

'A preliminary treaty being signed towards a peace, these are to direct and require you to reduce all artificers, riggers, labourers etc., to single days work. And as in further consequence of this, reduction may be expected to be made of such men whose inability, indolence and neglect of duty render them improper to be continued in the yards in time of peace. You are immediately to examine the state of the workmen at Chatham and send us an account of such as come within the aforementioned descriptions, distinguishing their occupation, age, time of service, and character. And you are in the meantime to give public notice in the yard that any artificer, rigger or labourers as desire it may be forthwith discharged and paid the arrears of wages due to them, and such men as apply are hereby directed to be discharged accordingly.'

For the *Victory* this simply meant that she was to remain in frame until the autumn of 1763 when work, once again, started upon her construction.

It was at this point that the *Victory* really began to take shape. First the planking was added, both an inner and outer skin being necessary. Next came the decks, the deck planking and the figurehead. This latter was not made within the dockyard, but by William Savage who resided in the town of Chatham. The

A commemorative stone which stands inside Chatham dockyard marking the site where *Victory* was built. She was, in fact, floated out from the Old Single (present No. 2) Dock in May 1765.

specifications for this figurehead were remarkably complicated, as it was intended to display the totality of British seapower. Hardly surprising, though, as the very ship, herself, had been named after the 'Year of Victories' — 1759. In that year, the British army had triumphed at Surat, Minden and Quebec and the navy at Lagos and Quiberon Bay. The design laid down was for a group figurehead depicting both King George III and Britannia, whilst smaller figurines represented Envy, Discord and Faction. The highly complicated nature of the original figurehead (it was replaced in 1801) can be gauged from part of the Admiralty specification:

'A new large figure for the head cut in front at the upper with a bust of His Majesty, the head adorned with laurels, and the body and shoulders worked in rich armour, and his George hanging before; under the breast is a rich shield partly supporting the bust and surrounded with four cherubs' heads and winds representing the four winds smiling, gently blowing our successes over the four quarters of the globe.

'On the starboard side of the head piece the principal figure is the large drapery figure representing Britannia, properly crowned sitting on a rich triumphal arch and in one hand holding a spear enriched and the Union flag hanging down from it, and with the other hand supporting the bust of His Majesty, with one foot trampling down Envy, Discord and Faction represented by a fiend or hag . . .'

76

Although this figurehead no longer exists, the original carvers' model can be inspected at the National Maritime Museum.

As the *Victory* neared completion, additional material was set aside. Anchors, masts, sails and rigging were all prepared; most of these items being manufactured within the dockyard, but some having to come from elsewhere. Such was the case with the larger anchors, one of which, a colossal item of eighty-seven hundred weight was shipped down from Deptford. Also, from the other dockyards came 150 tons of ballast, necessary to keep the ship correctly balanced and properly settled during her days in ordinary.

Clearly the long building task was nearing completion. At the beginning of 1764, the exterior of the ship was ready for painting. This was subsequently carried out in March, when a concoction of white lead and linseed oil was used. Later, the interior was to be painted red. This was a simple expedient designed to conceal the full horrors of battle. It simply meant that blood stains would be more easily hidden, and the crew would not be discouraged from their duties.

For 1765, her year of launching, a further £8,089 was set aside in that year's estimates. Most of this was for rigging and stores. At the end of April the Admiralty was informed:

'The Master Shipwright of His Majesty's Yard at Chatham having acquainted us that His Majesty's Ship *Victory* building in the old single dock will be ready to launch the ensuing spring tides; we desire you will acquaint the Right Honourable the Lords Commissioner of the Admiralty that we have ordered her to be launched at that time accordingly; which we hope will meet with their Lordships approbation . . .'

Thus, on 7th May the *Victory* was duly launched. Doubtless it was a memorable occasion, but possibly tinged by the knowledge that this particular ship was destined not to be commissioned, but simply placed in ordinary until her services were eventually required. Up to that point in time expenditure upon the *Victory* totalled £63,176. 3s. 0d.

With the launching of the *Victory* the dockyard at Chatham entered into a period of depression. For one thing, the number of ships under construction was limited due to a short fall in timber stocks, whilst restrictions on government expenditure led to warships being infrequently repaired. Lay-offs at Chatham were also severe. At the height of the Seven Years War, some eighteen hundred had found employment at Chatham, but shortly after hostilities had ceased, this number was curtailed to thirteen hundred. On top of all this was the continued reluctance to expend any money upon much needed improvements to the very fabric of the yard. This was, perhaps, the worst aspect of all. It meant, quite simply, that the dockyard at Chatham was unable to carry out the work for which it was designed. As a dockyard, it had insufficient dry docks for the number of ships needing repair; inadequate building slips; a ropehouse in the final stages of decay and sub-standard storehouses which were quite unable to cater for the large amount of stores which had to be housed. Not to put too fine

Two hundred years after her launch the dockyard celebrated its most famous ship. The building which was used to house various associated exhibits was the original No. 2 slip which, in 1966, was destroyed by fire.

a point on it, the dockyard was in a shambles. What is more, all this was adequately demonstrated during the crisis that occurred in 1770.

Towards the end of that year a controversy arose over the frequently contested Falkland Islands. In June 1770 a large Spanish force captured the Islands, wresting power from a handful of British settlers. News did not reach England for several months, whilst later negotiations demonstrated Spanish desire for an all-out conflict. That they eventually backed down, and ceded possession, was due entirely to French reluctance to enter any possible war. For several months, though, war appeared to be a very real possibility. The dockyards were instantly involved in preparing a fleet — Chatham was no exception. In September alone, Chatham dockyard received orders to commission nine warships for Channel service. Yet, despite the urgency of the situation, Chatham yard was quite unable to do anything with these ships until December.

At that time, Chatham had four dry docks, but not one of them was available. The number three dock was under repair, being treated for severe rot, whilst the number two dock was engaged in repairing the hulk, *Chatham*. The other two docks were occupied by *Panther*, then being re-caulked, and the *Mercury*. The real point, though, was that Chatham was so short of docks that ships lying in ordinary were frequently left to rot for great lengths of time. This, in fact, was why the *Mercury* was in for repair. Originally surveyed in 1765 she had been found to be in need of small repairs. By April 1770, when she was at last dry docked, these repairs were no longer minor and were being classified as serious. Thus, when any emergency arose there was simply such a collection of ships in need of repair — not to mention the docks — that ships waiting to be fitted out (and often in a state of disrepair) had to wait lengthy periods before being docked. During the autumn of 1770 the *Albion, Buckingham* and *Orford* were each ordered to be sheathed but, at that time, there was clearly no dock available. Their ability to join the fleet was subsequently delayed.

The situation at Chatham was further compounded by the additional absence of a hulk fitted with suitable lifting gear. A hulk, fitted with sheers, was the normal method used for the setting of masts in the great ships. As a major dockyard, Chatham would normally be expected to have two of these available. However, due to the steady deterioration of the dockyard hulks, a further false economy, neither the *Chatham* nor the *Winchester*, were considered strong enough for the tasks now demanded of them. In fact it was the *Chatham* which occupied one of the dry docks, and would not be ready until 18th December.

Interestingly enough, it was the crisis over the Falkland Islands that allowed the then very young Horatio Nelson, to take his first glimpse of his future flagship, the *Victory*. The *Victory*, of course, was still lying at anchor in the Medway, but soon to be brought into dry dock for repairs. Nelson, on the other hand, was a twelve year old midshipman about to board his uncle's ship, *Raisonnable*. During this, his first visit to Chatham, Nelson managed to lose himself and was forced to seek directions from a naval officer. As it happens, this officer was a friend of Nelson's uncle, Maurice Suckling, and so he took the young boy home. Food and hot tea were supplied, before a boat was arranged for the ferrying of Nelson to his ship. At sometime during the day, he must have seen the *Victory*.

For Chatham, the sudden end to the Falkland crisis brought no relief to the dockyard's rather depressed state. One report of this period declared:

'. . . those (buildings) now there have been very good when first built but as this was the yard that has had no considerable building in it, such as remain of those that were first built are in a very decay'd state and must by degrees, as money can be spared from other services, be pulled down and rebuilt.'

But all this amounted to no more than promises. Promises that, at sometime in the future, something would be done about the dilapidated condition of a once fine dockyard. In fact, Chatham had to endure another war, and it was only when this had ended that the government started to direct the necessary finances which were to take care of the renewal and improvement programme that Chatham dockyard required.

Chapter Eight

LABOURERS AND ARTISANS:
THE SOCIAL BACKGROUND

'That your petitioners have long labour'd under the severest hardships from the insufficiency of their wages, to support their familys at this time particularly from the exorbitant price of every article of provision . . .'
Part of a petition submitted by the Chatham shipwrights to the Navy Board in February 1772. The original is to be found on display at the Rochester Guildhall Museum.

Throughout the eighteenth century, the royal dockyard at Chatham was the largest industrial enterprise in south-east England. As already noted, it had a workforce which often exceeded fifteen hundred, and so gives the dockyard considerable historic interest. This, combined with the great wealth of surviving documents which relate to the yard during this period, allows a complete evaluation to be made of the prevailing administrative framework. Of, perhaps, even greater significance, though, is that this material also provides a good starting point for a study of early industrial working conditions, and the response of the employee to these conditions. In other words, it is possible to chart the early history of trade unions during their first and formative years.

In the very early days, groups of workers only came together during a crisis. During the seventeenth century this usually revolved around non-payment of wages. Governments, in those days, often found themselves very short of money and, as an economy measure, avoided paying the wages of those employed. At Chatham, wages were often held up for two or three years, and the dockyard workers had to organise demonstrations in order to draw attention to the extreme poverty into which they had fallen. Over the years, things became more organised and some groups of workers began to forge links with other yards. At the same time leaders began to emerge and patterns of action were set. However, before progressing any further on this theme, some consideration should be given to the actual conditions of work.

Employment within the dockyard was particularly arduous. The hours were long, and the money inadequate. During summer the day lasted from sunrise until sunset, whilst in winter the set hours were 6 am to 6 pm. Breaks for breakfast and lunch were, however, allowed. Yet it was also a long week, for Saturday was a working day, with Sunday providing the only rest day. Also missing were all but a few paid holidays. Of these, there were four: Coronation Day, the King's Birthday, 5th November and 29th May. Yet, even on these days the Navy Board expected some work to be completed, and workers reported at 6 am, then worked until midday.

It should not, of course, be felt that these hours were longer than those worked elsewhere. These were very much the traditional hours, and their eventual reduction was the result of long hard-fought battles waged throughout the nineteenth century. On the matter of wages, the Navy Board was somewhat less than generous. Dockyard rates were by this time far below those paid by other employers. Not that this was very surprising, whereas other employers put up their wages every decade or so, dockyard wage levels remained unchanged for nearly a century. Originally set in 1690, they were to remain essentially unaltered until the late eighteenth century.

Of the various dockyard workers, it was, not unnaturally, the artisans who received the highest wages, with ordinary labourers receiving a much lower rate. Basic day wages are listed below:

	s.	d.
Shipwrights	2	1
Caulkers	2	1
Joiners	2	0
House carpenters	1	10
Plumbers	2	4
Riggers	1	6
Sailmakers	1	10
Bricklayers	1	8
Pitch heaters	1	3
Labourers	1	1
Quarter boys		8
Oakum boys		6

In addition to these wages, more could be earned in the way of overtime. For a shipwright, a two and a half hour period of extra work (known as a 'tyde') gave him an additional 7½d. For a labourer this same period of overtime earned him 4d.

That dockyard wage levels were far behind other employers in North Kent can be attested by reference to various accounts held in both the Kent Archives Office and the Royal Engineers Library, Brompton. James Best, the Chatham brewer, was, in 1780, paying his labourers 1/10d per day, whilst labourers employed by the Royal Engineers in constructing the Chatham Lines were being paid 1/6d. Even farm labourers, a traditionally low paid sector of the economy, were usually earning 1/6d per day. Nor was it simply amongst the labouring classes that this disparity existed. Amongst artisans a similar situation prevailed. Whereas a dockyard bricklayer earned 1/8d, James Best was paying 4/4d, and those employed on the Lines received 3/-d. This was, again, the case with shipwrights. Those employed within the royal dockyard received 2/1d, but those in the private shipyards, such as Greaves and Nicholson of Frindsbury, could earn in excess of 3/-d a day.

Clearly, then, the Chatham dockyard worker could consider himself underpaid. Yet, despite this, large numbers chose to remain in the dockyard. They did so because of other factors which made the low wages just a little more palatable. These included job security and a newly introduced pension scheme.

Life during the eighteenth century was harsh. Survival depended on a man's ability to work. Failure to acquire a living wage would soon result in a one way journey to the poorhouse. The dockyard, whilst not paying a high wage, was considered to be a good employer. Once an artisan or labourer had been taken on to the establishment he was unlikely to be dismissed. This was clearly important. Other employers might pay well, but they had little compunction about dismissing an entire workforce once further work was unavailable. This was not the case in the dockyard. A larger than necessary workforce was retained so that it was always ready for any emergency that might arise.

The other main benefit of dockyard work was the pension scheme. First introduced in the 1760s, it allowed old and infirm workers to retire from the yard on two-thirds of the basic pay. In many respects it was a great step forward, for the idea of retirement was, then, an unknown concept. Prior to its introduction, older workers had been kept on in the yard, carrying out lighter and more menial tasks. Not everyone, however, following the introduction of the pension scheme, was eligible for retirement. A quota system operated, and those who were chosen were very sad cases indeed. One such was William Linthall, a seventy year old shipwright who, in 1775, was reported as being incapable of carrying out any work due to a broken collar bone. William Parker, a sixty-seven year old labourer, was also unable to work due to a number of broken ribs. All these injuries had been gained whilst working in the dockyard.

Dockyard employees were also eligible to the perquisite of 'chips', small pieces of timber which they were allowed to carry out of the dockyard. Used for building purposes or as fire wood, they were supposed to be useless for dockyard purposes; timber too small for constructing ships. A limit of three feet was placed on the length of this wood, whilst each man was restricted to what he could carry under one arm. 'Chips', however, caused much controversy, as some dockyard workers were inclined to carry out whole timbers or spend a great amount of time sawing up good timber. The Navy Board was certainly aware of what was going on and, in 1767, stated:

> '. . . the Privileges of carrying out of chips could never be intended to extend to the carrying out of slab or useful timber, or to authorize the sale of real chips, any workman who shall be concerned in any of those practices for the future is to be dismissed.'

The reason for this declaration was that members of the Navy Board had visited Chatham during the summer of that year and had observed many workmen collecting large mounds of 'chips' for purposes of holding sales within the dockyard. Members of the Board were shocked, and proceeded to reprimand a number of dockyard officers:

> '. . . that the officers of the yards have not been so attentive and diligent as they ought to have been in remedying the abuses arising from the privileges of

chips. Their Lordships hope that the Reproof and Injunctions given to them on this head will have their due effect. They recommend, however, future attention to this object; and as the abuse has been suffered to increase at Chatham Yard more than any other, particularly by the accumulation of a very great quantity of chips. Many of them unlawful ones, near the dock gate for sale . . .'

The neat bundles of 'chips' which dockyard workers were supposed to carry under their arms also might be used for smuggling stores out of the dockyard. Hemp, iron, bolts and sail cloth were all considered 'fair game'. This kind of theft was aggravated by low pay, and an accounting system which only allowed the dockyard worker to be paid on a quarterly basis. Even then they were frequently paid late. Certainly the theft of dockyard stores was well established and highly organised. If, however, the miscreant was discovered then he was liable to dismissal. That many dockyard workers avoided such punishment resulted from a lack of enthusiasm shown by those employed in searching the yard workers as they left the gate. It was the same porters who were open to bribes should they detect a worker with illicit stores. However, the numbers involved in this, and other aspects of fraud, is often inclined to be exaggerated and should not be overstated.

Those employed as clerical officers have also been labelled with the tag of corruption. To a certain extent this also appears to have been exaggerated, used as a means of explaining both inadequacies in the supply of material together with general financial problems. Yet a degree of dishonesty certainly existed, there being a number of documented cases of clerks and their officers being bribed by merchants. Such individuals would then overlook the arrival of poor quality or short measure stores. In fact, this was often known as 'hampering', for the usual way of bribing a clerk was to present him with a hamper of wine.

In 1786, the degree of corruption was noted in the dockyards when Charles Middleton, then comptroller of the Navy, stated that:

'. . . the public suffers in thousands for a trifling gratuity received by a yard officer.'

Also, during this period, a report was issued which went into more detail:

'Having great reason to apprehend that frauds have been frequently committed in some of the yards by making addition or alterations to the warrants and notes for the issue of stores after the full quantity demanded have been inserted therein and signed . . .'

Much government money was also lost through time wasting. The labour force may have been within the confines of the dockyard for the greater part of the day, but they were rarely engaged in constant work. Such physical exertion would have been impossible. Instead, the pace of work within the dockyard was generally rather slow. Moreover, a number of individuals probably managed to avoid working altogether. Certainly it was not unknown for a man to muster in the morning, and spend the rest of the day at home. Others had favourite corners of the dock-yard, such as the area to the south, where time could be spent away from patrolling officers.

Another important aspect of the dockyard was the means by which it was kept secure. During the day porters were on duty at each gate. They were sup-posed to search any man leaving the yard, whilst preventing labourers and artisans leaving during work time. Their failure to carry out these duties has already been explained. During the hours of darkness a different system was in operation. Marines patrolled the dockyard, whilst trusted workers were employed as watch-men, warders and rounders:

> 'Two rounders every night to be stationed at each end of the yards where the Guard Houses are, the times of their going round the yards to be so contrived, that the Posts may be under as frequent visitation as possible by some of them. The Rounders are to see the posts relieved at the appropriate time. Any rounder that evades watching in his turn without giving sufficient reason to the officer of the Guard . . . is to be discharged.'

This system did not, however, prevent thefts being carried out. The long, and somewhat cluttered, waterfront made an undetected entry into the dockyard particularly easy. Even during war years, security was not that efficient. It was, however, tightened up in 1776 after a pro-American incendiarism — James Aitkin — created a massive fire in the dockyard at Portsmouth.

The amount of theft associated with the dockyard is, of course, impossible to calculate. However, from the records it does appear that at least two or three major incidents occurred in every year. Once stolen, dockyard property would soon find a ready buyer. Philip Day, a blacksmith in Brompton, was one who was prepared to trade in stolen goods. In April 1790 the dockyard authorities had sufficient information to search his premises:

> '. . . searched a Workshop or Forge of Philip Day of Chatham aforesaid Black-smith situated in Brompton in the parish of Gillingham, found therein in the possession of the said Philip Day the iron screw bolt, two iron hooks, two iron clamp nails, two iron wedges and several pieces of iron nails all marked with the King's broad arrow and the fourteen iron clamp nails, six iron timber nails fifteen iron staples, iron Escutcheon and piece of iron bolt all unmarked or whose marks are defaced.'

It has already been noted that a particularly interesting feature of the dock-yard during these years is the high degree of organisation existing amongst the dockyard workers. Within the dockyard many features of the future trade union movement already existed by the late eighteenth century. Certainly, by this time, the yard workforce was fully aware that much could be gained by co-operation. Disputes which had their basis in one dockyard would soon spread to others, whilst mass demonstrations and strikes were frequently used, and often with some success.

The earliest recorded labour disputes revolved around the Navy Board's failure to ensure a regular payment of wages. This was in the mid-seventeenth century when government finances were in a truly appalling state. Whereas the dockyard worker might expect to have his wages paid one quarter in arrears, more often they were being held back for one or two years. In his autobiography Phineas Pett, then Master Shipwright at Chatham, mentions that in 1613 he accompanied 'the ordinary shipwright and other of Chatham to move the Lord Admiral about their pay being much behind hand.'

In December 1626 the men of Chatham were once again unpaid, and resorted to a petition:

'Having been kept in Kinges work 12 months without pay or allowance for meat and drink, many have pawned all they can make, others have been turned out of doors, and their wives and children are crying for food: pray that they may be paid.'

This appears to have had little effect as no payment of wages had been made by April 1627. In that year the men of Chatham felt forced, once more, to march upon London in order to demand their wages.

By the eighteenth century the industrial dispute began to take on a set pattern. The first move was invariably a petition, submitted to the Navy Board, and outlining the general grievances felt. It might, however, be several months before they received a reply and so, if a sense of urgency was felt, the aggrieved group might resort to a strike in order to gain more immediate attention. Such was the case in August 1739 when a major strike erupted over fines imposed upon five senior shipwrights. These fines, known as mulcts, were imposed by an officer of the yard when he concluded that insufficient work had been carried out upon a third rate, the *Nassau*, then being re-built at Chatham.

An immediate strike ensued, with virtually the entire shipwright force refusing to enter the dockyard. The following morning, 29th August, there was a mass picket of the main gate which, by all accounts, was fairly rowdy. The Commissioner of the dockyard, Thomas Matthews, appeared at the gate but was met with jeers and cat calls. He later stated that the men 'behaved with all the insolence imaginable'. The picket itself was only partially successful, stopping a number of wavering shipwrights, but having no effect upon other groups of workers. One officer recorded that the ropemakers 'would not be stopped by them and are at their duty'. The following day things became decidedly more serious. Another noisy picket was mounted in the morning, after which the Commissioner retaliated by dismissing eight ring leaders. Later, during the afternoon:

'. . . sixteen of the young men forced themselves into the gate, went to the chest, took out their adzes, went out again, swearing they would cut down any person that would oppose them.'

That evening the Navy Board itself became directly involved with the dispute when members of that august body arrived from London. Concerned about delays in the preparation of ships, and concerned that the strike might spread, they had come to Chatham in search of an immediate solution. Arriving outside the Commissioner's house at ten o'clock they were informed he was asleep. However, as the Commissioner's house was also being picketed at the time, it did afford members of the Navy Board an opportunity to talk with some of the strikers. As the official Navy Board minute later recalled:

> '. . . they seemed much pleased at Our Coming; and on our answering them, that we would do them justice; they promised that they themselves would go to work, and give notice to as many of the workmen, as they should meet with.'

News of the Board's arrival was quickly circulated. The following morning most of the yard's shipwrights were again gathered outside the dockyard gates, but refused to enter until the Board had repeated the assurances of the previous evening. Upon being given such assurances, the shipwrights entered the yard.

In fact, the outcome of this strike was a clear victory for the dockyard work-force. Later that day members of the Navy Board carried out a thorough enquiry in which they interviewed several people, including the officer responsible for imposing the mulct. After due consideration they decided that the fine was totally unjustified, and subsequently issued orders for its revocation. The Board did, however, indicate to the shipwrights that they:

> 'were extremely wrong in not applying themselves to Commissioner Matthews, when they first knew the mulcts was lay'd on them, as they and all others ought always to do, when they thought themselves injured.'

That this strike could have spread to the other dockyards was a very real possibility. The dockyard workers fully realised the advantage of such co-operation and shipwrights of Chatham, Sheerness, Woolwich and Deptford had particularly close contacts. Not that these contacts were limited to shipwrights. The ropemakers also appear to have had such links, and this was a feature of the strike that occurred in May 1745. On this occasion the ropemakers with, perhaps, some encouragement from Jacobite elements, struck over the matter of apprenticeships. A great fear then existed that too many apprentices were being appointed, and that this would lead to high unemployment upon the return of peace.

Events, once again, began with a petition, but to speed things along a strike was also called. On this occasion envoys were sent to the other dockyards, with a strike at Woolwich taking place shortly after. Despite this more widespread support, the ropemakers were not in such a strong position as the shipwrights had been. For one thing the war with France was coming to an end, and the rope-makers' skills were not in such great demand. The Navy Board felt secure in taking a tough line. On 18th May they sent a letter to the Commissioner at Chatham informing him that all ropemakers failing to return to work by the beginning of the following week were to be dismissed and would lose a year's back pay. Furthermore five of the ropemakers were immediately arrested, with troops readied for any possible trouble. These, however, were not needed as the Navy Board action effectively broke the strike.

Another dispute occurred in 1756 when a serious clash took place over the subject of 'chips'. In that year the Navy Board determined upon an all out effort at enforcing the instruction that these bundles should only be carried under the arm. Whilst this had been a long standing regulation, most were carrying large size bundles over the shoulders. The workforce was duly reminded of this order on Tuesday 15th June but chose to ignore the order. Led by a certain John Miller, a shipwright who marched some thirty feet in front of the main body, all refused to lower their chips. Miller was reported to have said:

'Are not the chips mine? I will not lower them.'

At this, a great mass of men pushed by, crowding the Master Shipwright and his assistant completely out of the gate. Once outside they gave three loud 'huzzas'.

For the rest of that week large groups of shipwrights, usually numbering between one hundred and fifty and two hundred, continued to force their way through the gates, refusing to lower their 'chips'. On the afternoon of 23rd June, however, events began to escalate when two hundred shipwrights assembled outside the Commissioner's house 'in a riotous manner'. Refusing to return to their work they talked of going out of the yard. Immediately the various dockyard gates were locked, but this only served to provoke the shipwrights for they proceeded to break open the main gate. Once out of the yard they gave three loud cheers.

The shipwrights were now on strike. Soon the original two hundred were joined by a great number of others. A petition was handed to the Commissioner on the 25th, and led to further rioting. On this occasion the Commissioner complained of much 'insolence'. Troops had to be used for the restoration of order.

Despite the high degree of trade solidarity accompanying the strike, it was but a short lived affair. The shipwrights soon realised that they were unlikely to achieve their demands. The Navy Board showed every sign of holding out, and fully indicated they were prepared to dismiss groups of striking workers. The result was a partial return to work on the 28th, with a complete return by the end of that week. On 5th July the Commissioner was able to report that the men were lowering their 'chips' and carrying them under arm.

It was not until 1775 that the dockyard found itself embroiled in another major conflict. This time the issue was task work, the Navy Board's term for payment by results — nowadays called piece rate. Navy Board officials wished to introduce this method of working which would increase output by encouraging all those employed in the dockyard to work that much harder. The promise of higher wages subsequently attracted many groups of workers, but the shipwrights chose to reject it. They feared dismissal should the Board find itself in need of fewer shipwrights, together with the suspicion that those chosen to work by task might find themselves in gangs of old and worn out workers.

The shipwrights at Chatham first began to work task in the early summer of 1775. In order to discover the results of this experiment, members of both the Admiralty and Navy Board arrived at Chatham just a few weeks later:

'In this yard they have formed them by task gangs, only four of which are presently employed, the others work on day as usual, but will take their turns on task when the job now in hand is finished, and when the experiment is finally approved and more work ready to set out, the number of working gangs will be increased. The men now seem perfectly easy and take to their work with great satisfaction and alacrity, as indeed they well may, for the average of their earnings seems to be 4 and 2 pence per day.

'The present state of the task at Chatham gives one great encouragement to hope for the entire success of this beneficial plan; for it is to be observed, that this is the yard in which the greatest difficulties have arisen.'

Yet, despite this hopeful sign, Chatham was, in fact, on the verge of a massive strike. The shipwrights were not at all happy with the scheme, submitting, in common with the shipwrights of several other yards, a petition to this effect:

'The humble petition of the Task Work companies in His Majesty's several yards at Chatham, Woolwich and Sheerness Humbly sheweth, that when the order for the present mode of working by task was sent by your Honourable Board, it was willingly entered upon, as it was hoped that it might prove a redress of their grievances, but instead thereof it has only added oppression to distress, and made them more miserable and wretched still.'

It was at this point that the high degree of organisation amongst the shipwrights began to show through. Emissaries began to pass between dockyards, as plans for strike action were hatched. The result was that, by the mid-summer of that year, groups of shipwrights were on strike at Plymouth, Portsmouth and Chatham. At Chatham the strike began on 5th July, and brought this immediate concession from the Navy Board:

'Many of the shipwrights in the several yards having expressed a dislike to the plan of task upon new works and considering it in a very different light from what it was intended have desired to be excused from working in that manner and that they may perform it in the usual manner by Day work.'

This, however, was rejected out of hand as the Chatham shipwrights wanted task work completely removed.

With the shipwrights' failure to adopt a more conciliatory attitude, the Navy Board began to adopt a tough policy designed to encourage an early return to work. Throughout July, therefore, a stream of instructions began to arrive which culminated, on the 14th, with an order for the dismissal of all striking shipwrights. And, although this was subsequently carried out, the Board must have realised that it was a most unrealistic policy. After all, there were some four hundred shipwrights on strike, and the dockyard could ill afford to lose such a high proportion of its workforce.

Despite the somewhat lengthy period in which the shipwrights remained on strike, no other group of workers chose to join them. Most of them continued to work task, and were highly satisfied with their increased wages. Moreover, the shipwrights themselves were eventually to be won over to this method of working. The process, however, was long and slow. Whilst not jumping at the opportunity to work the new system, many did feel the urge to obtain better wages and grudgingly accepted the benefits of task work. By 1782 the Earl of Sandwich, then First Lord of the Admiralty, was able to point out that since 1775:

'. . . by various managements, and pointing out quietly to the people the immense advantage the task men had over those who worked by the day, the four eastern yards, namely, Deptford, Woolwich, Chatham and Sheerness, have been brought to adopt this plan and are now eager in the execution of it.'

The introduction of task work, and its eventual adoption, did bring obvious advantages. For one thing, those employed by task were tripling their former day wages. This, of course, went some way in alleviating future wage demands. In 1801 a further increase in pay was brought about when the perquisite of 'chips' was abolished and each worker received an additional payment ranging from 2d to 6d depending upon his standing in the yard. Not that any of this brought earnings up to the level of those in the merchant yards, but it did help the dockyard worker cope with the problem of inflation.

The strike lasted for five weeks, but for the shipwrights it was to be a wasted period. The Navy Board, with the issuing of dismissal notices, had indicated its unwillingness to negotiate. They had made one concession, and they were prepared to go no further. This fact seems only to have dawned on the shipwrights after a considerable period of time had elapsed.

In mid-August the return to work began. But the Navy Board now had the upper hand. Each individual shipwright had to apply for re-entry into the dock-yard. The result was the failure of certain strike leaders to be so admitted. Furthermore, the yard authorities chose to reward those shipwrights who had not gone on strike by allowing them apprentices or 'in such other manner as shall be judged proper'.

Chapter Nine

AT WAR WITH NAPOLEON

'The new rope-house is very extensive, being 1140 feet in length; here large quantities of hemp are twisted into cables, some of them one hundred and twenty fathoms long, and twenty-inches round. In this yard there are four deep and wide docks, for docking and repairing large ships, in one of these the *Victory* was built, a first rate ship, the largest then in the universe, as it is said, carrying one hundred and ten guns. There are also six slips or launches, on which new ships are constantly building.'

Part of a description of Chatham dockyard written by Edward Hasted during the 1790s.

The latter years of the eighteenth century are generally considered to be the classic age of fighting sail. During this period the man-of-war reached perfection. The royal dockyards, as creators of the most powerful weapons then known to man, were particularly important industrial centres. Upon the six royal dockyards the nation depended. For, apart from their noted inefficiencies, and the occasional labour disputes, they produced outstandingly fine ships. Chatham was no exception. Of the twenty-seven ships-of-the-line at Trafalgar, four of them, *Victory*, *Revenge*, *Temeraire* and *Leviathan*, originated from Chatham. As much as anything, then, the victory gained in 1805 was a victory for the shipwrights at Chatham and the other royal yards.

For Chatham, the late eighteenth century was also a period of renewal. At the outset of the American war it was an ill-prepared dockyard. With only six slip-ways[1] and four dry docks, Chatham was quite unable to pace the demands of war. Rapidly the dockyard fell behind its given workload and, instead, numerous vessels had to be rigged and repaired in the many merchant yards sited along the Thames and Medway. Yet it was not just a lack of simple facilities. Many essential dockyard buildings were completely dilapidated, and could hardly be expected to operate at an efficient level.

Not surprisingly, once the American war had been brought to a conclusion, some consideration was given to improving the long neglected dockyard at Chatham. This started with the visitation of 1785, and the careful consideration which was given to the building fabric. A number of interesting recommendations were subsequently made, including suggestions for both demolition and repair work. The plank house, armourers' shop, treenail house, main store and rope-yard buildings were recommended for demolition whilst the mast houses, rigging house, hemp house and wharves were amongst those considered repairable. Up to this point, and as each year went by, huge sums had been required simply to keep these buildings in use so that by 1784 expenditure on this single item had

Amongst new buildings constructed towards the end of the eighteenth century were a number of timber drying sheds. This is one of two surviving groups that were completed in the 1770s and were used as a more efficient means of ensuring that newly arrived timber was properly seasoned.

reached the staggeringly high figure of £50,000. At that time, extensive repairs were also being carried out upon the anchor wharf.

In 1786 work started upon replacing the various condemned buildings. At the beginning of the year construction of a new storehouse was undertaken, whilst plans for the new ropehouse were finalised. The old ropehouse dated to the seventeenth century, and had witnessed but few alterations since that date. A central feature of this building was its extreme length, some eleven hundred feet in total, and made necessary by the demands of the ropemaking craft which required buildings to be as long as the longest piece of rope manufactured. Next to the ropehouse was the spinning house, which was equally as long, and also to be replaced. In fact, the newly designed ropehouse was to incorporate a spinning floor, adopting similar lines to one already built at Portsmouth. At this point it should, perhaps, be mentioned that the spinning floor was where the newly arrived hemp was spun into yarn. Once impregnated with tar it was transferred to the ropehouse laying floor where the yarns were spun into rope.

In April 1787, detailed plans for the new ropehouse at Chatham were dispatched to the dockyard via the Brompton coach. During the same month the Commissioner at Chatham was informed as to exactly how the work was to proceed:

Part of the double ropehouse which was completed in 1791. Unlike the seventeenth century ropery both the spinning and rope laying floors were combined into one building, so giving rise to the term 'double ropehouse'. Three storeys in height, the first and second floors were reserved for the spinning process whilst the heavier work of ropelaying was undertaken on the ground floor.

Interior view of the laying floor and from which the full length of 1,140ft can be more readily appreciated.

'. . . as it is intended soon to contract for the carrying on about one fourth part of the Double Ropehouse in this year . . . you are to begin with the south end, and take down the present Spinning House immediately, as far as is necessary for carrying on the same, and to proceed therein accordingly, taking care to preserve the old materials as much as possible and make use of as many as may be applicable to the new buildings.'

As the new ropehouse extended further back than the spinning house upon whose site it was now to occupy the Commissioner's garden was affected:

'And it being necessary to carrying this part of the Building to take down and re-instate the Commissioner's garden, also a part of the south wall of said garden in order to extend the present range with the projecting part of the said wall westward of the ropeyard.'

The work of constructing the ropehouse now went ahead, with most of the work being undertaken by the yard's own labour force although, in April 1787, it was necessary to employ two additional bricklayers. By December 1790 the ropehouse was substantially completed. It was some 1140 feet in length and divided into one hundred bays with two separate sections for the accommodation of the laying floor and spinning floor. Of brick construction it had a lead roof, with most of the lead coming from the old spinning house. Windows were originally unglazed to help reduce the amount of dust. The entire building was of three storeys, each of which had a separate laying and spinning floor (the heaviest rope being produced on the lowest floors only), whilst a cellar provided storage for tar. Attached to the north end of the ropehouse was a separate hemp storage house and a hatchelling house (this was used for combing out the hemp strands).

With completion of the new ropeyard, together with renewal work upon various other dockyard buildings, Chatham was virtually transformed. Other planned improvements, though, were not pursued owing to the outbreak of war with Revolutionary France. It was a war which was to last, on and off, for some twenty-two years and for the Chatham dockyard worker it was, as with all wars, to be a period of immense prosperity. The dockyard itself was also to benefit as the extreme duration of the war led to the construction of new mould lofts and a steam saw mill, whilst the dockyard chapel also dates to the latter years of the war.

Immediately before the outbreak of war there was a fairly serious fire within the dockyard. Fires, of course, were always a considerable danger in an area crammed with so much timber and other combustible materials. On this occasion there was some thought given to the possibility of the fire resulting from an arson attack as, six months earlier, a number of fire bombs had been found in the dockyard. Additionally, it was known that, with war imminent, a number of people were in the country who had 'evil designs' upon the various naval yards. The fire, which occurred during the night of 14th/15th November 1792 was on board the *Thunderer*, a 74-gun man-of-war, then in number four dry dock. Earlier

Chatham dockyard sometime towards the end of the eighteenth century. By this date a number of new buildings had been recently completed, these including the new double rope-house and stores that are to be seen to the south (or Chatham town end) of the dockyard.
(Ministry of Defence)

Ropeyard workers employed on the manufacture of cables during the eighteenth century. The equipment in use includes a stake for the support of the rope (v), a top cart (r) and several of the trade tools such as a woolder and a hand winder (x,g) which were both used for winding the rope together.　　　　　　　　　(Ministry of Defence)

Fire fighting machine similar to that used in the dockyard during the eighteenth century.

in the evening the usual checks had been made and no signs of fire had been discovered. Then, at half past one in the morning Thomas Curtes, a watchman at position number ten, observed smoke:

> '. . . arising out of the *Thunderer,* and on going up to her, discovered she was on fire apparently in the hold; he called to James Childe at post No. 9 to run up and give the alarm to the main Guard . . .'

Alarm bells were immediately rung, which brought help both from the marines and dockyard employees living nearby. This was part of a pre-arranged plan in which all those hearing the given alarm were to make their way into the dockyard. The shipwrights were to go direct to the scene of the fire, whilst labourers were to collect fire fighting equipment from the engine house. This was the building, sited in the centre of the yard, which housed various pumps and a mobile fire engine replete with familiar hand pumps common to this period.

The fire was happily contained, though considerable fear existed that it might spread to the rest of the yard. Damage was therefore limited to the *Thunderer* together with the dock apron. At the time some two hundred yard employees had entered the yard and a number were rewarded for their endeavours. This caused a serious grievance as the actual awards were inequitably distributed. At least one seditious note was placed outside the main gate and threatened more fires. An anonymous letter was also sent to the Commissioner:

> 'I hope you'll do whatever lies in your power to suppress those grievances that the whole yard now labours under for depend on it that note or libel, was stuck up by some Malicious, evil designing person, and if those Grievances are not redressed you may be careful to the consequences that may attend the same.'

The writer also noted the unequal distribution of rewards following the recent fire, giving the example of one person who received £5 for merely holding a candle, whilst others received nothing. The letter was signed 'A well wisher of the yard in general'.

War with France was declared in February 1793, with the dockyard workforce being rapidly expanded during the months leading up to the declaration. Thus, a workforce of 1,609 in September 1792 had reached 1,800 only a year later. The most urgent task undertaken was the preparation of ships for the coming war. Every week instructions came for further vessels to be brought out of the ordinary and each had to be surveyed, re-coppered[2] if necessary and rigged. Numerous contract riggers were engaged whilst crews had to be found for these same vessels. Not surprisingly the press gangs were extremely busy in the streets of Chatham.

In the two months leading up to war some twenty or more vessels were commissioned at Chatham, with riggers being put to work on such named ships as *Terrible, Vengeance, Audacious, Monarch, Medusa, Hermione* and *Suffolk*. In December 1792 *L'Aimiable* was brought into the yard at Chatham to receive stores and then to be rigged for Channel service. *L'Aimiable* was a thirty-six gun frigate, carrying a crew of 280, which, following repairs, had been launched on 14th December. These repairs had been carried out at Crump's yard in Rochester, one of the small merchant yards that then lined the river and occasionally benefited from the proximity of Chatham yard. Frequently such yards gained orders for the construction of lesser rated ships, or in the preparation of vessels during an emergency.

From February 1793 onwards Chatham was put under constant pressure as one crisis followed another. Battles such as St Vincent, Camperdown and Copenhagen meant a tremendous number of repairs and refits, providing the workforce with high wages brought by unlimited overtime. Not only this, but there was also a staggeringly high number of launches in these years with no less than thirty-three new vessels built at Chatham. Additionally there was the re-building of *Victory*. She entered dry dock in 1800 for what was termed a 'middling' repair. On inspection it was found that far more work would have to be carried out than had been initially anticipated. The 'middling' repair subsequently became a re-build and at a total cost of £70,933. Much of the hull and stern was replaced, rigging and masts renewed and modifications made to the bulwark. At the same time she was given a new figurehead, one probably on the same lines as the two cupids which she currently displays. The figurehead cost £50. *Victory* was undocked on 11th April 1803, being ordered immediately to Spithead where she was to wear the flag of Admiral Nelson.

The Battle of Trafalgar, fought in October 1805, may have removed the immediate fear of a French invasion, but it by no means reduced demands placed upon the navy. With ships stationed in every quarter of the globe, the dockyards were forced to work at an exhausting pace. For this reason much consideration was given to further improving the yard at Chatham. One especially important innovation was the steam powered saw mill designed by Marc Brunel.

A dramatic view of the dockyard that almost certainly dates to the 1780s. Drawn by Paton, who died in 1791, the mass of smoke that can be seen to the north emanates from the dockyard smithery. (Ministry of Defence)

An increased need for office space during the French Revolutionary and Napoleonic Wars was partially met by completion of this particular building in 1805. It was designed by Edward Holl, architect to the Navy Board from 1804, to accommodate the resident commissioner and his rapidly growing staff.

Surprising as it may seem, it was not until the latter years of the Napoleonic war that steam power was first introduced into the dockyard. That such an innovation was adopted at all was due, in no small way, to one Samuel Bentham. As Inspector General of Navy Works during the early nineteenth century, Bentham not only saw the advantages of steam power, pioneering certain projects, but he was also responsible for employing the genius of Marc Brunel.

Brunel was a French émigré whose first contract for the Navy Board was designing an advanced blockmaking machine for the dockyard at Portsmouth. Machinery of similar design was later installed at Chatham in 1807. Blocks, or encased pulleys, were used in the rigging of ships and provided simple mechanical power within the rigging system of a ship. Simple as the pulley might be, massive numbers were needed, with Chatham ships consuming over 10,000 a year. Indeed, a 74-gun ship used no less than 922. Made entirely by hand these pulley blocks consisted of several component parts which, Brunel felt, could easily be manufactured by machines. It was in April 1802 that he first submitted his design consisting of various steam powered machines which undertook the work of cutting and shaping, with the final product assembled by hand.

The blockmaking machine later installed at Chatham no longer exists, but the following description, which dates to 1862, gives a good indication of the process and machinery involved:

'The building containing the machinery for making ships' blocks cannot be always inspected by visitors, but in spite of all other machine attractions, this certainly strikes us as the most singular. The present mode of manufacturing these blocks has only been adopted since 1807, previous to which time they were made by hand, without the assistance of any machinery. The 'modus operandi' now, is first to cut by the steam saw the piece of elm of which they are made, to the requisite size. They are next perforated by three boring machines, with a hole through each to contain the centre-pin for the sheaves or pulleys, and as many other holes, in a perpendicular direction to the former, as are required for the number of sheaves it is to have. The mortises to contain sheaves are made by elongating the holes already made by the boring chisels. The corners of the blocks are then cut off by circular saws, which prepare them for the shaping machine, where they are shaped into elliptical form — and this machine is so constructed that a considerable number of blocks may be formed by one operation. The grooves to receive the ropes are next made, by what is called the "scoring machine", and the block is finished.'

Shortly after the installation of blockmaking machinery at Portsmouth, Brunel came to Chatham to consider possible improvements for the more efficient running of the dockyard. Almost immediately he turned his attention to the handling of timber stocks for here, indeed, there was much room for advancement. Chatham yard consumed over 12,000 tons of foreign timber in every year, but not one single stage of its use was mechanised. It was both shifted by hand, and later sawn by hand.

The earliest surviving covered slip to be found in the dockyard is No. 3 slip which was given a timber roof in 1838.

The solution to increased efficiency, Brunel decided, was in the construction of a steam powered saw mill, combined with an underground waterway which would bring timber directly into this saw mill. Added to this was an overhead rail system transporting the finished timbers to the appropriate storage area. Navy Board approval for such a plan was soon given, and construction work began in 1810. As a cost cutting exercise much of the Brunel designed complex was built by French prisoners brought to the dockyard from the various hulks moored in the Medway.

As completed, the mill consisted of a central building flanked by two wings. In one of these was the boiler house and, in the other, a cast iron water tank. A shaft connected the mill to the waterway, along which timber could be floated, and hoisted out by a steam powered crane. At this stage the timber would be placed on a rail car for delivery to the appropriate saw. Once sided the timber was again transferred to a truck which ran on an overhead rail system, standing five feet above the ground and supported on seventy-two double arched pillars. Powering the entire complex was a Maudslay built beam engine backed by two boilers. Towering above, and remaining to this day, is a brick chimney one hundred and forty feet high. Wildash, in his 'History of Rochester', gives the following description of the saw mill as it stood in 1817:

'At the north-east extremity of the yard some new works have lately been constructed, commonly called the sawmills, projected and executed by that modest and persevering mechanic, Mr Brunel, who has effected as much for the mechanic arts as any man of his time. The saw mills, as their name imports,

The rounded bow as developed by Robert Seppings whilst Master Shipwright at Chatham.

are employed in converting the fir timber used in the service of the yard into planks or boards; and are erected on an eminence about 35 feet above the level of the lowest part of the yard. To the ground on the north side of the mill, which is appropriated to the stowage of timber, balks are floated from the river by means of a canal which runs open about 250 feet; this canal on entering the rising ground becomes a tunnel in length about 300 feet, and empties itself into an elliptical basin the length of which is 90 feet, the breadth 72 feet, and the depth 44 feet. The operation of raising the timber from this basis is worthy of observation; and the steady, though quick motion with which it ascends is truly astonishing. We have witnessed a balk of 60 feet long, and 16 inches square, raised to the top of the standard 60 feet in the space of 20 seconds! The saw mill is constructed on a very extensive scale; and the mechanism of it may be reduced to three principal things; the first, that is the saw drawn up and down as long as is necessary, by a motion communicated to the wheel by steam; the second, that the piece of timber to be cut into boards is advanced by a uniform motion to receive the strokes of the saw; for here the wood is to meet the saw, and not the saw to follow the wood, therefore the motion of the wood and that of the saw immediately depends the one on the other; the third, that where the saw has cut through the whole length of the piece, the whole machine stops of itself, and remains immovable; lest having no obstacle to surmount, the moving power should turn the wheel with too great velocity, and break some part of the machine.'

Another important innovation brought into the yard at this time was the first of the covered slips. In 1813 the No. 2 slip was given a timber roof, so giving protection to vessels under construction. Unfortunately, although a good collection of covered slipways can still be seen in the yard, the No. 2 slip was destroyed by a serious fire in 1966.

Finally, before concluding the French War period, reference should be made to Robert Seppings who, as Master Shipwright at Chatham, introduced a number

101

of important design innovations to ships being built or modernised at Chatham. In particular, he turned his attention to giving ships-of-the-line increased strength when at sea. Most important, perhaps, was the 'Seppings System' of diagonal bracing which was first incorporated into the *Kent*, a large 74-gun third rate which had been brought to Chatham for dry docking. A vessel that was noted for her tendency to warp along the keel, it was considered that the new system would help solve her particular problem. Later, in 1810, Seppings was given permission to use this same system in the *Tremendous*, but this time he also included cross pieces between the various gun ports and additional timbers in the spaces between the lower frames. A second improvement that was also pioneered by Seppings during his period at Chatham was that of giving larger ships a round bow. This had the double advantage of providing greater strength, whilst providing more room for this traditionally under-gunned area of a warship. Both innovations, so it should be noted, were eventually to be incorporated into all new warships during the final years of the timber-built sailing warship.

1. Slip Nos. 5 and 6 were both added in 1772.
2. Ships of this period had their wooden hulls coppered, so protecting them from the 'Teredo Navalis' worm which ate through unprotected timbers.

A further group of offices that were originally built for the commissioner and his staff. Near this point, in the cashier's office, John Dickens found employment.

Chapter Ten

THE DICKENS CONNECTION

'It resounded with the noise of hammers beating upon iron; and the great sheds or ships under which the mighty men-of-war are built, loomed businesslike when contemplated from the opposite side of the river.'
Chatham Dockyard in 'Uncommercial Traveller', Charles Dickens (1863)

The eventual conclusion of a long drawn out war with France may well have been a period of jubilation for the nation as a whole, but for the inhabitants of Chatham it was very much a time of sorrow. No longer were the dockyard workers to receive high wages made available by the constant working of overtime; instead there was considerable unemployment throughout the Medway Towns. Within the dockyard, full time employment had been provided for something like 3,000 workers, but the years of peace very soon witnessed a one-third reduction in this number. Many had to throw themselves upon the parish. Hardly a surprising fact, as virtually every other industrial enterprise in the Medway Towns was also making drastic cuts amongst their respective workforces. Perhaps a few of these newly redundant men acquired jobs, but for most, this was an impossible task. The entire economy of the Medway Towns was geared to the needs of the navy. When there was no work for the dockyard, there was little work for anyone else.

Apart from the government dockyard, the largest source of employment within the area were the numerous private shipbuilding yards. These had shown a quite spectacular growth during those twenty or more years of war. Of these, the largest was clearly that of Josiah and Thomas Brindley whose yard was at Frindsbury. They built approximately twenty warships during those years, thriving almost entirely upon naval contracts. Amongst the vessels built at this yard was the *Shannon*, perhaps the most famous frigate of all time. Launched in 1806, she was to serve on the American station and, under the command of Philip Broke, captured the *Chesapeake* in an engagement which stirred the entire nation. That the firm of J. & T. Brindley could build such ships was no protection and, with the end of war, the yard was all but wound up. Other merchant yards which existed during the French wars were those of Crump at Rochester (responsible for repairing *L'Aimiable* in 1793), Greaves of Frindsbury (earlier they had built the 74-gun *Bellerophon)*, Nicholson of Rochester and Muddle of Gillingham. All these, and others, were now in serious financial difficulty.

Other employers were equally affected by the war. Those numerous merchants who supplied a great variety of commodities to the navy now found that their former source of profit was so reduced in size that such services were no longer required. Builders also suffered a rapid decline in trade when the demand for houses completely disappeared. In turn, this led to the closure of various quarries

103

and brickmaking concerns. Undoubtedly the only continuing business enterprises were the numerous ale houses where large numbers, now with so much time on their hands, began to flock in order to drown their sorrows — assuming they had the money!

To this somewhat depressed town there arrived, during the summer of 1817, a very young Charles Dickens. The son of a naval pay clerk, the future novelist was to spend a number of his childhood years in Chatham, using memories of these years to fill out the pages of numerous books. His father was John Dickens, a man in search of an opulent lifestyle, whose £200 a year salary rarely proved sufficient for such ambitious needs. In fact the future Micawber was very soundly based upon this one particular pay clerk.

That John Dickens moved to Chatham gives us, through the writings of his son, a unique glimpse into the life of a dockyard clerk. Receiving three times the wage of an artisan, such a clerk was relatively well off. The salary allowed him to rent superior property in the much sought-after Ordnance Terrace. It was a large house surrounded by fields, well away from the bustle of the dockyard. In all, the property John Dickens rented for £80 a year had three floors, a cellar and an additional outhouse which accommodated the kitchen. Furthermore, the family had two servants who lived in the basement which adjoined both the kitchen and cellar. One of these servants, Mary Weller, was to pass her name on to a member of the, yet to be formed, Pickwick club.

Ordnance Terrace had a truly rural setting. Behind stretched the chalk downlands of Kent, whilst in front, where Chatham station now stands, there was a wheat field. In this most respected street, John Dickens was considered a man of substance. As a clerk he could be considered the equal of any neighbour, and as a man in government employment he was considered extremely well placed. Later, in a series of essays entitled 'Our Parish', Charles Dickens described some of these neighbours who lived in such a superior area. At No. 5 lived a retired lady 'the best known and most respected among our parishioners . . . who resided in our parish long before our name was registered in the list of baptisms'. A naval captain, on half pay, also lived in this group of houses, as did a retired, but clearly very affluent, former London tailor.

The town of Chatham was a constant source of interest to the young Charles Dickens and, it is for this reason, the area was soon visited by members of the Pickwick club. It was Mr Pickwick who, supposedly, noted:

'The principal production of these towns appear to be soldiers, sailors, Jews, chalk, shrimps, officers and dockyard men. The commodities chiefly exposed to sale in the public street are marine stores, hardbake, apples, flatfish and oysters. The streets present a lively and animated appearance, occasioned chiefly by the conviviality of the military. It is truly delightful to a philanthropic mind, to see these gallant men staggering under the influence of an overflow, both of animal and ardent spirits; more especially when we remember that following them about, and jesting with them, affords a cheap and innocent amusement for the boy population.'

Pickwick goes on to describe an incident which happened the day before his arrival. Perhaps the incident is based on something that happened whilst Dickens was living in Chatham. The incident concerned a soldier who had been insulted whilst drinking in one of those numerous Chatham hostelries.

'The barmaid had positively refused to draw him any more liquor; in return for which he had (merely in playfulness) drawn his bayonet, and wounded the girl in the shoulder. And yet this fine fellow was the very first to go down to the house next morning, and express his readiness to overlook the matter, and forget what occurred.'

There can be little doubt that the dockyard also influenced some of the early writings of Charles Dickens. As much can be seen in 'Great Expectations'. Joe Gargary, the blacksmith, used to hum fragments of a song of which the refrain was 'Old Clem'. The original for this can be found in the dockyard, being sung by the yard blacksmiths:

'It was a song that imitated the measure of beating upon iron, and was a mere lyrical excuse for the introduction of Old Clem's respected name. Thus, you were to hammer boys round — Old Clem! With a thump and a sound — Old Clem! With a clink for the stout — Old Clem! Blow the fire, blow the fire — Old Clem! Roaring dryer, soaring higher — Old Clem!'

The young Charles Dickens probably saw a great deal of the dockyard in those days. It was on such visits that he witnessed the blacksmiths at work, and learnt their songs. Probably he saw the convicts at work upon a new dock, and subsequently wrote them, also, into 'Great Expectations'. But for a young boy, though, the one great treat must have been a visit to Sheerness made on board the naval yacht, *Chatham*. Accompanying his father who, as pay clerk, had frequently to visit Sheerness, the young Charles Dickens savoured the delights of sailing the Medway. The *Chatham* was a grand vessel for such a journey, being designed exclusively for dockyard use, replete with plush fittings and numerous small rooms. It was originally launched in the mid-eighteenth century, but underwent a re-build in 1793.

Life at Chatham ended rather suddenly. John Dickens may have earned a princely salary, but he could not live within its bounds. As the original Micawber he was a spendthrift, always heavily in debt. Within a few years he was quite unable to afford the annual rent demanded for the house they occupied in Ordnance Terrace; and this despite a considerable increase in salary. The result was that in March 1821 the Dickens family moved to far more modest accommodation provided by 18 St Mary's Place. This was a rather small cottage situated near the Brook, a rather fetid stream which carried the town's effluence. Much nearer the dockyard, it was a place that such a well paid clerk should really have avoided. But this particular dockyard clerk was only a step away from debtor's prison. Indeed, within a few years John Dickens was to be incarcerated in the Marshalsea Prison, having left Chatham in 1822. Sometime during the late

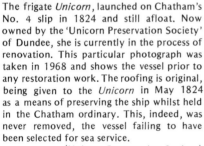

The frigate *Unicorn*, launched on Chatham's No. 4 slip in 1824 and still afloat. Now owned by the 'Unicorn Preservation Society' of Dundee, she is currently in the process of renovation. This particular photograph was taken in 1968 and shows the vessel prior to any restoration work. The roofing is original, being given to the *Unicorn* in May 1824 as a means of preserving the ship whilst held in the Chatham ordinary. This, indeed, was never removed, the vessel failing to have been selected for sea service.

(Unicorn Preservation Society)

Commemorative plaque noting the employment of Charles Dickens' father within the dockyard.

summer of 1822 Charles Dickens also left Chatham, in a coach 'melodiously called Timpson's Blue-Eyed Maid'. The journey of Pip, in search of his great expectations, was doubtless based on this one particular boyhood memory:

> 'So subdued I was by those tears, and by their breaking out again in the course of the quiet walk, that when I was on the coach, and it was clear of the town, I deliberated with an aching heart whether I would not get down when we changed horses and walk back, and have another evening at home, and a better parting.'

When Charles Dickens left Chatham on that particular occasion, the dockyard was still very much engaged in the construction of timber-built sailing ships.

Indeed, in that very year of 1822 five such vessels were launched. All were of the smaller type, being either sloops, brigs or fifth rates. Normally such small vessels would have been constructed in merchant yards but, with the return of peace, they were the only means of providing the dockyards with any form of work. The continued construction of such small ships also acts as a clear indicator to a changing role then being pursued by the Royal Navy. Rapidly, Britain's maritime arm was becoming the policeman of world affairs. Brigs and sloops were ideal for patrolling the slave coasts of Africa and the West Indies, whilst helping to reduce smuggling and other piratical activities nearer home. The larger naval vessel was to see only limited use during the years leading to the Crimean Campaign.

Yet, despite the continued dominance of the sailing ship, its days were clearly marked. Steam powered craft had already made their debut and were plying a regular commercial trade on a number of inland rivers. One of these, the *Margery*, fitted with a 10nhp side lever engine had operated on the Thames as early as 1815. The navy, for its part, was aware that such progress was being made, but had neither the funds nor the desire to innovate. The Royal Navy commanded the sea, it had a huge fleet which could be used to maintain this dominance, and hardly wished to encourage an alternative form of motive power which would soon make such a fleet obsolete. Apart from this, there were also sound practical reasons for rejecting the steam powered warship at this point in time. For a start, the earliest steamers were all paddle propelled with huge vulnerable wheels, set on each side, and severely restricting the number of guns that could be mounted. Moreover, in any battle these wheels could soon be shot to pieces, as could the equally vulnerable engine room situated on top of the hull.

Not that the navy totally ignored steam power, it simply took longer in accepting its arrival. Carefully feeling their way forward, the Admiralty adopted a policy of employing small paddle steamers, timber built and rigged for sail, in restricted harbour confines. It was, in fact, in 1822 that the navy first employed steam power when the *Comet* began service as a tug. In such a capacity the paddle steamer showed its advantages to the full. Extremely manoeuvrable, a paddle steamer could turn within its own length whilst remaining totally oblivious to wind direction.

Eventually small warships were to be given the benefit of steam, these being the early paddle sloops. One such example was the *Phoenix*, launched at Chatham in 1832. Additionally rigged for sail, she had limited sailing qualities owing to the hindrance of the stationary paddle wheel. Despite this particular drawback, such vessels were proving that steam did have an overwhelming advantage, thus paving the way for larger vessels to benefit. In 1842 Chatham launched her first steam frigate. This was the *Penelope*, formerly built as a sailing ship but converted in the dockyard. She was given a lengthened hull which allowed for the accommodation of a 650 hp engine, which was subsequently fitted by Seward and Capel at their East London yard. It was, of course, to become standard Admiralty policy for engines to be designed and constructed by private contract, although it was more normal for them to be fitted within the confines of the

The frigate *Unicorn* as she will eventually appear when completed by the Unicorn Preservation Society. Moored in Dundee's Victoria Dock, she is currently open to the public during the months April to September.   (Unicorn Preservation Society)

Visitors to the *Unicorn* at Dundee are rewarded by the opportunity of seeing a Chatham frigate that was constructed during a period of industrial transition. As can be seen from this photograph, iron has been used to support the deck beams. Another use of iron on board the *Unicorn* is that of the great iron strap bolted inside the hold and used in place of diagonal strengthening timbers.   (Unicorn Preservation Society)

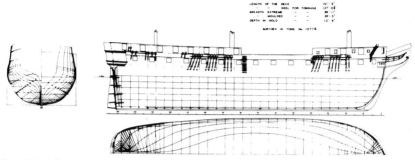

The original draught plan of two 'Leda' class frigates, *Diana* and *Latona*, both of which were built at Chatham. The *Unicorn* was identical in design. (Unicorn Preservation Society)

dockyard building the ship in question. This particular engine gave the *Penelope* a speed of ten knots, but necessitated a reduction of guns from forty-six to a mere sixteen. Subsequently the vessel returned to Chatham for fitting out and essential engine tests. It was in July 1842 that the 'Rochester Gazette' was able to report one such test carried out on the River Medway:

'In her passage down, not withstanding her great size, she gained upon some of the most rapid of the river boats; only three out of her four boilers were used, as it was found that sufficiency of steam could be generated from them . . . In trying her speed over the measured mile, she went over the distance up and down four times. In these trials she proved herself a vessel of extraordinary velocity . . .'

A rather curious vessel was launched at Chatham in 1844, the double fronted *Janus*, a small paddle sloop constructed with an identical stem and stern. Fitted with front and rear rudders, two figureheads and no bowsprit, she was designed by the Earl of Dundonald as a vessel able to reverse her course without turning. This was considered to be of particular use in intricate and narrow passageways. The *Janus*, though, proved to be of a poor design and was continually in dock for engine repairs, whilst her rigging also proved impracticable.

The obvious drawbacks that were associated with the adoption of steam power were invariably connected with the paddle wheel as a form of propulsion. Such problems were to be overcome by the submerged screw propeller. Hidden well away, such a device immediately became less vulnerable in battle whilst the removal of the paddle box would allow for a greater number of guns, all of which could be controlled by one person. Uncertainty, though, existed as to the power of screw propelled vessels, and this led to the famous trial between *Rattler* and *Alecto*. The *Rattler*, a screw ship, was built at Sheerness, and was tied stern to stern with the *Alecto*, a paddle sloop of similar displacement and horse power. With the *Rattler*'s engine stopped, the *Alecto* was allowed to proceed at full steam ahead. After a while instructions were given for the *Rattler* to start her engines. The result was truly shattering for the *Alecto* was not only brought to a standstill, but was actually towed backwards at a speed of two and a half knots.

109

An engraving of Chatham dockyard that first appeared in the Illustrated London News of 28th February 1846. Of particular note are the various slip and dock coverings that gave protection to those vessels that were either being constructed or repaired. At this point in time the dockyard was mostly engaged in the construction of smaller vessels of which rapid progress was being made on *Eurotas* and *Teazer*. Both were steamships, but neither were to be completed on time. Indeed, *Eurotas*, originally laid down as a sailing frigate, but since ordered for conversion to steam, was not finally engined until 1856.

Achilles, Chatham's first iron built warship, as she appeared immediately after her launch. This particular engraving shows the vessel moored in the River Medway and about to undergo her initial trials.

The first screw propelled ship to be built at Chatham was the *Bee,* launched in 1842 as an experimental design fitted also with paddles. Later, in 1846, the *Teazer* was launched. This was Chatham's first true screw vessel, being given a single gun and ordered for service off the coast of Africa. In later years, of course, larger screw vessels followed such as the *Horatio,* a 1,175 ton frigate launched in 1850. As with the paddle steamers, these vessels were also rigged for sail. It was not until the arrival of the compound expansion engine that steam became an economic process, with less coal being consumed. Thus, on these ships, whenever a favourable wind sprang up, canvas was set and all fires extinguished. To improve their sailing qualities, the screw vessel was given the facility of raising the propeller clear of the water in order to reduce drag.

Further progress now centred upon the development of high speed engines and the adoption of iron hulls. The former need not worry us unduly as much of the early work was carried out by private industry and, in particular, those engineering firms centred upon the Thames. Likewise, to begin with, the early development of the iron clad. The Royal Dockyards had little or no experience of iron working, whilst the private yards had built up a wealth of experience over the years. It was not until 1861, therefore, that Chatham received its first orders to construct iron clads, namely the *Achilles* and *Royal Oak.*

Iron clads, as the name suggests, were heavily armoured warships, initially wooden with belts of armour plate, but later of all iron construction. The pioneer was the French designer Dupuy de Lome who, in 1845, put forward plans for an iron fighting ship of 2,400 tons, but this was ahead of its time and never materialised. Later, in 1858, he did get the idea across to the French authorities and four steam powered iron clads were subsequently ordered. Only one, however, was to be iron hulled because France lacked the resources to smelt sufficient iron. The first to be completed was the *Gloire,* of 5,675 tons, with four inch armouring backed by 26 inches of wood. The need for such ships was, in itself, prompted by the changes occurring to the gun — that basic weapon of war. It was soon to be given an accuracy and range undreamed of but a few years earlier. The old muzzle loading cannon was being replaced by a new breech loader. These breech loaders had rifled barrels and fired a spinning shell which consequently gave it a smoother flight and obtained for it a much greater accuracy. In Nelson's day the heaviest gun could propel a 32-pound shot a few thousand yards, but the new guns could propel an 850 pound shell over ten miles.

The first British iron clads were laid down in private yards, but it was not long before similar orders were placed with the royal dockyards. Of these, the *Achilles* was to be the first iron hulled ship to be built by the Admiralty, and naturally led to numerous changes being made within the yard at Chatham. At the same time construction of the *Royal Oak,* a wooden hulled iron clad, was also put in hand. This vessel was originally planned as a conventional 90-gun battleship but while she was still in frame the decision was taken to cut her down, re-designing her as a 50-gun iron clad. It was a desperate attempt on the part of the Admiralty to reduce the French lead in this field, and to build up a fleet of iron clads as soon as possible.

Achilles under construction. Dockyard workers, during the spring of 1862, are seen employed upon the hull.

For the construction of these iron clads a considerable amount of new machinery had to be brought to the dockyard, including specialised bending, cutting and drilling equipment. Further, whilst the *Achilles* was being constructed in the No. 2 dock, the adjacent No. 1 dock was lengthened and transformed into a giant covered workshop. It was here that metal plates were assembled and then transferred to the *Achilles* by a newly installed tramway. As the iron plates being fitted both to the *Achilles* and *Royal Oak* were of 4½ inches in thickness, the shaping of these plates was carried out by 'a ponderous machine weighing nearly twenty tons' and delivered to the yard in January 1862. The following month saw the arrival of the new drilling machines. Close to the No. 7 dock, where the *Royal Oak* was under construction, a special work shed was erected and slotting machines installed.

Being a completely new venture for the dockyard work, predictably enough, fell behind. Constantly the delivered iron plates had to be rejected, failing to

The stern of *Achilles* which was considered, at the time, to be a splendid specimen of iron forging. Supplied by the Thames Iron and Shipbuilding Company, it weighed in excess of 20 tons.

meet the high standards demanded by the Admiralty. Yet every effort was made at maintaining the most rapid building pace possible. All other work in the dockyard was frequently brought to a standstill, allowing absolute priority to the iron clads. If shipwrights were unable to be employed on one ship, then they were transferred to the other. Such was the situation in February 1862 when the majority of shipwrights were engaged upon the building of the *Royal Oak*. According to the 'Rochester Gazette', 'the officials of the yard being apparently determined to spare no effort in order that she may be as far as possible advanced by September, the time fixed for launching her'. Indeed, this particular deadline was adhered to, with the *Royal Oak* being launched on 10th September. That week's Gazette reported the event:

> 'As this was the first launch of a vessel of this class from the Chatham dockyard — and in fact from any of the Royal Dockyards — great interest has been excited by the event . . . An immense staging was erected in the head of the slip; it was tastefully decorated with flags. Admission to this was only to be gained by ticket . . . At half past one o'clock labour was suspended in the Yard, and already a large crowd was greatly increased by the flocking to the spot by hundreds of workmen.'

Once launched, the *Royal Oak* was transferred to the No. 3 dock where she received an 800 hp engine built by the Henry Maudslay company. Eventually, in April 1863, she was commissioned.

With the launching of the *Royal Oak*, a large proportion of the dockyard workforce was transferred to the *Achilles*, with 1,300 being employed upon this one ship. As new processes were involved, the Admiralty was forced to engage an increased number of iron smiths together with boilermakers, a class of worker not previously engaged by the royal dockyards. Frequent industrial problems resulted, however. The boilermakers struck for increased pay, whilst the iron smiths, on a completely separate occasion, also struck, objecting to the assistance they were being given by shipwrights. The Admiralty reply to both these disputes was the dismissal of all workers involved, together with their total replacement by shipwrights. For the Admiralty this proved a satisfactory arrangement and, from then on, they chose to train shipwrights in the art of iron shipbuilding. Thus, from that time forward constructional work in royal dockyards upon the hull of iron and steel ships has been entrusted to the shipwright. For her part, the *Achilles* was launched in December, receiving 1,250 hp engines in the early part of the following year.

At the time of her completion the *Achilles* was the largest ship in the world. She had a total length of 380 feet and displaced some 9,820 tons. This may not sound much in this day of the supertanker, but suffice it to say that the *Achilles* dwarfed the *Victory*, together with any other ship previously built at Chatham. Like others of this age, the *Achilles* was a hybrid, having a steam powered engine below, and rigging above. Replete with canvas sufficient to cover a total area of 50,000 square feet, she also had 750 tons of coal in her bunkers. With thirty miles of rigging cordage on board, she had fitted to her stern a 12½ ton screw propeller. Because of the great amount of deck clutter produced by four masts and two funnels, her considerable array of guns were mounted in the broadside pattern. It was not until masts and rigging could be totally dispensed with, that central turrets were introduced to the upper decks. Originally the guns mounted on board the *Achilles* were 100-pounder smooth bores, but they were soon replaced by 7 inch and 8 inch rifled muzzle loaders. Having, as they did, a much greater range and accuracy they were not to be, however, the final armament. In 1874 she was to receive a total of fourteen 9 inch guns. That such large calibre guns could be mounted on the lower gun deck is due simply to the small barrel which was just a little over twelve feet. Later barrels of this calibre would measure two, three or even four times this length.

While the *Achilles* was still under construction, she was visited by Charles Dickens who was somewhat older than that twelve year old boy who departed Chatham in 'Timpsons Blue Eyed' Coach. He was returning to some of his boyhood haunts and, as such, was considerably impressed with the many changes that had been brought to the dockyard. Entering by the main gate, standing 'like an enormous patent safe', he came upon the *Achilles*.

'Ding, Clash, Dong, Bang, Boom, Rattle, Clash, Bang, Clink, Bang, Clatter, Bang Bang BANG! What on earth is this! This is, or soon will be, the Achilles, iron armour-plated ship. Twelve hundred men are working on her now; twelve hundred men working on stages over her sides, over her bows, over her stern, under her keel, between her decks, down in her hold, within her and without, crawling and creeping into the finest curves of her lines wherever it is possible for men to twist. Twelve hundred hammerers, measurers, caulkers, armourers, forgers, smiths, shipwrights; twelve hundred dingers, clashers, dongers, rattlers, clinkers, bangers bangers bangers!'

Later in his essay upon his visit he refers to other work in progress and notes 'certain unfinished wooden walls left seasoning on the stocks, pending the solution of the merits of the wood and iron question'.

'Everywhere as I saunter up and down the Yard, I meet with tokens of its quiet and retiring character. There is a gravity upon its red brick offices and houses, a staid pretence of having nothing worth mentioning to do, an avoidance of display, which I never saw out of England. The white stones of the pavement present no other trace of Achilles and his twelve hundred banging men (not one of whom strikes an attitude) than a few occasional echoes.'

Further pursuing his wanderings, the novelist reached the sawmill with its 'tram road supported by pillars, is a Chinese Enchanter's Car, which fishes the logs up, when sufficiently steeped, and rolls smoothly away with them to stack them'.

Impressed as he undoubtedly was, Charles Dickens was also aware that work within the dockyard was aimed in one direction. It was aimed towards war, and in war, man suffers. Where men, on that day, were employed in building ships, on another they might be dying. Referring but once more to the *Achilles*, Dickens summed up his true feelings:

'Yet all this stupendous uproar around the rising Achilles is as nothing to the reverberations with which the perfected Archilles shall resound upon the dreadful day when the full work is in hand for which this is but note of preparation — the day when the scuppers that are now fitting like great, dry thirsty conduit pipes, shall run red.'

Chapter Eleven

THE NINETEENTH CENTURY

'The committee agreed last year to the enlargement of Chatham dockyard, and I have no doubt it will become one of the wonders of the world.'
Report of a speech by Lord Paget, Chatham News, 1st March 1862

In 1862 work began on a massive plan at Chatham, designed to both expand and modernise the dockyard. It was to be the most complete renewal programme ever carried out at Chatham, with a 380 acre extension added to the already existing 97 acres. Much of the new work was concentrated on St Mary's Island, recently purchased for just such a project. Included in the new construction work were three basins for the refitting and repairing of ships, large numbers of machine shops and four graving docks. Total expenditure amounted to £3m, with building work essentially completed by 1885. All this, of course, attached much renewed importance to the dockyard at Chatham, particularly as Woolwich and Deptford yards were both closed during this period. The result was that Chatham became the only major eastern yard, taking on a considerable increase in repair work.

Since the end of the Napoleonic war only the most limited of reconstruction work had been undertaken at Chatham. A new dock had been added in 1820 whilst, over the years, a number of the slipways were roofed. The new dock, being positioned between the old second and third docks, led to a renumbering of the dock sequence. It also meant that, for a time, Chatham had five dry docks and not four. However, this was only a temporary situation as, shortly after, the old fourth dock (new No. 5) was converted into a building slip.

The erection of covers over the building slips started during the Napoleonic war when the No. 2 slip was given a timber roof (see chapter nine). The process of covering the remaining slips was taken in hand after the French wars. There is some evidence to suggest that all of the dockyard slips were covered by 1832, but the existing covers are somewhat later. Thus, the timber roof to the No.3[1] slip dates to 1837 and, owing to a disastrous fire of 1966 which destroyed Bentham's cover to the No. 2 slip, is the only extant example of a timber covered slip. It was between 1845 and 1847 that slips 4, 5 and 6 were roofed with a cast iron structure. Finally, in 1853 the seventh slip was given a covering designed by Colonel G.T. Greene of the Royal Engineers.

Changes within the dockyard during the post-Napoleonic war years were not directed entirely towards improving the docks and slipways. Advances in the science of shipbuilding necessitated additional buildings able to prepare and handle new materials. Certain alterations to the dockyard have already been noted with regard to the *Achilles* and the new workshops built in the area of the No. 2 dock.

The dockyard in 1869. Amongst buildings visible are the former police section house, the No. 7 slip as originally covered and several storehouses. Also to be seen, and just a little beyond the boundary wall, is the since demolished overhead trackway that carried sawn timber from Marc Brunel's famed saw house. (R.E. Library)

Other changes though had already preceded the building of the *Achilles*. In 1817 a new lead and paint mill was constructed immediately to the east of the ropery. Powered by steam, it was used for rolling lead sheet and producing the lead paint needed by Chatham and other royal dockyards. Later, in 1836 a new smithery was also built, allowing greater use of iron within the dockyard.

As well as alterations to the design of the dockyard, this was also a period of administrative changes. Traditionally, responsibility for governing dockyards had been vested in the Navy Board, a body which closely liaised with the Admiralty. A civilian body, the Navy Board held regular meetings in London and these generated a flow of instructions to Chatham and the other naval dockyards. In the case of Woolwich and Deptford, however, the Board chose to administer these direct, but with regard to Chatham, a more distant yard, a resident commissioner was appointed. He was the man on the spot, the one who directed the day to day running of the yard, implementing any issued instructions. Under him were the various dockyard officers such as the Master Shipwright.

This, then, was the prevailing administrative framework, and it was one which had lasted a good many years. Indeed, Chatham's first resident commissioner had been Phineas Pett, whilst Samuel Pepys had been a member of the Navy Board. Now such time honoured institutions were under review. What's more, in 1832 the Navy Board, together with any appointed representatives, was abolished. In its place was inserted a much expanded Admiralty. Up to this point in time, the Board of Admiralty had only ever taken responsibility for the Navy. As such it had worked hand in hand with the Navy Board. It was never superior to this Board, but merely a senior partner in the governance of maritime affairs. If more ships were needed, or a particular vessel was in need of repair, then the Admiralty simply requested the Navy Board to undertake the desired task. Whilst the Admiralty could criticise the Navy Board, and sometimes demand, it could never instruct. A ship in the hands of the dockyard was Navy Board property, but once at sea it belonged to the Admiralty. All this changed in 1832. The Navy Board had grown far too complex. Responsible for dockyards both home and abroad, it was also liable for stores, hospitals and barracks, all of which were growing in ever multiplying numbers. With an administrative organisation long out of date, inefficiencies within the Navy Board had become a byword. The result was that the Board of Admiralty, following an Act of Parliament, took over the Navy Board's role. Immediately four naval lords (the future sea lords) were given combined responsibilities for both the Fleet and the dockyards. Under them a new administrative system was created, whose direct link with the dockyards was via naval superintendents. It was they who replaced the resident commissioners. Always to be drawn from serving naval officers they were not, in the case of Chatham, to be of a lower rank than that of captain.

A further administrative change occurred in 1834. On that occasion dockyard security was handed over to the newly formed Dockyard Police Force. Prior to the setting up of this body, security within the yard had been the duty of specially appointed groups of workers. Known as porters, rounders and watchmen they had, since 1686, undertaken all of the basic duties necessary for the securing of the dockyard. Whilst rounders undertook regular nightly patrols, watchmen remained on duty at various watch boxes whilst porters did duty on the gate at day time. In certain periods this essentially civilian force was strengthened by patrols mounted by marines. The Dockyard Police Force, as such, had only a limited period of existence. In 1860 it was replaced by the Metropolitan Police (Dockyard Division) who, in turn, were superceded in 1934 by the Royal Marine Police. A further change occurred in 1949 with the creation of the Admiralty Constabulary and, finally, in 1971 the Ministry of Defence Police took over the task of dockyard security.

In 1843 a further landmark in dockyard history was reached with the establishment of the Dockyard Apprentice School. This was an institution whose object was that of training the dockyard apprentices in a scientific manner. Previously the training of apprentices had been left to individual artisans. These artisans had received payment for this task, but no overall check was maintained as to the quality of training that each individual apprentice received. At one time Chatham had pioneered an evening school in which apprentices — most of whom could not read or write — were trained in the most basic of skills. The dockyard school, established in 1843, was different from this early school at Chatham in that it was held during daylight hours and was restricted to technical subjects. Eventually, entry into the Dockyard School was by examination.

Having briefly dealt with administrative changes, it is necessary to undertake some further discussion of the immense extension to Chatham dockyard on which construction began in 1862. Preparations for this extension can be dated

The dangers of dockyard work. In September 1857 the No. 4 caisson collapsed, allowing water to flood into the dock. The vessel inside, *Beacon*, suffered considerable damage, but no dockyard workers were injured as the accident happened early in the morning.

to the early part of the nineteenth century. In the years 1820, 1847 and 1854 large areas of land were purchased for just such a scheme. Yet, even earlier, in 1814, the engineer John Rennie proposed an extension to the dockyard which would have considerably increased the size of the yard. Unlike the eventually adopted plan, his idea was for a south-westerly expansion of the dockyard in which the Chatham and Limehouse Reaches of the River Medway would have been converted into large wet docks. As such a plan would have meant blocking off the entire Medway river, a ship canal would have been built between Upnor and Rochester. The adoption of such a scheme would have denied much of the Medway Towns its river frontage and it was for this reason, combined with the high costs involved, that the scheme was never pursued.

The subsequent extension programme dates to the 1860s, although some general rebuilding was started in 1855. In that year the second dock was completely rebuilt, considerably increasing its length and so allowing it to accommodate the very largest of warships. Improvements were also made to several other docks at this time, whilst a new mast house and mast slip were also constructed. At the same time early preparations for the future extension were made when work was begun on a sea wall round St Mary's Island. An unusual aspect of the construction work of this time was the considerable utilisation of convict labour, used in an attempt to reduce building costs.

Convicts, with their warders, are seen in 1883 on the steam collier dock unloading a barge that had brought construction materials for the yard extension.　　　(R.E. Library)

Work proceeds upon the massive extension. Amongst those employed were numerous convicts from Chatham Prison. One of the tasks they were given was the manufacturing and shifting of bricks.　　　　　　　　　　　　　　　　　　(R.E. Library)

That a need existed for an expanded dock at Chatham had been agreed for some time. The ever increasing size of ships, together with the attendant difficulties of fitting huge pieces of machinery into these vessels, clearly required a purpose-built dockyard. Chatham was well suited for such a scheme having suitable land readily available. The recently purchased St Mary's Island offered endless possibilities and, even today, is largely undeveloped.

The extension scheme eventually adopted required the construction of three specialised basins situated along the line of the old St Mary's Creek. Each of these basins was to be concerned with a different aspect of dockyard work, allowing ships to be refitted or repaired whilst still in commission. Of the three basins the largest was to be the twenty-eight acre refitting basin, whilst adjacent to it was to be the twenty-one acre factory basin and then the twenty-one acre repairing basin. Leading out of the repairing basin, which was designed to accommodate ships newly launched or stripped for repair, were four dry docks each of a uniform 469½ feet in length. Around the various basins numerous steam cranes, designed to carry 100 ton loads, were to be located. Other structures included in the extension plan were factory buildings, a pumping station and hydraulic capstans. The basins themselves, were to be linked by passageways and vessels could enter either at Gillingham or opposite Upnor. The Upnor entrance though, has since been blocked.

Much of the early work upon the extension scheme concerned reclamation work on St Mary's Island. This had originally started life as a tidal swept marshland of a seemingly unsuitable disposition. During the 1860s the island site was completely drained and then built up an additional eight feet, with sure foundations being dug for the numerous projected buildings. Most of this work was carried out by convicts. At one time there were over one thousand prisoners working the site, and being accommodated in a newly constructed prison which had replaced the prison hulks. Escape attempts were numerous. One prisoner, for instance, upon answering his name during an evening muster, immediately detached himself from the main party and buried himself up to his neck, in mud. It was some hours before his absence was noticed, and he was eventually found when preparing to swim across the Medway towards Upnor.

Another task given to the convicts was that of preparing and then operating a twenty-one acre brickfield built to the north end of St Mary's Island. This produced most of the bricks used in the extension and is said to have been responsible for the manufacture of 110 million bricks by March 1875.

The first phase of the dockyard extension was completed in 1871. At that time two of the dry docks were complete, whilst in June of that year the repairing basin was officially opened. This was the basin immediately opposite Upnor, and built with an entrance into the Medway river. The entrance, sealed by caissons — a kind of dock gate — separated the two bodies of water. As part of the opening ceremony, the iron clad *Invincible* was brought to Chatham so as to demonstrate the advantages of the new basin:

A special coffer dam that was erected for purposes of assisting work upon the three basins to be constructed on St Mary's Island. (R.E. Library)

'As she passed through none who saw her grand and graceful proportions — her deck alive with officers and men — but must have admired the spectacle. The great ship had her course turned when she had entered the basin, and she proceeded towards No. 1 dock. In a short time with hauling and very slow steaming, she was got safely into No. 1 dock where she will undergo repair — the dock will henceforth be 'the Invincible Dock'. The fine ship having been placed in dock, the caisson to close its mouth was placed into position, and preparations made for emptying the water in the dock — a process which at present takes a considerable time, as there are only temporary engines for the dock; hereafter all the docks can be emptied in four hours by the powerful machinery to be provided.

'When the *Invincible* had passed into the basin, immediate preparations were made for replacing the caisson at the entrance. By means of capstans and hawsers it was hauled into position, and then sunk into the groove into which it fits, water being admitted into the caisson to depress it.'

'Chatham News' report of 24th June 1871.

It was a proud day for Chatham, and the paper duly gave the opening a full spread. To prevent any confusion it should be pointed out that 'the Invincible dock' was, in fact, the first of the new docks and was to be later designated No. 5. Like the other fitting basin docks it had a watertight caisson preventing the entry of water from the basin, whilst the pumping gear referred to was completed in 1874, and driven by a 250 hp steam engine. In its comment column the 'Chatham News' went on to extol the virtues of the extension scheme:

'Those who do not love Chatham, or have a jealousy of her, have been ever ready to prophesy that the new dockyard must be a failure — that the works attempted must tumble in — that if basins and docks were made ships could not get up the river to enter them, and so on. Well — a grand basin, 21 acres in area, with a depth of 33 feet of water, has been successfully constructed; ships have steamed through it; a fine iron clad vessel with her guns etc, on

122

Invincible in No. 5 Dock. She was the first warship to make use of the new facilities being built at Chatham. (R.E. Library)

board, has safely come up the Medway, has passed through the wide and deep entrance of the uppermost basin, has traversed the basin, and is now in one of the enormous graving docks which abut on the basin, another dock is ready to receive the largest ships in the Navy; many ships of the first class could lie in the far stretching basin. Thus much HAS BEEN accomplished. There have been difficulties but they have been overcome. At no distant period a second basin of nearly the same size will be completed. The two great docks in hand will be finished rather later — a glance at these in their present state impresses one with the magnitude of the work, and proves how much time must necessarily be occupied in carrying it out. A few years later the third and largest basin may be expected to be completed . . .'

As noted in the 'Chatham News' report, work had begun on the two other basins as well as the second pair of dry docks. It was in November 1872 that the No. 8 dock was finally completed, with the No. 9 dock being finished in 1873. Next was the factory basin and finally, in 1883, the fitting out basin. Considerable convict labour was used throughout. The fitting out basin also provided the means of access from the Medway, through the caisson gates of the Bull's Nose — so named because of its shape. This is situated at the Gillingham end of the dockyard, and consists of two locks sealed by the caissons already mentioned.

123

Launch of *Alexandra* from No. 7 Dock on 7th April 1875.

The Upnor entrance was also available for use, but this was built as a secondary or emergency entrance. With the fitting out basin coming into use, work was concentrated upon erecting the final building around this basin, together with the huge cranes. This took a further two years, with the extension being brought officially into use sometime towards the end of 1885.

The transit of goods in and out of the dockyard during this period was eased when, in February 1877, a railway branch line into the dockyard was officially opened. Built as a joint venture with the 'London, Chatham and Dover Railway Company', it joined the main line just to the east of the present Gillingham station. Within the dockyard, a railway system connects most of the important working areas, and was once served by a series of industrial steam locomotives. Prior to closure, the stock of engines, although resembling their steam predecessors, were diesel powered. Modern British Rail diesels also entered the yard when necessary.

Once completed, the extension works totally revitalised the dockyard, allowing the refitting of a greatly increased number of ships whilst encouraging the Admiralty to use Chatham for the building of numerous battleships. This, of course, led to a considerable increase in the dockyard workforce. Whereas in 1860 the labour force stood at 1,735 it had, by 1885, and completion of the extension works, reached 4,199. Of the ships built at Chatham, each class of battleship was larger than its predecessor. In 1875 Chatham launched the *Alexandra* then the largest ship ever built within the dockyard. Displacing just over nine thousand tons it exceeded by nearly twice the tonnage any previous ship built within the dockyard. Yet, not ten years later, the *Rodney*, displacing over ten thousand tons, was launched. Others followed in quick succession.

124

Fourteen thousands tons had been reached by 1891 with the launching of the *Hood*, followed by the fifteen thousand ton *Venerable* in 1899.

These launchings, of course, provided a general point of interest for all those who lived in the Medway Towns. It was something to be proud of, with many hundreds being present at the various launchings. Sometimes these launchings were given additional importance when they were accompanied by a royal visit. Such was the case in September 1885 when the *Rodney* was launched. Built in the No. 7, or Alexandra dock, she was a battleship with an immense hitting power provided by her 13.5 inch guns mounted in pairs both fore and aft of the superstructure. In addition, she had a broadside armament of six inch guns. As a further indication of progress in this period, her armouring was made up of alloy steel plates 18 inches in thickness. Her 'christening' was performed by the Duke and Duchess of Edinburgh which, for the town of Chatham, was an event to be celebrated. The entire afternoon was declared a holiday. The royal party, arriving at Chatham railway station, were met by various civic dignitaries before being escorted to the dockyard. Most of Chatham turned out for the occasion, with the entire route bedecked with flags. At the railway station, itself, the wooden pillars supporting the roof were enveloped in red cloth whilst on each side of the platform a pyramid of flowers was arranged. Further along the route the railway bridge had been converted into a victory arch whilst above shops in the High Street was affixed the motto: 'Success to HMS Rodney, may she always carry the British flag to victory'. Not surprisingly, large numbers entered the dockyard to actually witness the launching. According to the 'Chatham News':

'Stand accommodation was provided at the head and halfway down the slip for some 4,000 visitors who had been provided with tickets, the Royal stand being immediately in front of the vessel. This was handsomely decorated with flowers, hot house plants etc, and presented a very attractive appearance. The launching apparatus, with the gaily decorated bottle of wine, was in the centre of the stand, the cabinet containing the launching apparatus having some handsome flowers upon it.'

A number of speeches were made, commissioned photographs of the royal party were taken and music played by the bands of the Royal Engineers and the Royal Marines:

'Shortly afterwards, Her Royal Highness, accompanied by the Duke and their son . . . advanced to the cabinet containing the launching apparatus, and the working of the wheel was explained to Her Royal Highness by Mr Warren[2]. When this was done it was announced that the tide was sufficiently high for the vessel to leave the dock, the amount of water to launch her requiring a rise in the tide of sixteen feet.

'Her Royal Highness then took the miniature wheel with both hands, and with considerable dexterity turned it round to the indicated point. There immediately followed a tremendous thud caused by the knocking away of the last dog-shoe. At this moment, the greatest anxiety prevailed to see if the

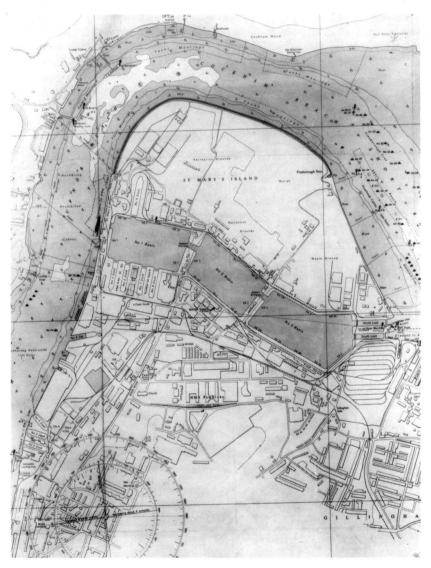

A general map of the dockyard (c1981) showing the area of the Victorian extension. A second entrance on the Upnor side of the river was sealed in 1906.   (Ministry of Defence)

vessel would start, but the anxiety was at once allayed, as the board holding the gaily decorated bottle of wine, and which was attached to the vessel, was seen to tighten, and as the vessel moved the bottle was dashed against the bows of the vessel, the Duchess at the same time naming the vessel 'The Rodney'. Starting very slowly at first, the vessel quickly increased her velocity, and with a crashing of the blocks on which she had rested, and the cheering of the vast multitude, the vessel went down the ways in splendid style, and took the water as gracefully as a vessel of much smaller weight and draft could do. The bands present played the national anthem and 'Rule Britannia', and when the vessel was fairly on the bosom of the Medway, Admiral Rice called for three cheers for the Rodney. They were most lustily given.'

The ever-increasing size of battleships very soon produced problems at Chatham. The dockyard extension scheme was a product of the 1860s, and no one at that time could possibly envisage the massive size that ships were eventually to reach. The 'Dreadnoughts', frequently ships in excess of 19,000 tons, could neither be built nor properly refitted at Chatham; only the smaller class of warships could be dealt with. Important in themselves, these ships were not the reason the extension had been built, and it was a disappointing period for all those connected with shipbuilding at Chatham. Many, indeed, even feared for their jobs. But the solution came from a rather unexpected direction. In 1906, amid great secrecy, the C.17 was launched. For Chatham dockyard this meant a new specialism and the beginning of a new era.

1. Formerly the No. 5 dock.
2. Warren was the Chief Constructor. He was the most senior technical officer in the yard, and second only to the superintendent of the dockyard. Although the title was new, having been created in 1875, it was simply the new name given to the Master Shipwright.

A 160-ton crane as once used for the fitting out of warships at Chatham.

The expansion of the dockyard into Gillingham resulted in a considerable building boom. These houses, situated in Malvern Road, were typical of those once occupied by skilled artisans.

Chapter Twelve

A NEW SPECIALISM

'Ever seen a dockyard Matie run
Yes, I've seen it done,
At the sounding of the Bell
Dockyard Matie runs like hell'
A traditional Dockyard rhyme

The major extension which so totally transformed Chatham dockyard during the nineteenth century had an equally dramatic effect upon the Medway Towns. Prior to the 1860s, the entire Medway valley had fallen into a period of severe economic depression. A whole series of lay-offs within the dockyard had seriously reduced local buying power, forcing large numbers to contemplate a move to the metropolis. The extension works changed all this, revitalising the area by increasing employment opportunities and allowing the frequent working of overtime. Whilst the dockyard was able to employ 5,000 workers in 1885, this number had increased to 10,000 in 1903.

During these years Chatham dockyard attracted large numbers of new workers. Many came from outside the Medway Towns, choosing to move into an area offering guaranteed employment. Amongst them were large numbers from Deptford and Woolwich, dockyard workers seeking new opportunities following the closure of these two Thames-side yards. Others came from South Wales. They too had experience of dockyard work, being formerly employed at Pembroke, a run-down government dockyard.

Consideration of the census figures ably demonstrates the effect of dockyard employment upon the Medway Towns. Between 1861 and 1891, the initial period of expansion, the Towns saw a forty-nine per cent population increase. Most were choosing to settle in either Chatham or Gillingham, with the latter seeing the greatest rise in population. This is hardly surprising. The extension works now brought the dockyard well inside the parish of Gillingham, and to an area which could accommodate much new housing. Chatham, on the other hand, was heavily built up, having provided homes for dockyard workers since the seventeenth century. The immediate result was that two areas now witnessed a building boom. One was lower Gillingham, adjacent to the new gate, and the other was Luton, a part of Chatham still able to offer considerable room for housing. Whilst Chatham witnessed a 28% rise in population during those thirty years, Gillingham's population increased by 91%. Even more staggering is that during the ten years after 1891 Gillingham saw a further increase in its population of 53%[1]. Such population increases were a simple reflection of activity within the dockyard. They were years of full employment, with large numbers of warships coming off the slipways as the Admiralty made a determined effort to equip the Navy with ever more sophisticated ships.

In Gillingham the hundreds of small terraced houses located within a short walking distance of the newly completed extension provided ideal accommodation for yard workers. Such houses could be rented for three or four shillings a week and, although sparse, were at least comfortable. With four or five rooms plus a kitchen, outside toilet and garden, such houses were a considerable improvement upon the tenemented and back to back housing which had so characterised earlier building booms in Chatham. Naturally the erection of these houses took on a logical sequence. In lower Gillingham, the majority of houses date to the 1865 to 1900 era. Chatsworth Road has a long row of terraced houses dating to 1865, whilst the more exclusive Kingswood Road was built during the late 1880s. Franklin Road (once part of Gillingham Road) has a whole range of building dates, becoming appreciably later as the distance from the dockyard increases. Finally, of course, the lower Gillingham area became totally saturated and building land was acquired on the far side of the High Street. Roads such as Balmoral and Windsor date to the mid-1890s, whilst Gillingham Road is of the 1897 to 1910 period.

The tremendous number of terraced houses were not simply restricted to yard workers. Gillingham was a mixed community with railwaymen, shop workers and farm labourers all living in similar accommodation. Yet some roads were clearly more sought after than others. Labourers, with a lower income and a less predictable wage, found themselves in the least desirable roads. The lower end of Franklin Road was just such an area. Here, a mass of property opening straight on to the streets was soon to become one of Gillingham's slum areas and has since been demolished. The more select areas, those occupied by shipwrights and other artisans, had houses with small forecourts and bay windows. Such housing carried an element of prestige, distinguishing the occupier as a member of the working class elite. Additional to all these were roads, few in number, which offered either larger or semi-detached residences. Often occupied by dockyard officers, these fetched a much higher rent and identified the occupier as middle class. Station Road, with houses set well back and often occupied by officers of the Royal Engineers was one such example.

Balmoral Road, Gillingham, has particularly interesting associations with the dockyard. Many of the houses in this road were owned by a former dockyard shipwright, James Croneen. Long since having given up the trade, he had turned his skills to building, reaping huge profits from the local housing boom. Indeed, he is believed to have become the richest man in Gillingham. Amongst the houses he owned were a group opposite Balmoral Gardens. The cost of building each of these houses was £99, and the particularly large front doors, made of teak, came from the old timber warships brought to Chatham for breaking up.

The end of another day. Dockyard 'maties' race for trams outside Pembroke Gate.
(Medway Fine Arts Studio)

Despite massive employment, poverty still existed in the Medway Towns. For all but established workers, seasonal lay-off was still a common feature of dockyard employment and labourers, in particular, were often in a very unpredictable situation. Added to the factor of seasonal unemployment, there was the problem of the permanently unemployed, those with large families or where the breadwinner was either unable to work, or had died. Like any community, the Medway Towns had its share. Street singers were common, as was begging. For these wretched people, the dockyard workers certainly did what they could. During times of great hardship a soup kitchen existed in the yard, supported by donations from both officers and men. Another feature was the queue of ragged children outside the dockyard gates, waiting for any uneaten midday meals.

That the dockyard dominated the Medway Towns can hardly be doubted. Any visitor to the area would receive ample proof from witnessing the massed crowds of workmen making their way to the dockyard in the mornings. Each dressed with a remarkable degree of similarity; collarless shirt, cloth caps and a lunch carried in a red spotted handkerchief. Often, though, a heated lunch might be brought to the dockyard gate at a later hour. The working day began early (around 7 am but it varied by season)[2] and at the appointed time a seething mass of humanity marched towards the dockyard. At ten minutes before the start of work, the bells at each of the gates would be rung by a member of the dockyard police. Later, to indicate five minutes, the bell would be rung again

131

Main Gate during the early years of the present century.

The Royal Navy barracks which were officially opened in 1903.

and, as time progressed, it would start a more regular tolling. Once this occurred the 'maties stampede' took place as the late risers tried to reach their respective station offices. Here each man collected a work ticket, replacing it at the end of the day. Failure to reach the office on time meant an immediate deduction from the week's pay with a series of late arrivals leading to dismissal.

Because the dockyard at Chatham was such an important employer, most of the local elementary schools had special dockyard classes. These were designed to help pupils pass the civil service exam which restricted apprenticeship entry into the yard. For those of a working class background, a dockyard apprenticeship was highly prized. They provided excellent opportunities, being the only means of acquiring establishment status. An established worker was reasonably safe from dismissal, being eligible for a pension should a lay-off occur. Apprentices were expected to attend the dockyard school, and would finally take an exam, the results of which governed entry into the trade. Those receiving the highest grades were eligible for a shipwright apprenticeship or the very new trade of electrical engineering, whilst those doing less well could become joiners, carpenters, pattern makers and so on.

The final years of the nineteenth century witnessed the building of a new naval barracks adjacent to the dockyard. It occupied that area formerly taken up by the old convict prison. This area had recently become vacant as, with completion of the extension works, the prisoners had been dispersed elsewhere. Part of the prison was subsequently demolished and construction work upon the barracks began in May 1897. Completed six years later, and at a cost of £425,000, the barracks could accommodate 4,742 officers and men. Previous to this time, ratings based at Chatham had been housed in hulks laid up in the River Medway. The name of one of these, *HMS Pembroke,* was used as the official title for the new barracks which were situated close to the dockyard's Pembroke gate.

Although the naval barracks provided a certain degree of civilization, the usual complaint was one of insufficient facilities. Most of the ratings posted to Chatham preferred, instead, to spend their evenings in the Towns. At this time many of the Chatham pubs were dominated by the 'blue jackets', whilst the gaiety theatres proved an equally popular venue. Like any naval town, Chatham also had its resident prostitutes. Pubs in the Brook area, such as the 'Dover Castle', were a regular stomping ground for the Chatham business girls, and they seem to have had a fierce reputation. A common naval ditty of the time refers to them:

> 'I've fought with the Russians,
> I've fought with the Boers,
> But never no more with an old
> Chatham whore.'

To tempt ratings away from such delights, a Royal Navy Mission was established in the Brook. It provided classes, meetings and entertainment of a religious, social and educational character. Should the 'blue jackets' not appreciate this,

LAUNCH OF H.M.S. "AFRICA," CHATHAM, 20th MAY, 1905.

LEAVING THE WAYS.

WATERBORNE

ON THE WAY TO "FITTING OUT" BASIN

A sequence of pictures which show the launching of HMS *Africa* from the No. 8 slip. *Africa* was to be the last battleship launched at Chatham. The No. 8 slip was added to the yard between 1898 and 1900.

there were also a number of rest homes. These were designed as alternatives to the pubs and brothels, having a pub atmosphere minus the alcohol. Both the Methodist church and the Salvation Army ran such homes, and they provided sleeping accommodation, billiard games, reading rooms and canteens. The site of one of these homes, 'Navy House' in Clover Street, can still be identified, as its weather worn sign is still very visible.

Another popular venue was 'Barnards Palace of Varieties'. This was an old-fashioned gaiety theatre in which acts were introduced by a board brought onto the stage. Over the years it put on a great number of shows, with both Marie Lloyd and Gracie Fields visiting. Next door to Barnards was a Chatham pub with a somewhat questionable reputation. Theatre chorus girls had made it their home and were prepared to supplement their meagre wages by offering themselves for five or ten shillings. Those with homosexual leanings were also known to frequent this pub.

Inside the barracks discipline was harsh. Uniforms had to be spotless, messes were frequently out of bounds and the parade ground was always to be crossed at a run. Infringement of these, or any one of a great number of other regulations, meant an immediate spell of confinement. Daily life within the barracks was extremely monotonous. Sometimes a group of ratings would be detailed to assist the dockyard workforce in urgent refit work but, more often, ratings were given the unpopular task of peeling 'spuds'. Apart from this, another 'soul destroying' task was that of cleaning the parade ground. On such occasions a long line of ratings would be continually marched up and down, picking up every small piece of litter. After lunch the whole exercise was repeated.

From consideration of the barracks, a return to the dockyard should now be made. The distance between the two might be short, but in every other respect they were worlds apart. Furthermore, a strange relationship existed. In one respect the dockyard 'matey' admired the 'blue jackets'. They always celebrated any victory or achievement — especially if a Chatham ship was involved — but on the other hand they would never contemplate the navy as a suitable career for a son. Moreover, the dockyard worker resented the de-humanizing ways of the navy. The 'do that', 'do this' mentality was one that they totally rejected. For their part, naval personnel thought of the yard worker as a rather lazy individual always in search of a quiet corner. It was by no means a correct assessment, but one built up over the years and fed by grossly exaggerated stories. Most yard workers were hard working, conscientious individuals who took a great pride in producing the best warships in the world.

For the dockyard, those years leading up to World War One saw a number of changes. It was the period in which submarines were first constructed, whilst the dockyard's last battleship was also launched. In 1897 work started on a new dock, with a new slip being constructed a year later. At the time of its completion the new dock, No. 9, was the largest in the world, being 650 feet long*. It meant that for a short time Chatham was still in a position to re-fit the largest ships in the navy. The newly built slip, completed in 1900, was also larger than earlier slips, designed for the building of battleships. As it happens, only one was ever to be constructed on this slip. This was the *Africa*, the last battleship ever launched at Chatham. She was a pre-Dreadnought, King Edward VII class, displacing 16,350 tons. Her main armament was four twelve-inch turret mounted guns, supported by additional 9.2-inch and six-inch broadside guns. Large for her day, she was quickly to be superceded by the Dreadnoughts, a class of battleship far too large for Chatham. Water depths and difficulties in entering the yard, meant that the battleship would, in future, have to be built elsewhere. The launching of the *Africa* was duly reported by the local press. The 'Chatham News' noted that a special train was laid on, to bring various dignitaries from London, and that the ship was launched by the Marchioness of Londonderry. She was responsible for severing a chord which:

> 'released two heavy weights each weighing 5 cwt which fell, knocked away the dog shoes and released the vessel, but the great leviathan showed no sign of moving and two hydraulic presses, each capable of moving 200 tons, were immediately brought into play to start her, but with little or no effect. A lift frame hydraulic ram, exerting a pressure of 1,000 tons, however had the desired effect, and sent the vessel on her course.'

Within a few years of the *Africa*'s launch, Chatham yard was engaged upon the construction of a strange new revolutionary vessel — the C.17. This was a

---

* Adjacent to the No. 9 Dock was the No. 9 machinery shop, under construction in 1904, whilst Nos 1 and 2 generating stations were also being built at this time.

C17, the first of fifty-seven Chatham built submarines.   (RN Submarine Museum, Gosport)

submarine. The first of a kind which was to become a specialism of the yard. By later standards, of course, the C.17 was a somewhat crude design. Extremely small, conditions for the crew were made far worse by the danger of fumes emitted from a twelve cylinder petrol engine which powered the craft when surfaced. Submerged, an electric engine took over this role. Constructed on the No. 7 slip, the C.17 was subjected to a great cloud of secrecy. At one point the launch, which was in August 1908, was even planned for midnight:

> 'The so-called moonlight launch of a submarine from the slipway at Chatham yard caused quite a commotion in the London Press, which appeared to have overlooked the fact that submarines were being built at this port. As for secrecy this has been strictly observed at all the launches of submarines from the slips of private firms, whereas at Chatham, the workmen employed in building them are bound to secrecy. The Admiralty were bound to construct some of these little craft in the Royal dockyards, if they desired to keep a necessary check on the charges of contractors, and Chatham has been selected because all other new constructions had ceased, except that of a few barges and small craft. Apparently the work has been performed so expeditiously and cheaply, under many handicapping conditions, that their lordships have decided to build other submarines at the Medway ports, and Chatham will do the work.'

After the launch, C.17 was taken to No. 2 dock where she was fitted with engines and other machinery, all of which was constructed within the dockyard. In September the 'Chatham News' was reporting:

136

'The first two of the four submarines being built at Chatham, will be ready for trials in a few weeks, probably, and there will then be an opportunity of comparing the Dockyard work on this kind of vessel to that done by private firms. Chatham Dockyard was entrusted with the first pair of this type of craft to be built in the Royal Dockyards and apparently the Admiralty are quite satisfied with the progress that has so far been made, as a second pair of similar craft have been put in hand, and will no doubt be pushed forward as fast as possible.'

The second of these submarines to be built at Chatham was the C.18. She was launched in October 1908, also being built in the No. 7 slip. The second pair of submarines referred to were the C.19 and C.20, both launched in 1909. These, together with a further two C-class submarines built at Chatham, saw a full commitment during the coming war years, operating mostly in the North Sea and Baltic areas.

As with any weapon of war, particularly one so completely new, the submarine was constantly subjected to various design improvements. As a result Chatham soon began work on two D-class submarines. These were much larger than the C-class, being twice the size, and designed for longer distance patrol work. Instead of the petrol engine, motive power on the surface was provided by a diesel, which produced increased power whilst reducing the threat of accidental explosion. The greater size also permitted a more powerful electric motor to be installed, whilst a W/T unit was incorporated into the basic design. A few years later Chatham was producing E-class submarines. These were similar to the Ds, but half as large again. They were to be used throughout the war and, like the D-class, saw service in the Mediterranean and Dardanelles. The Es were the last of the pre-war submarines, with Chatham required to build four.

The years leading up to World War One were not entirely restricted to the building of submarines. Numerous other vessels were also launched and, in particular, cruisers. Amongst the cruisers was the *Chatham*, name ship of its class. From the laying of her keel to final completion was a two year task, indicating the pace to which Chatham was working. In 1912, the year of *Chatham*'s launching, there was clearly a strong sense of urgency about any work undertaken. Built at a cost of £349,358 the *Chatham* was immediately commissioned and dispatched to the Red Sea area, remaining there until the outbreak of war.

Between 1911 and 1914 Chatham dockyard was fully employed in all of those tasks so essential for the maintenance of a fleet on the verge of war. In this four year period the yard constructed eight submarines, four cruisers and five other vessels. In 1914 a great variety of orders was placed with the yard, but the main concentration was on refitting and getting ships ready for sea. By the early summer, with war about to be declared, large numbers of older ships were taken out of the Medway anchorage. They were inspected, coaled and loaded with essential supplies. Some of them were little more than rusting hulks. Such was the case with the *Hogue, Aboukir* and *Cressy*. Built at the turn of the century,

137

Medway Floating Dock, near Sheerness.

In the summer of 1912 an Admiralty Floating Dock (*AFD 4*), was brought into the Medway for the purpose of dry docking the new 'dreadnought' battleships. Previously Chatham had not been in a position to dock such large vessels, the yard's permanent dry docks being too small. The picture, which was taken on 2nd September 1912, shows first use of the new floating dock by the 19,250 ton *St Vincent*.

they were vessels clearly obsolete. As armoured cruisers they had been ordered to join the seventh cruiser squadron. Within a few weeks of war being declared they were to bring a startling reminder to the Medway Towns of just how brutal war could be.

1. A breakdown of census returns for the Medway Towns 1861 to 1901

	Strood	Rochester	Chatham	Gillingham
1861	3,915	12,311	24,650	14,608
1871	4,186	12,806	26,184	19,936
1881	5,395	14,254	26,525	20,644
1891	7,796	15,611	31,594	27,872
1901	10,006	17,613	36,944	42,643

2. Dockyard working hours 1905
   Summer: 7 am to 12 pm and 1.30 pm to 5.30 pm (Saturday 7 am to 12 pm) mid-winter: 7.30 to 12 pm and 1.30 to 4 pm (Saturday 7.30 am to 12.30 pm).
   313 days worked in the year with an average of eight hours per day. Apart from Sundays, holidays were also granted on Good Friday, August Bank Holiday, the King's Birthday and Christmas Day. Boys employed in the yard, under the Factory Act, also received Easter Day and Boxing Day.

Chapter Thirteen

INTO THE TWENTIETH CENTURY

'Dockyard mateys' children, on the old Dockyard wall.
Watching their fathers doing damn all.
When they grow older, they'll be dockyard mateys too.
Just like their father, nothing to do!'

Traditional dockyard rhyme

Declaration of war, in August 1914, was an inevitable fact of life. For a considerable number of years European politics had been so finely balanced that any real expression of surprise must relate to the length of time preceding hostilities. By 1914 the various western nations were well prepared. Britain, continuing a long adopted policy, relied heavily upon the Royal Navy. During these years the Admiralty built up a fleet of dreadnoughts, backing them with a massive array of smaller ships. The Medway anchorage was crammed to capacity, providing for vessels on permanent standby.

Amongst those warships peacefully at rest in the Medway anchorage were the cruisers of the seventh squadron: *Cressy, Aboukir, Hogue, Bacchante* and *Euryalus*. All were of the same class, armoured and mounting 9.2-inch guns. Built at the turn of the century, they were nearing obsolescence. Indeed, if truth be permitted, they were little more than rotting hulks, fit only for the breakers yard. But the Royal Navy needed ships, and the Cressy class cruisers did at least float.

Each year the dockyard workforce religiously surveyed the various vessels lying at anchor. Defects were noted and acted upon. Little, however, could be done about the problems of rust. It was the same with all the ships in reserve. There was certainly nothing special about the Cressy class, and with the rest of the ships in reserve they were to receive their test on the outbreak of war. In the summer of 1914 orders were issued for the formation of various warship groupings, and the seventh cruiser squadron was instructed to patrol the southern North Sea, keeping an eye on enemy shipping movements, keeping the channels free of mines. At all times they were to operate with a destroyer screen. To man these various cruisers, large numbers of naval reservists were called up. In addition, regulars from Chatham barracks were also directed to these ships. Not surprisingly, when these cruisers sailed, they had a large proportion of Chathamites on board. After all, a number of regular sailors, knowing that their ships frequently put into Chatham, had moved their families into the area.

The seventh cruiser squadron left Chatham the day war was declared. Before heading towards the potentially hostile North Sea, they spent a number of days manoeuvring off Queenstown as part of a shake-down cruise. It was the only

The funeral procession of those killed on board the Chatham built *Arethusa*. Their final resting place is in Woodlands cemetery.

opportunity that the numerous ratings had of familiarising themselves with this class of ship. On 21st August, Commodore Roger Keyes, having boarded the *Bacchante*, expressed his surprise at the poor state into which these vessels had been allowed to fall. He witnessed the crew engaged in the removal of rust from the sides, whilst the newly painted decks did little to conceal the true age of these much dated vessels. He was later to write: 'For heaven's sake take the Bacchantes away. How can the atmosphere be the right one?'

For a six week period, the various ships of the seventh cruiser squadron patrolled an area close to Dogger Bank. Rarely were all the ships together. The monotony was frequently broken by re-coaling, carried out at Sheerness. This was never a popular exercise, as it involved the entire crew in the shifting of coal. At such times, both ship and men were a uniform shade of black. Furthermore, actual patrol duties were looked upon with some considerable suspicion. Out in the middle of the North Sea, these old cruisers were highly vulnerable to attack, it was even felt that the squadron had been placed there as bait. Certainly they were within easy striking distance of German battle cruisers, and maybe the Cressy class were to be sacrificed. That there was no basis for such a rumour is adequately confirmed by new orders withdrawing all cruisers from North Sea patrols. These instructions however were never fulfilled. Even before the orders could be issued, three of the Cressy class were lying at the bottom on the North Sea.

On the morning of 22nd September the cruisers, *Aboukir*, *Hogue* and *Cressy*, were patrolling their normal territory. The *Euryalus*, flagship to the squadron, had returned to Sheerness for coaling, whilst the *Bacchante* was at Chatham receiving engine room repairs. Severe storms over the last few days had left the cruisers without any destroyer screen, but these were shortly to be dispatched from Harwich. Visibility at first light was good, a fact which undoubtedly aided a German intruder. Unknown to the British cruisers, they were well within torpedo range of the German unterseeboht, U-9. At 6.20, the U-boat had been successfully manoeuvred into a firing position and its commander, Kapitan Leutnant Otto Weddigen, confidently pressed the firing button. A great swoosh of water indicated that the first tube had successfully released its charge. Thirty seconds later a muffled explosion indicated the morning's first kill. The *Aboukir*, hit fully amidships, begun to list to port. No one on board had seen the submarine, whilst any wake produced by the torpedo had also gone undetected.

As men began to pour into the cold dark waters of the North Sea, most speculated upon the *Aboukir* having hit a mine. Nobody suspected a submarine at this point. The *Hogue* and *Cressy*, oblivious of any danger, moved towards the stricken cruiser. It was a bad move on their part. At 6.55 the U-9 fired two torpedoes, completely shattering the *Hogue*. Aboard the *Cressy*, the single remaining cruiser, something approximating the truth began to dawn. The sea must be full of U-boats. Numerous guns opened fire. Every bit of driftwood was seen as an enemy submarine. Later, crewmen interviewed by the press were to talk of five submarines, with at least one sunk. But this was nothing like the complete truth. Only one submarine was in the area, the U-9, and she remained unscathed. At 7.17 she fired another torpedo. This time the target was *Cressy*, with the ship being hit close to the boilers. Water suddenly flooded in, and the seventh cruiser squadron had ceased to exist.

Incredibly, with hardly a shot being fired, the Royal Navy had suffered a major defeat. Three thousand British sailors had been forced to leave their sinking ships, and 1,500 of them were never to see England again. It was a shock for the nation, and a tragedy for Chatham.

As a naval stronghold, the Medway Towns had already suffered their first casualties in what was to be a long and bitter war. Amongst the crew of the *Pathfinder*, already sunk by an enemy U-boat, Chatham personnel had sacrificed their lives. Despite this, however, the town had been rejoicing. A successfully fought action off Heligoland Bight had involved the *Arethusa*, a ship built in the Chatham dockyard, crewed by Chatham sailors and now returned to the area for repairs. The *Arethusa*'s crew, though, were less inclined to rejoice. They had seen just how bloody war could be. Upon the ship's return, two crew members assaulted a police officer. Brought before the courts, they were given a month's hard labour. More than a little aggrieved, and encouraged by the hardships they had suffered, one of the ratings threw down a blood stained naval collar. It was a legacy from the battle, a reminder of the bitterness of war, and a plea for the madness to end.

Sometime around midday on the 22nd, rumours first began to spread the length and breadth of Chatham. The country had suffered a naval defeat, and three Chatham ships had been sunk. The names of three Cressy class cruisers were circulated, but so were the names of various other ships. The source of these rumours was the dockyard. At the town hall, then a central recruiting office, hundreds of distraught women began to gather outside. At first the authorities could say nothing, but eventually an official statement was posted outside. It merely confirmed the loss of the *Aboukir, Hogue* and *Cressy.*

Large numbers chose to remain outside the town hall. They awaited a list of survivors. With brothers, sons and loved ones known to be on these cruisers, there were few in Chatham who did not have a cause for concern. It was to be four days before such a list could be assembled. On 25th September numerous sheets of paper, listing survivors who had been brought into Harwich, were pasted up. To provide illumination during hours of darkness, six arc lamps were also erected.

At 9 pm on 25th September, the first of the survivors reached Chatham, being brought by train from Harwich. The news of their imminent arrival spread and crowds congregated at the station. But the train was not to stop. Instead it passed right through the station, being directed into the dockyard, where three hundred ratings made their way to the barracks. A further two hundred arrived the following day.

For Chatham this was only the first of a number of wartime horrors. On 26th November 1914, some residents in the Medway Towns actually witnessed a distant naval tragedy. A London class battleship, the *Bulwark*, blew up in the Medway. At the time she was anchored in Kethole Reach and had just finished early morning coaling. Although not a Chatham based ship, there were a number of Chatham ratings on board. The cause of the explosion was undoubtedly accidental, being aided by a design fault notorious to that type of battleship. The 'Chatham News', in its edition of the following week, carried a full report and noted that many Chatham residents had heard the explosion, whilst those on higher ground had actually seen the flash. Of a crew of 753, only twelve survived.

Even worse was to follow. On 27th May 1915, a fast mine layer, the *Princess Irene,* was also destroyed by an internal explosion. She, too, was anchored in the Medway. Many, of course, felt that this, together with the *Bulwark* explosion, were the result of sabotage, but little evidence points in this direction. At the time, the *Princess Irene* had been loaded with five hundred mines, any one of which could have been faulty. The explosion completely destroyed the ship and killed all but one of the crew. On this occasion, doors and windows in both Rochester and Chatham were shaken. According to the 'Chatham News':

'The force of the explosion was terrific. To many it seemed louder than the *Bulwark,* and that shook many houses to their foundations. The spectacle for a few moments was terrible in its grandeur — one who has seen Vesuvius in an eruption likened it to that spectacle for a moment, flames and smoke belched forth in great volume.'

In fact, the force of the explosion was so great that many people instinctively assumed that it had emanated from within the dockyard. Large numbers gathered outside the main gate and it was some time before they could be convinced of their mistake. Of the *Princess Irene*'s crew, many had been drawn from the barracks, being mostly fresh recruits. Only a few, therefore, were actually Chathamites. This, of course, makes it no less a tragedy but did take some of the pressure away from an already hard hit town. In Sheerness, though, the disaster was heavily felt. Amongst the dead were seventy-six dockyard workers from that town. They had been carrying out last minute refit work, being due to return to their homes that evening.

Apart from those wartime disasters which more directly affected Chatham, the war years also saw a number of Chatham-built vessels destroyed. One such casualty was the *Arethusa*, a hero of the Heligoland Bight, wrecked in 1916 after hitting a mine. But it was the submarines which received the severest mauling. Of the twenty C to G-class submarines built at Chatham prior to 1917, five were destroyed during the war years. These were the C.33, C.34, E.1, E.7 and E.8. R-class submarines, built at Chatham in 1918, were too late for entering hostilities. As submarines, though, they were an interesting class, being designed for anti-submarine duties. Displacing 410 tons, they were highly manoeuvrable underwater, having a submerged speed of fifteen knots. Fitted with advanced hydrophone gear and six bow torpedo tubes they would have been a match for any U-boat they came into contact with.

On 17th September 1917, emphasis upon ship losses was completely overshadowed by an air raid which caused considerable loss of life within the naval barracks at Chatham. Four German Gotha bombers, intending to attack the dockyard, indiscriminately bombed the Medway Towns. One bomb, a 110-pounder, crashed into the naval barracks, exploding within the drill hall then being used as sleeping quarters. One hundred and thirty-six naval ratings were killed, giving this bomb the gruesome record of causing more loss of life than any other single bomb dropped throughout the entire war. A clock, later found smashed on the parade ground, gave the time of the explosion as 11.12 pm. Most of the deaths resulted from flying glass, with a great number of the injured trapped in the debris.

Apart from the naval barracks, bombs also fell on the inner lines, Trinity School, Chatham cemetery and Mallerigh Road. A further bomb fell on the High Street, damaging a number of shops. But these bombs compared as nothing with the death and destruction brought to the barracks:

'All through the night the work of rescue went on. It was a sad spectacle in the moonlight — officers and men carrying the dead bodies of comrades into buildings which had been transformed into a mortuary and the seriously wounded cases into motor ambulances which sped to the hospital.'

With this raid, Chatham found itself in the front line of the war. Not only were numerous residents constantly in fear of a War Office telegram, but now had the

The naval barracks drill hall showing the spot where the fatal bomb exploded. Its original target had been the dockyard.

additional worry of further bombing raids. The dockyard, of course, was a natural target. The River Medway, pinpointing the exact position of the dockyard made it an incredibly easy target. Quite early on, night raids by Zeppelins had been considered a very real possibility. A primitive early warning system was evolved, in which a number of telephones within the dockyard were to be constantly manned. When an air raid warning was given, members of the electrical department were to be informed immediately. They, in turn, rang through to the power station so that all lights could be extinguished at source. On the night of 17th September the warning system only partially worked. A practice alert was in operation and only a few realised a real air raid was in progress. Most thought that the given warnings were all part of the practice.

As might be expected, the war was a busy period for the dockyard. Of all the work undertaken, however, one task, the construction of the *Zubian*, has always been looked upon with special pride. The *Zubian* was a tribal class destroyer which originally started life as two separate destroyers — the *Zulu* and *Nubian*. In late October 1916 the *Nubian* was torpedoed whilst cruising off the Belgian coast. With most of her bow section destroyed she was carefully towed to a safe harbourage. A few weeks later the *Zulu* was mined, losing most of her stern section. Both ships being of the same class, it was decided to join the two. This was the task undertaken by Chatham dockyard, and it was completed by June 1917, with the join being made between the third and fourth funnels.

Another of the major tasks undertaken at Chatham was that of preparing a number of ships for a raid upon Zeebrugge. This was to be an extremely imaginative operation, carried out in April 1918, being designed to block both Ostend harbour and the Bruges canal at Zeebrugge. Had it been successful, the plan would have seriously undermined German U-boat operations, as both Zeebrugge and Ostend were key submarine bases. Three blockships, in reality the hurriedly converted cruisers *Thetis, Iphigenia* and *Intrepid,* were to be scuttled at the mouth of the Bruges canal whilst two further cruisers, *Sirius* and *Brilliant,* were to be placed at the entrance to the Ostend harbour. To help ensure success, and to provide a massive diversion, numerous ratings and marines were to be landed on the Zeebrugge mole, to create as much havoc as possible. Finally, communications were to be severed by two submarines, loaded with high explosives, and designed to destroy a railway viaduct linking the mainland with the defensive mole.

Although carefully planned, the completed operation fell short of the desired objectives. Undertaken on the night of 22nd/23rd April, the basic element of surprise was lost when an earlier attempt had been abandoned due to adverse weather conditions. Only one submarine was able to reach its target, the block ships were very badly positioned and the marines were decimated even before the planned landing. The result was that Zeebrugge harbour was only partially blocked.

Chatham's role was in adapting many of the ships subsequently used in the raid. Between February and April 1917, major work was undertaken upon six ships. The *Vindictive,* a former cruiser, and the vessel used to land the marines, was given much additional armament in the form of howitzers, mortars and flamethrowers. The *Thetis, Iphigenia, Intrepid, Sirius* and *Brilliant,* blockships, had a great deal of their equipment removed whilst each was filled with 1,500 tons of concrete. Lesser alterations were carried out on other ships, including the careful placement of explosives in the submarines C.1 and C.3.

By November 1918 the workforce at Chatham was in excess of 11,000. Because of the demands of war, a proportion of this figure was diluted labour. Large numbers of those in the lesser trades had either volunteered or been conscripted for military service and their jobs taken over by an older man. This, of course, was a wartime expediency and to last only for the duration of the war. With the return of peace, the conscripted men were to be given their jobs back — or at least this was the theory. In practice, whilst the dockyard authorities were usually prepared to offer a job, it was not always one of such a high grade. Mr F.R. Scott, a trained wireman and a member of the Electrical Trades Union, was one such victim. He had left the dockyard in 1918 having volunteered, he was duly sent to France where, with the war brought to a sudden conclusion, he was transferred to the army of occupation. Upon returning to Chatham in 1920 he was given the alternative of joining the Construction Department as a labourer, or that of collecting his cards. Naturally he chose the former, but also sought help from his union. They indicated a complete inability to help him, and so he tore up his union card, joining the Transport and General Workers Union instead.

During this period of their history, the dockyard unions were in a very weak position. Denied the right of strike, they had few other sanctions to level at the

Vindictive, a second class cruiser that was originally launched from Chatham's No. 2 dock in 1897. In later years she was prepared at Chatham for the raid upon the Belgian port of Zeebrugge.

dockyard authorities. Prior to World War One the largest of the unions was the 'Government Labourers Union'. A dockyard branch of this union had been formed as early as 1889 and in 1914 it had a recorded membership of 1,574. It was, however, only a local union and, for this reason, the decision was taken in 1919 to dissolve the branch. Members, instead, joined either the 'Transport and General Workers Union' or the 'Municipal and General Workers Union'. Another of the early unions, and the largest of the craft unions, was the Associated Shipwrights Society. It had two dockyard branches, one of which had been established in the 1880s and the other in 1896. In 1919 the Whitley Councils were established. They allowed union leaders, within the dockyard, the right to discuss pay and conditions, but they were really part of an elaborate government operation to further weaken the power of unions. For this reason Whitley councils were largely rejected outside of the civil service.

A great deal of antagonism existed between the unions and the dockyard management. It was not uncommon for members of the dockyard police (CID section) to take up position outside a union meeting and to note the names of all those who entered. In 1926, the dockyard unions felt unable to give any support to the General Strike and work proceeded as normal within the dockyard. Indeed, the yard was used as a centre for strike breaking. Large amounts of coal, destined for various power stations, was constantly despatched by train. This was dockyard coal which had originally been brought to the yard both for powering ships and also much of the yard machinery. Mr S.R. Stears remembers seeing a number of 'Southern Railway' engines coming into the yard to collect loaded coal wagons. Pulled by two engines at a time, some of these loads numbered two hundred wagons and stretched from the Gillingham Gate down to the No. 8 slip — some 2,000 feet. At the time, Mr Stears was employed in the dockyard as an engine driver. On such occasions, he was given the task of 'bumping' the trucks from the rear in order to help the overloaded trains up the incline immediately outside of the yard. Also in connection with the 1926 strike, it should be mentioned that a great number of naval ratings were sent to various ports in the country to help keep services open.

The post-war years were a difficult time for the dockyard. Admiralty orders for the construction of new warships were immediately cancelled, whilst work on the *Warren*, a W-class destroyer under construction, was suspended. This, the only destroyer ever to have been ordered for construction at Chatham, was never completed, being scrapped in 1919. At the same time, the Navy was also being run down and the Medway was crammed with ships being paid off. The numerous creeks were filled with unwanted torpedo boats, whilst destroyers and cruisers were anchored in mid-river positions, awaiting delivery to the breakers yard.

To provide some work, the yard labour force was employed upon completing a number of partially finished ships. These were vessels originally launched in private yards but having no engines or other equipment. In 1922 the cruisers *Enterprise* and *Despatch* came to the yard, as did the V and W-class destroyer *Whitehall*. The submarines L.23, L.53 and K.26 were also fitted out at Chatham, whilst the submarines K.24, K.25 and K.28 were to have been brought to Chatham, but were scrapped instead.

The K-class submarines were an unusual design, being steam powered and intended for operating with the fleet. The basic layout left a great deal to be desired, for although the powerful steam engines allowed the vessel a speed of 24 knots, the problem of having a funnel on board a submarine went largely unsolved. When surfaced the funnel was far too low, and high waves frequently entered the boiler room through the funnel. When submerged the submarine was powered by an electric motor, with the funnel lowered. A watertight compartment was supposed to prevent the entry of water into the boilers, but the seals proved inadequate. At least one K-class submarine was lost when water entered the boilers during submersion. This, however, was but a minor problem. Far more serious was the difficulty of operating such craft with the fleet. Submarines naturally have a low silhouette and are difficult to observe, as a result of which they were frequently involved in collisions, either with each other or various other ships.

Chatham dockyard began work upon the K.26 in 1921. The hull had been completed by Vickers in 1919 and the red oxide coated frame was brought to Chatham shortly after. An improved system for closing the funnel and air intakes was provided whilst modifications were made to the arming of the submarine. A somewhat unlucky design, its reputation continued with the K.26. Even whilst at Chatham two dockyard men were killed due to a blow back of steam in the boiler-room. Later, the K.26 did operate with the fleet after its

The ill-fated *K26*.   (RN Submarine Museum, Gosport)

Odin, launched from the No. 7 slip in May 1928.

commissioning in 1923, but was scrapped in 1931 after the Admiralty was finally convinced that the whole concept of submarines operating with the fleet was a failure.

Over four years elapsed before a completely new vessel was to be constructed at Chatham. In 1923 the experimental submarine, X.1, was successfully launched. It was a craft well in advance of its day, displacing 2,780 tons, and the largest submarine ever built at Chatham. It was designed as a submarine cruiser, armed with four 5.2-inch guns and six torpedo tubes, she had the ability, should the need arise, to engage an enemy destroyer on the surface. The whole concept, however, was a little too far in advance of its day. Operating such a large submarine was to prove extremely difficult. The main engine, built in the factory at Chatham, proved totally unsatisfactory and was for ever breaking down. Nor did the vessel have any obvious use. On the surface it was too slow to operate with the fleet, whilst an alternative role of commerce raiding was heavily frowned upon. As a result, the X.1 was laid up within five years of her launch.

The launching of the X.1 coincided with the first of a series of lay-offs that now occurred within the dockyard. During the 'twenties and early 'thirties the dockyard was heavily under utilised, with rumours abounding as to its imminent closure. Even with the redundancies many of the retained gangs found themselves under employed. It was not unusual for labourers, upon entering the yard in the morning, to be sent straight for the magazine. This was not for purposes of work, but simply that chargemen should know where they were if they should be needed. In 1924 the number of yard discharges accelerated, with unemployment for a large group only being saved by two Admiralty contracts. Chatham yard was given the go-ahead on building a submarine, the *Oberon*, and a cruiser, the *Kent*. Immediately three special gangs were shoaled, two for the cruiser and one for the submarine.

The *Oberon* was one of a new class of patrol submarines. Constructed on the No. 7 slip, it was a conventional design, built with Pacific operations in mind. The *Odin*, launched at Chatham in 1928, was also of this class. To save money, the *Oberon* was to be launched with her batteries already fitted. This produced a problem, as the launch way had not been designed for the increased weight. On the original day set for the launch, a number of the blocks became jammed, with one becoming totally immovable. Two shipwrights were, in fact, under the submarine, trying to remove this block, right up to the time of the launching ceremony. Eventually the ceremony had to be cancelled, with the *Oberon* launched the following day. As so often happens, the slipway caught fire on this occasion owing to so much of the grease which had been placed on the ways being squeezed out by the vessel's excessive weight.

Both the *Oberon* and the *Kent* were substantially completed by 1926. Much of the fitting was undertaken after the launch, but for the shipwrights their job was complete. With the Admiralty placing no further orders at this time, redundancies were again introduced. Indeed, dismissals were to continue right into the early 'thirties, with the dockyard labour force down to 7,000 in 1933. Bill

149

Humphreys, a former shipwright who had been employed upon the *Oberon*, was one of those dismissed. He received his cards in 1927, a victim of post-war economies. More fortunate than most, he initially took up building work in Rainham. Others, however, had to search further afield. Many of those formerly employed at Chatham moved to Tilbury, finding employment in constructing some of the docks there. Some shipwrights managed to re-enter the dockyard as casual labourers. At the time Admiralty oil boats were coming into the yard, with a number of shipwrights being made responsible for both cleaning out and repainting them. It was hardly work for a skilled man, but then, of course, times were desperate.

In many respects shipwrights found it a lot easier than most groups to obtain alternative employment. Whereas most tradesmen had fairly restricted skills, noticeably boilermakers, coppersmiths and patternmakers, shipwrights had a great wealth of skills. They could turn their hands to anything. Labourers, though, were even less fortunate. Thrown out of the dockyards in large numbers they invariably had to turn to state assistance and had little money with which to support their families.

The depression, then, hit Chatham as much as anywhere. Relying heavily on one industry, no improvement in the fortunes of the Medway Towns could possibly come about until the Admiralty sanctioned a new building programme. A move which did not occur until the mid-1930s when the spectre of German fascism made such a move inevitable. Somewhat unfortunately, though, Chatham's salvation came as a direct result of a new war. From 1934 onwards a whole programme of S-class submarine construction was begun, whilst the cruisers *Euryalus* and *Arethusa* date to the immediate period before the outbreak of war. Again, the world had failed to learn from an earlier folly; war, once more, was about to be declared.

Chapter Fourteen

WORLD WAR TWO

'The dim dark sea so like unto death
That divides and yet unites mankind.'

Longfellow

For Chatham, like so many other working-class towns, the years of depression were painfully felt. The years of high unemployment left a deep scar. Fear of the workhouse was desperately felt in all quarters, and there were few in the dockyard who were not worried about the next round of 'cut backs'. Yet a certain humour still managed to surface, with unemployment euphemistically known as 'being on the big firm'. It was perhaps the children of the unemployed who suffered most, kitted out in ill-fitting clothes, denied even the most modest of luxuries and reared on a somewhat spartan diet. Bread and dripping, or bread and jam was the main food item of the day; with jam being the most favoured simply because it was cheap. Numerous farms existed in the Kentish countryside and youngsters were regularly sent out to purchase fresh fruit for jam making.

Within the town of Chatham a noticeable gulf existed. On the one side were those with a secure job, on the other stood the unemployed. Mrs H. Brenchley (née Lemmon) vividly recalls these years. Her father was Henry James Lemmon, an iron caulker at the dockyard. He was fortunate, remaining employed for the entire period. But even for his family, life was no bed of roses. Earning £2.7s.6d he had to support a wife and five children. Each Friday he gave his wife £2 for the housekeeping, retaining for himself the additional 7/6d together with any overtime money earned. Of the £2, some 12/- was immediately spent on groceries with the rest being set aside for rent, clothes and savings for an annual holiday taken in Ramsgate. To this extent the Lemmon family could be considered a little better off than most. An annual holiday was one luxury that a good many had to do without. As a dockyard caulker, Henry Lemmon took his holidays during the first week in August as, during the 'twenties and 'thirties, the dockyard had begun closing down for one week in every year. Even so, Henry Lemmon was not paid for holidays and it was a tremendous strain supporting such a large family away from home. Despite this, it was an event to be looked forward to. So as to economise, the journey was made by bus, with changes being made at Sittingbourne, Faversham and Canterbury. This, of course, was no easy task for such a large family. The numerous suitcases, together with a pushchair in tow, produced considerable problems.

Henry Lemmon worked mainly on submarines. For this reason he usually acquired tickets so that his children might see most of the launchings. Another treat for the children was that of taking their father's dinner to work. Mrs

151

It was during the inter-war period that Chatham dockyard was first thrown open to the public in the form of Navy Week (later Navy Days). A special attraction for the year 1929 was a newly constructed replica of HMS *Kent*, an eighteenth century ship-of-the-line.

Lemmon would put stew and vegetables into a china pudding basin, placing a plate on top. This was then tied up with an obligatory red spotted handkerchief. The children walked to the yard, but were given one penny for the tram fare back. Hundreds would be queuing outside the yard gates by the time they got there, as nobody was allowed in until midday was chimed. Then there would be a concerted rush, with the men coming to meet the children. Usually Henry Lemmon gave his own children a quick tour of the ship upon which he was working, followed by a cup of tea. Mrs Brenchley, who is now a housewife living on the Hoo Peninsula, remembers that such moments made her feel very 'grown up', sitting round an open fire with her brothers and sisters, drinking tea boiled in an empty fruit tin. As always it was pitch black and covered in scum.

In 1934 the dockyard saw the launching of the *Arethusa*. A name class cruiser, she displaced 5,000 tons and was designed for protecting the trade routes. A product of the 1931 naval estimates, her construction cost the country £1¼m. That she was built at Chatham was a relief for a great many. It kept two gangs of shipwrights, and many additional workers, fully occupied during the years when the depression was hitting hardest. Finally completed in 1935, No. 8 slipway was again in use when work started upon the *Euryalus*. Amongst the shipwrights employed upon this cruiser was Bill Humphreys. He had returned to the yard several months earlier, taking the opportunity to train as a shipwright welder, a relatively new skill. Whilst welders had been present during the construction of the earlier O-class submarines, it was at that time all rather primitive. When the welder needed power, all the lights in the vicinity dimmed as the dockyard power-house was not designed to produce the large amounts of localised electric current

MODEL OF H.M.S. "KENT",
CHATHAM NAVY WEEK, AUG, 1 - 8, 1931

Another attraction for the 1929 Navy Week was a model of the recently launched cruiser that also carried the name of 'Kent'. As it happens, the real HMS *Kent* had been launched in the yard just three years earlier.

which was required. Improvements, however, were on the way, and before long welding had completely replaced riveting. As a shipwright welder, Bill Humphreys was the first welder to start work upon the *Euryalus.*

The *Euryalus,* following in the wake of the *Arethusa,* meant that large numbers could again find employment within the dockyard. But, as well as this, increased orders were being placed for the construction of submarines. From about 1934 onwards, two further building slips were permanently employed in this kind of work. Once built, of course, these vessels also had to be fitted out. Thus, the dockyard not only needed large numbers of shipwrights, caulkers and others more directly related with shipbuilding, but also large numbers of skilled labourers who were employed in the factory. The factory, originally built in the 1880s and sited close to the Upnor wall, was responsible for manufacturing the many component parts. Within the factory there were several sections each having its own specialisation; these being submarines, steam propulsion, torpedo tubes and aircraft catapults. The largest was the steam section, responsible for the manufacture of turbines, dynamos, propellors, auxiliary machinery and anything to do with the actual propulsion of a steam powered ship. The torpedo tube section, as the name implied, manufactured torpedo tubes whilst the aircraft catapult section manufactured launching devices for aircraft then being carried on board warships. In the 1930s many ships were undergoing modernisation programmes which often included the addition of a catapult, whilst vessels like the newly built *Arethusa* were purpose-built to carry a small seaplane which was stored between the funnels. Finally, in the submarine section, the large diesel engines were manufactured. This end of the factory was particularly noisy as, on completion, engines were test run, at four-fifths power, for seventy-two hours. Later, they were also given an eight hour test at full power.

Arethusa, launched in March 1934 and built on the No. 8 slip.

Apart from the construction of new ships, re-fit work on older vessels was accelerated. From 1937 onwards a number of C-class cruisers, ships originally built during World War One, were brought to Chatham for conversion into Anti-Aircraft gun ships. Amongst this batch of vessels was the *Coventry*. Much of her upper deck was removed and her six-inch guns replaced by 4-inch, high angle, anti-aircraft guns. Ships like these were later to see heavy deployment amongst the various Atlantic convoys and were to have quite a high loss. Later, with the outbreak of war, the yard found itself engaged in the fitting of degaussing gear to numerous smaller vessels, so neutralising their magnetic attraction to mines.

The dockyard's transfer to wartime duties was fairly smooth. Already by 1939 numerous dug-outs had been constructed, whilst most of the personnel had been issued with gas masks. In September 1939, the yard was subjected to a number of air raid alerts and, as nothing came of these — other than a great waste of time — the whole business was streamlined. Instead of having thousands of men sitting in shelters for hours on end, dockyard personnel were to be given two warnings. The first indicated a raid approaching whilst a series of pips meant an attack was imminent and that immediate cover should be taken. Apart from all this, there were a number of practice alerts in which female clerical staff, employed in the clock tower offices, had to spend entire mornings typing whilst wearing gas masks.

As in the First World War, the dockyard witnessed considerable dilution of labour. A number of the craft unions agreed to unskilled workmen carrying out the work of artisans, and allowing these workers to be dispersed to other yards. In addition some two thousand women entered the yard during this period. They undertook crane driving, machine operating and various unskilled jobs. Within the factory about one hundred women were employed in each of the two shifts and were responsible for operating most of the automatics. Also within the factory, the Amalgamated Engineering Union specifically agreed to skilled labourers undertaking the work of fitters — but only for the duration of the war. Previous to 1939 the wage structure within the yard had been set so that a top rate skilled labourer received the equivalent wage of a bottom rate fitter. For the six years of war, all these careful wage divisions were scrapped, as unions and management pooled their resources in the fight against fascism.

Early in 1940 the cruiser *Ajax* entered the yard following upon her River Plate exploits. All in all she was not too badly damaged, although a number of dockyard workers recall her funnels having been thoroughly pierced by shrapnel. For the Germans she was to become a propaganda target. With the sinking of the *Graf Spee*, Hitler would very much like to have seen the destruction of such ships as the *Ajax*. Certainly the Germans were aware of her having entered Chatham yard, and at least one attempt was made to destroy her. This was when a lone German aeroplane, a Dornier 17, carried out a surprise raid and unloaded a series of bombs onto the yard. At the time, the *Ajax* had just come out of No. 9 dock and was lying next to the Upnor wall. Workers on the *Euryalus*, also undergoing a minor re-fit, saw the bombs coming and felt sure that one of them had gone down the *Ajax*'s funnel. As it turned out it was a near miss, the bomb had hit the jetty, killing a crane driver.

To fool the Germans, the *Ajax* was quickly returned to No. 9 dock and her place alongside the Upnor wall was taken by a C-class cruiser. This was one of the ships undergoing conversion to that of anti-aircraft gun ship. Her upper decks were all burnt away and she looked a complete wreck. Naturally, upon the return of a German reconnaissance aeroplane, this ship was mistaken for the *Ajax*. Within a few hours 'Lord Haw Haw' was proclaiming the loss of this first rate cruiser.

Over the coming months, the dockyard was subjected to a number of damaging raids. Of these the worst undoubtedly occurred in late 1940, when the factory was bombed. Within that building a two shift system operated, with 600 workers in each shift. It was 8 pm double British Summer Time that the Medway area was subjected to a more than usually intense raid. A number of bombs fell in the vicinity of the dockyard, one exploding inside the factory. With a large number of workers inside, and shrapnel flying everywhere, numerous injuries resulted. In all, there were twenty-three fatalities, most of which were caused by the great glass roof falling in. On later occasions both the smithery and saw mill were also bombed.

One incident which most dockyard men recall is that of the *Arethusa* returning to Chatham during the autumn of 1940. Being a relatively new cruiser, she was well protected against air attack. Included in her armament were eight 4-inch anti-aircraft guns. These had an incredible range and the captain was determined to use these guns upon any bombers seen to be approaching London. Having entered dry dock the workforce was duly informed that the guns were going to be used and that the wedgings were to be made absolutely firm. Many of the yard workers did not in fact believe the *Arethusa* would open fire in dry dock as such an idea had always been totally unimaginable. Anyway, within a few days some forty to fifty bombers were sighted and the 4-inch guns opened fire. A curtain of exploding shells proceeded to force many of the bombers to alter course, with the action doing a good deal to raise morale within the dockyard. Nor did this incident go unnoticed by those responsible for the defence of London, the *Arethusa* being subsequently moored close to Tower Bridge.

In May 1940, a dockyard Home Guard battalion was formed. Originally the 14th (Medway) Kent battalion, it later became the 31st Battalion under the command of Lt. Col. H.B. Forbes. It was the largest of the Kent battalions, membership being compulsory for all males working in the dockyard. Platoons and companies were organised around specific work areas, such as the factory. Over the years various training sessions were organised with imaginary parachutists landing on St Mary's Island and mock battles with Royal Navy personnel. Apart from the Home Guard, the dockyard also organised itself into various first aid units whilst a strengthened auxiliary fire service operated a number of 1914 vintage Merryweather fire engines.

A particularly hectic period for the dockyard was at the time of the Dunkirk evacuation. Chatham was the nearest major naval base and many returning destroyers, heavily damaged, were directed to the Medway. Many only just managed to reach the dockyard, for they were all but sinking. Subsequent repairs had to be rushed. Instead of removing all of the damaged plates, gaping great holes were simply covered so that the destroyer might be returned to action, and room made for others. One such damaged destroyer, the *Pelican*, considerably battered, brought home the true shock of war when the dockyard 'maties' discovered the remains of several dead crew members.

As a dockyard, Chatham played a valuable role during the war years. Employing a workforce of 13,000, of which 2,000 were women, it had a tremendous output. In all, twelve submarines, four sloops and two floating docks were laid down during these years, whilst 1,360 re-fits were carried out. Additionally the dockyard supplied stud welding equipment for tanks and other fighting vehicles, fitted out over 1,200 shore establishments and, in December 1944, supplied and started a shore carrier service to naval bases and parties on the continent. A number of two-man submarines were built at Chatham, fitted with lorry diesel engines and dustbin-like torpedo tubes. Of the larger re-fits, the cruiser *London* was plated with armour and *Scylla* was converted to an escort carrier flagship. The final months of the war also saw Chatham busily engaged in fitting out part of a fleet destined for the Far East and the continuing war against Japan.

Chapter Fifteen

A PHOENIX FROM THE ASHES

Undoubtedly the main thread that runs through the entire post-war history of Chatham dockyard is that of it being under constant threat of closure. Compared with those other royal dockyards at Portsmouth, Devonport and Rosyth, the yard at Chatham was considerably under-utilised and witnessed a great number of cut backs and general lay-offs. Within a few months of World War Two having ended a number of Admiralty contracts were cancelled, whilst work on the submarine *Adept* and sloops *Nonsuch* and *Nymph*, all at that time still on the slipways, was never to be completed.

Admittedly the 1950s did see a general improvement in the situation, with the yard receiving orders to construct the *Oberon*, first of a new class of patrol submarines. Laid down on the No. 7 slip in November 1957, she was not to be finally completed until February 1961. Indeed, during her early period of construction a number of unforeseen problems were encountered, these frequently resulting from a lack of recent submarine construction experience and the need for earlier lessons having to be relearnt.

Eventually six 'Oberons' were built at Chatham, of which three were constructed for the Royal Canadian Navy. These latter received enlarged de-icing and air conditioning systems, so preparing them for the extremes of climate they were likely to meet. The *Okanagan* was the last of these to be launched and represented an important landmark for Chatham. She was the very last warship to be constructed there, with the dockyard thereafter concentrating upon re-fit work. Indeed, in February 1966, only seven months before the launch of the *Okanagan*, work began on construction of the nuclear complex which allowed Chatham to handle work upon the Fleet class nuclear submarines.

The building of Chatham's nuclear complex was first announced in March 1965, and at a time when renewed fears existed as to the possible closure of the naval base. The last of the 'Oberons' was nearing completion and no new orders had been received. All in all, the future looked bleak as Chatham had then only the ability of re-fitting conventional submarines. The nuclear complex, naturally enough, changed all this. A dockyard within a dockyard, the site chosen for its construction was between the old Nos. 6 and 7 docks, these two docks being strengthened to allow for the erection of a particularly large cantilever crane.

Yet even this failed to save Chatham. Despite the expenditure of several million pounds upon the nuclear re-fit complex, the dockyard was still to face final closure. Indeed, the eventual loss of the complex was to cause severe problems for the navy, leading to the early scrapping of a number of submarines that would normally have been dry docked at Chatham for the replacement of used

An aerial view of the dockyard taken during the final years of naval occupancy. In the immediate foreground, and easily identified by its huge cantilever crane, is the now demolished nuclear refit complex whilst moored in the No. 1 basin is *Blake*, a former helicopter cruiser.
(Kent Messenger Group)

The Fleet Class submarine *Courageous* passes through the Bulls Nose entrance. She was about to undergo a re-fit in the nuclear complex.
(Ministry of Defence)

The launch of *Okanagan* on 17th September 1966. Built on the No. 7 slip, she represents the last major launching at the Chatham yard. (Mr A. Morris)

reactor cores. Amongst these was *Dreadnought,* a submarine that was actually awaiting her re-fit during the period in which the dockyard was being run down.

As for that much feared announcement, this was to be made by John Nott, the Secretary of State for Defence, in a statement to the House of Commons on Thursday 25th June 1981. It was a truly shattering piece of news and one that has since helped make unemployment in the Medway Towns amongst the highest in the south-east.

Whilst numerous individuals campaigned to keep the dockyard open, others were planning on how best to use the land once the inevitable had occurred. For such purposes, three separate organisations were either created or otherwise brought into into the Medway area, with each taking responsibility for a separate section of the former dockyard.

First to become operational was the Medway (Chatham) Dock Company, a body which had been established under the auspices of the Medway Ports Authority. Taking over the No. 3 basin some three months before the official departure of the Navy, a thriving port complex has since been created. In all, the new company is responsible for a 100 acre site and has used this space for the creation of eight separate berths.

The first commercial vessel to take advantage of the new port at Chatham was the *Vibrence.* Owned by Crescent Shipping, this low air draught short sea trader brought in a packaged cargo from Kalmar, Sweden. From that small beginning, Crescent have gone on to develop a fully operational cargo terminal port with Roll-on/Roll-off (Ro/Ro), Lift-on/Lift-off (Lo/Lo) and Stow-on/Roll-off (Sto/Ro) facilities based on berths 3 and 4.

Amongst the companies that operate from the newly created Chatham Docks is Kent Line. This particular vessel, one of two that are regularly to be seen in the No. 3 basin, is the *Duke of Anglia*. She has a capacity for eighty-eight trailers. (Kent Line)

Other companies that operate within the newly established Chatham Docks are Kent Line and Honigs. The first of these, Kent Line, is based around the No. 2 berth and operates a twice daily Ro/Ro service to Zeebrugge. Honigs, on the other hand, are a warehousing and stevedoring firm that specialises in the unloading of forest products. Around No. 8 berth they have established a Sto/Ro ramp and additional Lo/Lo facilities. A final company worth mentioning is that of Chatham Shiprepair which opened at the entrance to No. 3 basin in 1985. Offering repair facilities for dredgers, sludge carriers and Ro/Ro ferries, they also provide emergency repairs for ships trading in the Medway.

It was not until 31st March that the Royal Navy officially abandoned responsibility for the yard. On the following day both English Estates and the Chatham Historic Dockyard Trust became the new owners of that part of the dockyard which was not already occupied by the Medway Dock Company.

In general terms, English Estates currently occupy the central dockyard area that includes Nos. 1 and 2 basins together with the site of the former Nuclear Refit Centre. Charged with the task of completely redeveloping the entire area, they were the subject of much local criticism when they undertook a wholesale demolition of numerous buildings that they considered to have no further use. Retained however, is the No. 8 Machine Shop, the Boilershed and the Machine Shed, all of which began life at Woolwich and were brought to Chatham sometime after the closure of that particular dockyard in 1869.

160

As for their precise plans for the future, English Estates, having engaged a firm of consultants, allowed public access to these ideas during the summer of 1985. Backed by a fanfare of publicity, it was indicated that an entire community was to be created, and one that was designed to meet the nation's three most pressing needs, those of jobs, homes and leisure. In keeping with this new face of the twentieth century, the word dockyard was abandoned and, instead, the term 'Chatham Maritime' was introduced.

Designed to be completed sometime during the mid-1990s, the entire scheme hinges upon a massive amount of private investment. New industry, so it is hoped, will be attracted into the former dockyard area by a recent acquisition of 'Enterprise Zone' status. To further encourage such a move, English Estates are currently developing a basic infrastructure that will consist of a spine road, a new link bridge across the basins and factory buildings.

As noted in their publicity handouts, the hub of this redevelopment programme will be centred around the two basins, with one of them reserved for water sports and the other more simply used for yachts and basic instruction in small boat sailing. Around both of these basins there will also be established up-market housing and a shopping arcade. Complementing all this, further low-density housing is planned for St Mary's Island, the occupants being given fine views of the river. Playing fields will be retained and a primary school is also planned.

Obviously an exciting venture, it will doubtless bring great prosperity to the area. However, it is not beyond criticism. Whilst the Medway Towns has a fine working class tradition, the Chatham Maritime area will be ferociously middle class. Gerald Hinks, editor of the 'Chatham News', is just one of many who has directed a limited amount of criticism towards the scheme. Whilst generally giving it his support, he went on to declare in a comment entitled 'A future for all — or a rich man's paradise?' that:

'. . . some people otherwise enthusiastic — and count me among them — have some reservations about the prospects of creating an elite community within a community. English Estates would dismiss the elite notion and tell us that the homes for the dockyard are wide-ranging.

But really we are looking here at up-market homes. The most desirable executive residences with delightful river views are going to be in the £200,000 bracket.

Not everyone will be able to afford the unique Chatham Maritime experience.'   ['Chatham News', 7th June 1985]

A third and final area of the dockyard, as already noted was placed under the charge of an historic trust. Government funded, the officially entitled Chatham Historic Dockyard Trust was given a once and for all grant of £11.3m. As the first chairman of the Trust, Lt. Gen. Sir Steuart Pringle, soon discovered this money was quite inadequate, being only sufficient for the basic upkeep and maintenance of the numerous historic buildings that it was now responsible for managing.

Artist's impression of how English Estates hope to develop their own particular section of the former dockyard. The focal point is a 900-berth marina. Also to be noted are the office/high technology premises in the foreground and set in small, landscaped, 'business parks'. Housing is to be seen around the planned marina and river bank. The acquisition of Enterprise Zone status offers those who choose to invest in the scheme a 100% capital allowance, rate free benefits until 1996 and simplified planning procedures.   (English Estates)

In all, this third section of the dockyard, comprising an area of 80 acres, stands immediately beyond the dockyard Main Gate and approximates the original area of the yard prior to the Victorian extension. Of considerable historic importance, it is a complete dockyard in its own right, the area having within its bounds the original covered ropery and attendant buildings, numerous offices, the covered slipways, three dry docks, timber seasoning sheds, mast house, sail loft and residences. Most of them constructed during Georgian or early Victorian times, they all carry listed status.

This area of the dockyard will eventually become a living museum in which various traditional trades and skills will be practiced in the midst of an historic setting. It is already open to the public with a visitors' centre in operation.

Restoration work is shortly to begin on the mast house and mould loft. Once completed, this fine eighteenth century building will also encompass a gallery that will depict the development of the wooden warship. Similarly, the No. 1 Smithery, which lies close by, will have the purpose of demonstrating the rise of the iron clad.

Slightly more controversial is the decision to integrate modern houses into the overall scheme. These will be situated close to the officers' terrace (also to be refurbished), establishing a nine acre area for private residence. The Trust, however, is at pains to reassure its critics that any new development will be designed to blend with the surrounding environment.

Within the area administered by the Historic Trust there also exists the dockyard museum which, to further complicate matters, is owned and operated by the Chatham Dockyard Historic Society. Originally established while the dockyard was still in naval hands they were, at that time, allowed use of the old lead and paint mill. In itself a building of considerable importance, it is an early example of a completely fire proofed building and it currently houses a varied collection of artefacts and photographs.

With so many plans and ideas being put into operation, the future of the Medway Towns no longer looks as bleak as it did in 1981. Admittedly long-term employment levels within the dockyard will never compare with earlier decades, but new jobs are certainly being created, providing the possibility of a renewed affluence. The local community must, nevertheless, remain alert. In particular, entry into the former dockyard must be carefully monitored, with thought being given to an improved and expanded rail network. Already a number of local access roads are heavily congested and will be quite incapable of handling the likely increase in tourist, commercial and residential traffic. Whilst the construction of new roads would not be impossible, this is hardly a real solution. Apart from encouraging even more cars and lorries, it would inevitably shatter the quality of life for those already living in the Medway Towns.

Despite such potential problems however, the continuing story of the dockyard is a positive one. The bleakness of 1981 has been replaced by a great new future. The Medway Towns have already gained a large port complex and a museum with unrivalled potential. These facilities, combined with the soon to be developed 'Chatham Maritime', clearly show that it is to be full steam ahead into the twenty-first century.

What more could be asked?

Appendix One

BUILDINGS OF INTEREST

1. AREA OCCUPIED BY CHATHAM DOCKYARD HISTORIC TRUST

Main Gate

Completed in 1720, it is a three storey brick building displaying the royal coat of arms on the outside face. The latter is dated 1812 and signed 'Coade and Seeley'. A further coat of arms, dating to 1720, exists on the inside of the main gate.

Original Outer Wall

Part of the original dockyard wall that was built 1718-1722 remains, being visible just inside the present wall. Also to be seen are two watch towers.

Bell Mast

Early nineteenth century. Originally erected so that the workforce might be more easily summoned it is, in effect, a tall mast with a base of five small octagonal columns.

Police Offices

One long single storey eighteenth century building. The front consists of an open-sided passage supported by ten wooden Doric columns.

Royal Dockyard Church

Built between 1808 and 1811 at a cost of £9,000, the church is in the classic style and typical of its building date.

Figurehead (opposite church)

Bust of Wellesley and originally taken from HMS *Wellington.*

Lead and Paint Mill

Designed by Edward Holl, this building was completed in 1819 and supplied much of the navy's lead and paint needs. Because of the inflammable nature of these particular materials, the building was fire-proofed through the use of brick outer walls, stone paving on the upper floors and iron trusses, window frames and doors.

Rope House

One of the longest buildings in the country, it is still being used for the manufacture of rope. Of red brick, with a slate roof, it was completed in 1791. Much

Lead and Paint Mill. Standing close to the Main Gate, it now houses a dockyard museum that is run by the Chatham Dockyard Historical Society.

original machinery is extant, including a Maudslay laying machine dating to 1811. Also, in the same area, can be found the ropery offices, tarring house, black yarn store, white yarn house and hatchelling house, all of which date to the same period. The hemp house, on the other hand, is part of the earlier ropery, being completed in 1729.

Assistant Harbour Master's Office
Early nineteenth century and currently serving as a small cafeteria it stands adjacent to the Queen's Stairs.

Medway House
This plum coloured brick house was erected in 1703 for the accommodation of the resident-commissioner of the yard and is a fine example of its period. Amongst its more notable features is that of a painted ceiling by Thornhill which depicts Neptune crowning Mars. It is suggested that the painting was originally destined for *Royal Sovereign*, a first rate that had been launched at Woolwich a few years earlier.

Officers' Terrace
Twelve red brick houses all of which were completed between the years 1722-1731 and constructed in order to accommodate dockyard officers.

Chimney of Brunel's saw mill as completed in 1814.

Sail Loft
Dating from the 1720s, this building was originally used for the manufacture and storage of sails. The upper floor, completely free of structural supports, allowed sails to be fully laid out. The oldest surviving sail loft in a royal dockyard, it was also used for the manufacture of flags.

Cashier's Office
Originally a single storey office dating to the late eighteenth century.

Stables
Authorised in 1737 and remaining much as completed.

Admiral's Office
Dating to 1809, it was designed by Edward Holl and originally included a mould loft.

Clocktower Building
Mid-1720s, it was designed as a storehouse with a mould loft on the upper floor. The clock, sitting in a central turret, is of 1802 as are the upper floors.

Dry Docks

A great number of dry docks are to be found throughout the area of the former dockyard, with Nos. 2, 3 and 4 being amongst the oldest.

Dock Pumping Station

Dating to 1858, it was designed to pump water from the adjoining No. 2 dock. This building once housed a Boulton and Watt beam engine.

Covered Slipways

A quite unique collection of slipway coverings are to be found at Chatham and, between them, they demonstrate a number of developments that took place throughout the nineteenth century. For instance, the earliest to be seen is the timber built No. 3 slip covering that was completed in 1838. Further along can be seen slip Nos. 4, 5 and 6 which were completed with metal roofs in 1847, followed by No. 7 slip covering which was completed in 1855.

Mast House and Mould Loft

Originally constructed in 1753 the upper floor contained a further mould loft for the laying down of ship's lines and the subsequent cutting of templates.

No. 1 Smithery

Constructed in 1808 to an Edward Holl design, it is mentioned by Charles Dickens in 'Uncommercial Traveller'. It originally consisted of three ranges set around an open courtyard, but was subsequently rebuilt and enlarged. The courtyard was probably covered sometime around 1860.

Timber Seasoning Sheds

Built during the 1770s these were designed to make better use of dockyard timber, allowing newly arrived stocks to be stored properly.

Saw Mill

Built between 1813 and 1814 to a design by Marc Brunel, this was part of a complete unit for the transporting, cutting and storing of dockyard timber. An early example of iron framing, the remaining structure was subsequently used as a laundry.

Apprentice School

Constructed during the nineteenth century it is soon to be demolished.

2. AREA OCCUPIED BY ENGLISH ESTATES

No. 8 Machine Shop

Originally a covered slipway, dating to 1865, it was removed from Woolwich dockyard shortly after that particular yard was closed. Subsequently re-erected in 1880, it is a large iron framed building that is surmounted by a clock. Current plans by English Estates will see the retention of this building and its conversion into a covered shopping centre.

Machine Shed

Another survivor from Woolwich, this was also re-erected at Chatham sometime after 1869. Originally dating to 1865, it has cast iron frames and corrugated iron cladding.

Boilershop

Erected in 1876 this building is a further survivor from Woolwich and also has cast iron frames and corrugated iron cladding.

Combined Ship Trade Office

To the rear of No. 8 Machine Shop this is a cast iron framed building that dates to 1880.

Basins

All three basins were originally constructed as the centre piece of the Victorian extension that was finally completed in the 1880s. Only Nos. 1 and 2 are administered by English Estates, No. 3 basin being within the province of the Medway Dock Company. All three basins, together with adjoining docks, are to be retained.

Canteen

Built sometime around 1905 it has a distinctive stripped baroque style. It is to be found on the south side of North Road.

Motor Depot

Although situated in the former area of the dockyard this was the drill block and drill shed to *HMS Pembroke* and was completed in 1905.

Pembroke Barracks

Within the area of the former naval barracks, and also administered by English Estates are a large number of buildings and other structures that were all completed at the beginning of the century. Amongst these are included the chapel, various barrack blocks, the captain's house, main gate, railings, stairs, lamps and bridge. From a slightly earlier date, 1869 to be precise, is the stone and marble memorial to French prisoners-of-war.

Appendix Two

SHIPS BUILT AT CHATHAM
(Compiled by J.J. Colledge)

Ships noted in this appendix as having been 'rebuilt' were older vessels that had been dry-docked at Chatham and then rebuilt as new. All existing timbers were removed and only re-used if found to be in good condition. Frequently the opportunity was also taken to enlarge these vessels.

Tonnage bm until 1869; Displacement from 1870; Standard displacement from 1926.

Launched	Name	Rating	Guns	Tons
1586	*Sunne*	Pinnace	5	56 (Baker, Sun (Sonne) Hard)
1586	*Seven Stars*	Pinnace	5	140 (Baker, Sun (Sonne) Hard)
1602	*Moon*		9	100 (Gunwharf site)
1604	*Answer*		21	200 (rebuilt)
27. 2.1613	*Phoenix*		20	246
1615	*Vanguard*		36	665 (rebuilt)
1623	*Henrietta*	Pinnace	6	70
1627	*Maria*	Pinnace	6	70
1647	*Dragon*		32	556
1652	*Merlin*		14	129
1653	*Fairfax*		52	745
1655	*Norwich*		30	265
1656	*Blackmoor*	Sloop	14	90
7.1656	*London*		64	1104
1657	*Cygnet*	Sloop	8	58
1657	*Parrot*	Sloop	6	60
1658	*Bradford*		24	294
1658	*Lion*	4th Rate	48	(rebuilt)
1659	*Towing Galley*	DY craft		
1660	*Sovereign*	1st Rate	100	1545 (rebuilt: formerly *Sovereign of the Seas)*
1665	*Little Victory*	5th Rate	20	175
1665	*Unity*	DY craft		68
1665	*Prosperous*	DY craft		68
1666	*Victory*	2nd Rate	82	1029 (rebuilt)
3.1667	*Monmouth*	2nd Rate	66	856
1670	*Prince*	1st Rate	100	1395
1671	*Queenborough*	Yacht	4	27
1673	*Chatham*	Sloop	4	50
1673	*Chatham Double*	Sloop (experim.)	4	50
1673	*Hound*	Sloop	4	50
1673	*Sheerness*	DY Smack		18
1674	*Katherine*	Yacht	8	131
1675	*Montagu*	3rd Rate	62	764 (rebuilt)
1675	*Defiance*	3rd Rate	64	898

1677	*Mary*	Yacht	8	155
1678	*Anne*	3rd Rate	70	1051
1679	*Berwick*	3rd Rate	70	1041
1679	*Pendennis*	3rd Rate	70	1051
1682	*Britannia*	1st Rate	100	1708
1685	*Royal Sovereign*	1st Rate	100	1683 (rebuilt: formerly *Sovereign* of 1660)
1687	*Sedgemoor*	4th Rate	50	633
1687	*Salamander*	Bomb	10	184
17.12.1689	*Experiment*	5th Rate	32	370
29. 3.1690	*Dolphin*	Fireship	8	267
1690	*Royal Oak*	3rd Rate	74	1154 (rebuilt)
1691	*Adventure*	4th Rate	44	438 (rebuilt)
1691	*Towing Galley No. 1*	DY craft		91
1691	*Towing Galley No. 2*	DY craft		91
20. 4.1691	*Supply*	DY Hoy		94
20. 4.1691	*Chatham*	4th Rate	48	686
1692	*Royal William*	1st Rate	100	1568 (rebuilt: formerly *Prince*)
15. 3.1693	*Rochester*	4th Rate	48	607
11. 4.1693	*Sussex*	3rd Rate	80	1203
24. 6.1693	*Serpent*	Bomb	12	260
25. 6.1693	*Mortar*	Bomb	12	260
19. 8.1693	*Unity*	DY Hoy	4	79
11.1693	*Maidstone*	5th Rate	24	250
19. 3.1694	*Lizard*	5th Rate	24	250
9.1694	*William & Mary*	Yacht	10	152
9.10.1694	*Chatham Hulk*	DY sheer hulk		714
10.12.1694	*Squirrel*	Yacht	4	37
6. 3.1695	*Chichester*	3rd Rate	80	1210
1695	*Victory*	1st Rate	100	1486 (rebuilt: formerly *Royal James*)
5. 4.1695	*Serpent*	Bomb	4	140
16. 9.1695	*Swift*	Brigantine	4	80
11.12.1695	*Royal Transport*	6th Rate	18	220
10. 7.1697	*Flamborough*	5th Rate	24	252
7. 8.1697	*Lowestoffe*	5th Rate	32	357
2. 3.1698	*Triumph*	2nd Rate	90	1482
31. 5.1698	*Somerset*	3rd Rate	80	1263
30. 4.1698	*Resolution*	3rd Rate	70	902 (rebuilt)
1699	*Eagle*	3rd Rate	70	1099 (rebuilt)
1699	*Expedition*	3rd Rate	70	1116 (rebuilt)
1699	*Stirling Castle*	3rd Rate	70	1087 (rebuilt)
29. 9.1699	*Tilbury*	4th Rate	48	691
30. 9.1699	*Merlin*	Sloop	2	66
30. 9.1699	*Swallow*	Sloop	2	66
1701	*Prince George*	2nd Rate	90	1421 (rebuilt: formerly *Duke*)
1702	*Northumberland*	3rd Rate	70	1096 (rebuilt)
1702	*Falkland*	4th Rate	48	638 (rebuilt)
16.12.1702	*Nightingale*	5th Rate	24	251
12. 5.1704	*Mary*	3rd Rate	64	914
1704	*Union*	2nd Rate	90	1348 (rebuilt: formerly *Albermarle*)
10. 3.1705	*Fowey*	5th Rate	32	414
21. 9.1705	*Stirling Castle*	3rd Rate	70	1122

Date	Name	Rate	Guns	Tonnage
1706	London	1st Rate	100	1685 (rebuilt)
3. 7.1707	Salisbury	4th Rate	54	703
18.10.1708	Chester	4th Rate	54	704
20. 1.1709	Lion	3rd Rate	60	906
2. 8.1710	Vanguard	2nd Rate	90	1551 (rebuilt)
19. 9.1711	Bonaventure	4th Rate	54	703 (rebuilt)
21. 4.1712	Sandwich	2nd Rate	90	1573 (rebuilt)
25. 4.1712	Rose	6th Rate	20	273
18. 7.1716	Chatham	Yacht	14	60
29. 7.1717	Newark	2nd Rate	80	1283 (rebuilt)
20. 5.1718	Norwich	4th Rate	48	703 (rebuilt)
13.11.1718	Suffolk	3rd Rate	70	1129 (rebuilt)
25. 3.1719	Swallow	4th Rate	50	711 (rebuilt)
1721	London	2nd Rate	96	1711 (rebuilt)
26.10.1721	Colchester	4th Rate	54	682 (rebuilt)
30. 6.1721	Edinburgh	3rd Rate	70	1119 (rebuilt: formerly Warspite)
23.11.1721	Hawke	Sloop	8	103
2. 8.1722	Plymouth	4th Rate	60	955 (rebuilt)
19. 9.1723	Lennox	3rd Rate	70	1128 (rebuilt)
30. 4.1724	Sunderland	3rd Rate	60	951
1725	Little London	DY smack		16
1725	Supply	DY Hoy		122
19. 5.1725	Anglesea	5th Rate	48	601 (rebuilt)
8. 2.1726	Union	2nd Rate	90	1578 (rebuilt)
1726	Albemarle	2nd Rate	90	1578 (rebuilt)
28. 9.1728	Royal Sovereign	1st Rate	100	1883 (rebuilt)
15. 2.1730	Greenwich	4th Rate	54	756 (rebuilt)
1732	Marlborough	2nd Rate	90	1567 (rebuilt: formerly St Michael)
25. 8.1732	Spy	Sloop	14	201
2. 6.1733	Tilbury	4th Rate	60	963
1734	Chatham Lighter No. 1	DY craft		73
24. 7.1735	Strafford	4th Rate	60	1067
29.11.1737	Elizabeth	3rd Rate	70	1224 (rebuilt)
1739	Chatham Longboat	DY craft		23
11. 8.1740	Guernsey	4th Rate	50	863 (rebuilt)
1.10.1741	Chatham	DY Yacht	6	74
22. 4.1742	Stirling Castle	3rd Rate	70	1225
31. 5.1744	Edinburgh	3rd Rate	64	1285 (rebuilt)
27. 8.1747	Newark	2nd Rate	80	1521 (rebuilt)
18. 7.1748	Somerset	3rd Rate	70	1436
8. 8.1750	Prince	2nd Rate	90	1677 (rebuilt)
21.10.1752	Speedwell	Sloop	8	142
24. 5.1754	Wolfe	Sloop	8	141
3. 3.1756	Namur	2nd Rate	90	1813
25. 9.1756	Union	2nd Rate	90	1781
5. 5.1757	Burford	3rd Rate	70	1424
23. 7.1757	Hussar	6th Rate 28	28	586
30. 9.1757	Actaeon	6th Rate 28	28	585
13.12.1757	Dorsetshire	3rd Rate	70	1436
25. 2.1758	Lennox	3rd Rate	74	1759
22. 6.1758	Panther	4th Rate	60	1285 (built by Henniker)
14. 4.1759	Sandwich	2nd Rate	90	1869

10. 8.1759	*Valiant*	3rd Rate	74	1799
19. 2.1760	*Bellona*	3rd Rate	74	1615
21. 4.1761	*Ocean*	2nd Rate	90	1833
27. 3.1762	*Pearl*	5th Rate	32	683
15. 4.1763	*Ramillies*	3rd Rate	74	1619
26. 7.1763	*Exeter*	3rd Rate	64	1340 (built Henniker's yard)
8.10.1763	*Ferret*	Cutter	6	83
7. 5.1765	*Victory*	1st Rate	100	2150 (now preserved at Portsmouth)
13. 1.1766	*Aurora*	5th Rate	32	679
25. 4.1766	*London*	2nd Rate	90	1894
30. 7.1768	*Barfleur*	2nd Rate	90	1947
10.12.1768	*Raisonnable*	3rd Rate	64	1386 (first ship upon which the future Adm. Nelson served)
2.10.1769	*Salisbury*	4th Rate	50	1051
13. 7.1770	*Kingfisher*	Sloop	14	300
1771	*Lighter No. 1*	DY lighter		130
8.1772	*Augustus*	Gun vessel		
31. 8.1772	*Prince George*	2nd Rate	90	1955
28. 4.1774	*Roebuck*	5th Rate	44	886
28. 6.1775	*Stirling Castle*	3rd Rate	64	1374
20. 4.1776	*Camilla*	6th Rate	20	433
27.12.1776	*Ariadne*	6th Rate	20	429
27.12.1776	*Pegasus*	Sloop	14	300
20. 8.1777	*Formidable*	2nd Rate	90	1934
27. 5.1778	*Nymphe*	Sloop	14	300
22.10.1778	*Alfred*	3rd Rate	74	1638
28. 8.1779	*Montague*	3rd Rate	74	1631
1. 7.1780	*Leander*	4th Rate	50	1044
27.12.1780	*Amphion*	5th Rate	32	678
10. 3.1781	*Dolphin*	5th Rate	44	879
13. 2.1782	*Atlas*	2nd Rate	90	1931
19.12.1782	*Diadem*	3rd Rate	64	1376
12. 3.1785	*Mooring Ltr. No. 9*	DY craft		120
19.10.1785	*Mooring Ltr. No. 10*	DY craft		120
15. 9.1788	*Royal George*	1st Rate	100	2286
15. 4.1790	*Queen Charlotte*	1st Rate	100	2279
9.10.1790	*Leviathan*	3rd Rate	74	1707
2.1791	*Goodwill*	DY lighter		115
7. 1.1791	*Rattlesnake*	Sloop	16	321
1793	*Chatham*	DY Yacht		93
28. 6.1794	*Stag*	5th Rate	32	776
12. 7.1794	*Unicorn*	5th Rate	32	776
1794	*Anson*	5th Rate	38	1360 (cut-down from a 64)
17. 7.1795	*Ville de Paris*	1st Rate	110	2332
1796	*Medway*	DY Hoy		116
26. 3.1796	*Clyde*	5th Rate	38	1002
26. 3.1796	*Tamar*	5th Rate	38	999
11. 9.1798	*Temeraire*	2nd Rate	98	2121
14.12.1799	*Active*	5th Rate	38	1058
	Princess Amelia	3rd Rate	74	1906 (laid down 1.1.1799, canc. 3.1800)
11. 4.1800	*Victory*	1st Rate	100	2164 (rebuilt)

Date	Name	Type	Guns	Tons	Notes
18.11.1800	*Leda*	5th Rate	38	1071	
13. 4.1805	*Revenge*	3rd Rate	74	1954	
24.10.1805	*Thames*	5th Rate	32	662	
25.11.1806	*Meleager*	5th Rate	36	875	
16.11.1807	*Warspite*	3rd Rate	74	1890	
26. 4.1808	*Iphigenia*	5th Rate	36	870	
25. 6.1808	*Merope*	Brig-sloop	14	252	
23.10.1808	*Muros*	Brig-sloop	14	252	
1. 8.1810	*Impregnable*	2nd Rate	98	2264	
20. 6.1811	*Orlando*	5th Rate	36	876	
11. 4.1812	*Tenedos*	5th Rate	38	1085	
11. 4.1812	*Briton*	5th Rate	38	1080	
2. 4.1813	*Chatham Hulk*	Sheer hulk		1691	
17. 4.1813	*Bacchus*	Brig-sloop	18	384	
14. 7.1813	*Lively*	5th Rate	38	1080	
1814	*Mud Boat No. 1*	DY craft		58	
1814	*Mud Boat No. 2*	DY craft		58	
1814	*Sheerness Boat No. 1*	DY craft		54	
2.1814	*Prompt*	5th Rate	32	660 (unframed and sent to Canada)
2.1814	*Psyche*	5th Rate	32	660 (unframed and sent to Canada)
3.1814	*Colibri*	Brig-sloop	18	382 (unframed and sent to Canada)
7.1814	*Goshawk*	Brig-sloop	18	382 (unframed and sent to Canada)
	Julius	3rd Rate	74	1750 (on order 1815, cancelled)
28. 3.1815	*Howe*	1st Rate	120	2619	
25. 4.1815	*Defence*	3rd Rate	74	1754	
5. 9.1815	*Hercules*	3rd Rate	74	1750	
16. 1.1816	*Diamond*	5th Rate	38	1076	
15. 4.1816	*Minotaur*	3rd Rate	74	1726	
3. 5.1817	*Starling*	Cutter	10	151	
1818	*Mud Boat No. 3*	DY craft		58	
1818	*Mud Boat No. 4*	DY craft		58	
12.12.1818	*Bustard*	Brig-sloop	10	237	
10. 2.1819	*Brisk*	Brig-sloop	10	237	
25. 6.1819	*Blanche*	5th Rate	46	1074	
1820	*Open Barge No. 1*	DY craft		100	
1820	*Tank Schooner No. 2*	DY craft		107	
26. 7.1820	*Trafalgar*	1st Rate	106	2404	
1821	*DY Barge No. 2*	DY craft		100	
16. 6.1821	*Latona*	5th Rate	46	1071	
8. 1.1822	*Diana*	5th Rate	46	1083	
26. 3.1822	*Rattlesnake*	6th Rate	28	503	
26. 3.1822	*Weazle*	Brig-sloop	10	237	
7. 5.1822	*Basilisk*	Cutter	10	161	
21. 6.1822	*Procris*	Brig-sloop	10	238	
12. 4.1823	*Prince Regent*	1st Rate	120	2613	
21. 8.1823	*Thames*	5th Rate	46	1088	
20.11.1823	*Rainbow*	6th Rate	28	503	
1824	*Van*	DY barge		132	
30. 3.1824	*Unicorn*	5th Rate	46	1084	
14. 5.1824	*Aetna*	Bomb	12	375	

22.10.1824	*Hearty*	Brig-sloop	10	228
1825	*Fly*	DY barge		108
1825	*DY Barge*	DY barge		43
20. 2.1825	*Lapwing*	Brig-sloop	10	228
19. 5.1825	*Formidable*	2nd Rate	84	2289
16. 7.1825	*Harpy*	Brig-sloop	10	232
30. 7.1825	*Mermaid*	5th Rate	46	1085
28.10.1825	*Crocodile*	6th Rate	28	501
26. 1.1826	*Sulphur*	Bomb	12	375
25. 4.1826	*Fairy*	Brig-sloop	10	233
9. 5.1826	*Espoir*	Brig-sloop	10	233
21. 6.1826	*Powerful*	2nd Rate	84	2296
19. 8.1826	*Calypso*	Brig-sloop	10	233
16.11.1826	*Acorn*	Sloop	18	455
16.11.1826	*Mercury*	5th Rate	46	1084
23. 8.1827	*Childers*	Brig-sloop	18	385
22. 9.1827	*Royal George*	1st Rate	120	2616
20.12.1827	*Africaine*	5th Rate	46	1173
1828	*Dove*	DY lighter		135
19. 1.1828	*Cruizer*	Brig-sloop	18	385
19. 2.1829	*Eurotas*	5th Rate	46	1170
1. 8.1829	*Algerine*	Brig-sloop	10	230
13. 8.1829	*Penelope*	5th Rate	46	1091
27.11.1829	*Delight*	Brig-sloop	10	230
12. 1.1830	*Thalia*	5th Rate	46	1082
23. 6.1830	*Lark*	Cutter	4	109
4. 8.1830	*Jackdaw*	Cutter	4	108
	Orpheus	5th Rate	46	1215 (ordered 9.6.25, cancelled 2.31)
	Vestal	6th Rate	28	709 (ordered 29.10.30, cancelled 8.12.31)
24. 8.1831	*Hornet*	Schooner	6	181
22.11.1831	*Seagull*	Schooner	6	279
	Vesuvius	Bomb	12	372 (ordered 30.8.28, cancelled 10.1.31)
2. 2.1832	*Conway*	6th Rate	28	652
2. 5.1832	*Castor*	5th Rate	36	1293
15. 6.1832	*Scout*	Sloop	18	488
17. 7.1832	*Rover*	Sloop	18	590
28. 8.1832	*Forrester*	Brig-sloop	10	229
11. 9.1832	*Griffon*	Brig-sloop	10	231
25. 9.1832	*Phoenix*	Paddle sloop		802 (first steam vessel built at Chatham)
	Charon	Paddle sloop		802? (ordered c 5.31, cancelled 11.32)
18.12.1832	*Monarch*	2nd Rate	80	2255
4.1833	*Mud Barge No. 8*	DY craft		79
4.1833	*Mud Barge No. 9*	DY craft		79
10. 6.1833	*Waterloo*	1st Rate	120	2718
30. 9.1833	*Gulnare*	Paddle vessel		306
26.11.1833	*Rochester*	DY craft		154
5.1834	*Blazer*	Paddle vessel		525
10. 7.1835	*Wanderer*	Brig-sloop	16	428
23. 9.1835	*Spider*	Schooner	6	183

24. 9.1835	Devon	DY craft		154
4. 4.1836	Bat	DY Hoy		75
4. 4.1836	No. 1	Mooring lighter		168
5. 4.1836	No. 2	Mooring lighter		169
13.10.1836	Wolverine	Brig-sloop	16	428
7. 2.1837	Mercury	DY tender		70
19. 5.1837	Tank vessel	DY craft for Malta		119
12. 9.1837	Widgeon	Paddle Packet		164
5.12.1837	Dasher	Paddle Packet		260
13. 6.1838	Hydra	Paddle Sloop		817
30.11.1838	Aid	DY store carrier		154
14. 1.1839	Hecla	Paddle sloop		817
30. 3.1839	Hecate	Paddle sloop		817
30. 5.1839	Fantome	Brig-sloop	16	483
7. 9.1839	Alecto	Paddle sloop		800
5. 5.1840	Maeander	5th Rate	46	1215
28. 9.1840	London	2nd Rate	92	2607
28. 9.1840	Polyphemus	Paddle sloop		800
12. 2.1841	Ardent	Paddle sloop		801
20. 7.1841	Growler	Paddle sloop		1059
28. 2.1842	Bee	Screw and Paddle Vessel		42
25. 7.1842	Virago	Paddle sloop		1059
25. 7.1842	Goliath	3rd Rate	80	2599
21.10.1842	Cumberland	3rd Rate	70	2214
5. 4.1843	Penelope	Paddle Frigate		1616 (conversion)
6. 2.1844	Janus	Paddle sloop		763
20. 4.1844	Espiegle	Brig-sloop	12	443
20. 4.1844	Mutine	Brig-sloop	12	428
2. 7.1844	Retribution	Paddle Frigate		1641 (originally named Watt, at time of launching largest steamship in RN)
8. 5.1845	Raleigh	4th Rate	50	1939
8. 5.1845	Calypso	6th Rate	20	731
19. 7.1845	Active	5th Rate	36	1627
2.10.1845	Bulldog	Paddle sloop		1124
	Nankin	4th Rate	50	2049 (ord. 26.1.46, frames to Woolwich DY 22.2.46)
25. 6.1846	Teazer	Screw Gun Vessel		296 (first screw vessel built at Chatham apart from Bee above)
31. 3.1847	Arab	Brig-sloop	16	481
27. 9.1847	Elk	Brig-sloop	16	484
27. 9.1847	Heron	Brig-sloop	16	482
7. 2.1848	Vivid	Paddle Packet		352
1. 7.1848	Mars	3rd Rate	80	2576
8. 2.1849	Elfin	Paddle Yacht		98
	Challenger	Corvette	18	810 (ordered 8.8.44, cancelled 22.3.45)
	Highflyer	Screw Frigate		1150 (ordered 25.4.47, transferred to Woolwich Dockyard 30.11.49)
	Biter	Screw Gun Vessel		296 (ordered 26.3.46, cancelled 22.5.49)
	Boxer	Screw Gun Vessel		296 (ordered 26.3.46, cancelled 22.5.49)

1.12.1849	*Tiger*	Paddle Frigate		1221
17. 6.1850	*Horatio*	Screw Frigate		1175 (converted from 5th Rate)
	Chesapeake	5th Rate	36	1622 (ordered 10.12.34, cancelled 1850)
	Coquette	Corvette	18	731 (ordered 27.3.34, cancelled 1851)
2. 6.1851	*Brisk*	Screw sloop		1073
25.11.1851	*Despatch*	Brig-sloop	16	483
31. 8.1852	*Kangaroo*	Brig-sloop	16	481
21. 7.1853	*Cressy*	Screw Ship	81	2539
5.10.1853	*Euryalus*	Screw Frigate		2371
1.12.1853	*Majestic*	Screw Ship	81	2566
6.11.1854	*Orion*	Screw Ship	91	3281
20. 3.1855	*Hawke*	Screw Ship	60	1754 (conversion from 3rd Rate)
27. 9.1855	*Chesapeake*	Screw Frigate		2377
23.11.1855	*Mars*	Screw Ship	80	2573 (conversion from 3rd Rate)
24. 1.1856	*Severn*	4th Rate	50	1986 (last sail warship built at Chatham)

All below are screw ships unless otherwise stated:

5. 4.1856	*Aetna*	Floating Battery		1588 (first ironclad built at Chatham)
20. 5.1856	*Cadmus*	Corvette		1466
28. 3.1857	*Renown*	(Battle)ship	91	3319
25. 4.1857	*Racoon*	Corvette		1467
30.11.1857	*Goliath*	(Battle)ship	80	2596 (conversion from 3rd Rate)
15. 4.1858	*Hero*	(Battle)ship	91	3148
13. 8.1858	*Mersey*	Frigate		3740
21. 3.1859	*Trafalgar*	(Battle)ship	90	2900 (conversion from 1st Rate)
4. 5.1859	*Hood*	(Battle)ship	91	3308
1. 6.1859	*Charybdis*	Corvette		1506
27.10.1859	*Irresistible*	(Battle)ship	81	2642
11. 1.1860	*Rodney*	(Battle)ship	90	2770 (conversion from 2nd Rate)
23. 6.1860	*Orpheus*	Corvette		1705
21. 7.1860	*Atlas*	(Battle)ship	91	3318 (never completed)
1. 1.1861	*Undaunted*	Frigate		3039
25. 5.1861	*Bombay*	(Battle)ship	81	2782 (conversion from 2nd Rate)
9. 7.1861	*Rattlesnake*	Corvette		1705
9. 8.1861	*Arethusa*	Frigate		3141 (conversion from 4th Rate)
	Pitt	(Battle)ship	101	3716 (ordered 5.3.60, cancelled 13.2.62)
10. 9.1862	*Royal Oak*	Ironclad		4056
19. 5.1863	*Salamis*	Paddle Despatch Vessel		835
	Pomone	Frigate		3039 (ordered 5.3.60, cancelled 12.12.63)
	Boadicea	Frigate		3353 (ordered 3.61, cancelled 12.12.63)
	Falmouth	Corvette		1857 (ordered 5.3.60, cancelled 12.12.63)
	Ganymede	Corvette		1857 (ordered 5.3.60, cancelled 12.12.63)
	Albatross	Sloop		695 (ordered 25.3.61, cancelled 12.12.63)
	Tees	Sloop		952 (ordered 5.3.60, cancelled 12.12.63)

Date	Name	Type	Tonnage / Notes
	Diligence	Sloop	952 (ordered 3.61, cancelled 12.12.63)
23.12.1863	*Achilles*	Battleship	6039 (first iron built battleship at Chatham)
	Belvidera	Frigate	3039 (ordered 8.4.59, cancelled 16.12.64)
	Menai	Corvette	1857 (ordered 5.3.60, cancelled 16.12.64)
26. 4.1865	*Bellerophon*	Iron Battleship	4270
27. 5.1865	*Lord Warden*	Ironclad Battleship	4080
29. 3.1866	*Reindeer*	Sloop	952
5. 6.1867	*Myrmidon*	Sloop	695
17. 8.1867	*Blanche*	Sloop	1270
17. 8.1867	*Beacon*	Gunvessel	464
10. 2.1868	*Hercules*	Battleship	5234
25. 5.1868	*Monarch*	Battleship	5102
31. 5.1870	*Sultan*	Battleship	5234
8. 3.1871	*Glatton*	Coast Defence Ship	4910
9. 3.1871	*Woodlark*	Gunvessel	663
25. 3.1871	*Scourge*	Gunboat	254
25. 3.1871	*Snake*	Gunboat	254
29. 2.1872	*Frolic*	Gunvessel	610
29. 2.1872	*Kestrel*	Gunvessel	610
12. 3.1872	*Rupert*	Coast Defence Ship	5444
12. 3.1872	*Fidget*	Gunboat	254 (never placed in commission)
13. 3.1872	*Badger*	Gunboat	254
24. 9.1872	*Ready*	Gunvessel	610
20.11.1872	*Rifleman*	Gunvessel	610 (last RN ship to round Horn under sail)
11. 2.1873	*Ariel*	Gunboat	438
11. 2.1873	*Zephyr*	Gunboat	438
1. 3.1873	*Raleigh*	Frigate	5200
27. 4.1873	*Albatross*	Sloop	950
27.11.1873	*Flying Fish*	Sloop	950
7. 4.1875	*Alexandra*	Battleship	9490 (originally laid down as *Superb*)
9. 5.1876	*Temeraire*	Battleship	8540
30. 6.1876	*Garnet*	Corvette	2120
31. 1.1877	*Euryalus*	Frigate	4130
12. 9.1877	*Cormorant*	Sloop	1130
17. 9.1879	*Agamemnon*	Battleship	8510
2. 3.1880	*Doterel*	Sloop	1130
9. 6.1880	*Constance*	Corvette	2380
15. 6.1881	*Polyphemus*	Torpedo Ram	2640
8. 9.1881	*Conqueror*	Battleship	6200
	un-named	Torpedo Ram	2640 (ordered 30.12.81, cancelled 10.11.82)
7. 6.1883	*Calypso*	Corvette	2770
29. 1.1884	*Warspite*	Armoured Cruiser	8400
8.10.1884	*Rodney*	Battleship	10300
	un-named	Battleship	6200 (ordered 31.12.84, cancelled 1885)

HMS *Warspite* (1884)

HMS *Hood* (1891)

Date	Name	Type	Tonnage	Notes
31. 3.1885	*Mersey*	Cruiser	4050	
	Adventure	Torpedo Ram	2640	(ordered 6.3.85, cancelled 8.1885)
29. 9.1885	*Severn*	Cruiser	4050	
27.10.1885	*Hero*	Battleship	6200	(first Chatham warship to abandon sailing rig)
7. 6.1887	*Immortalite*	Armoured Cruiser	5600	
9. 6.1888	*Medea*	Cruiser	2800	
11. 8.1888	*Medusa*	Cruiser	2800	
4.12.1888	*Research*	Paddle Survey Vessel	520	
30. 3.1889	*Sheldrake*	Torpedo Gunboat	735	(first torpedo gunboat built at Chatham)
30. 4.1889	*Skipjack*	Torpedo Gunboat	735	
31. 5.1889	*Salamander*	Torpedo Gunboat	735	
31. 5.1889	*Seagull*	Torpedo Gunboat	735	
23.11.1889	*Blake*	Cruiser	9000	
14. 8.1890	*Andromache*	Cruiser	3400	
10. 2.1891	*Apollo*	Cruiser	3400	
11. 3.1891	*Hawke*	Cruiser	7350	
30. 6.1891	*Hood*	Battleship	14150	
10. 8.1892	*Barfleur*	Battleship	10500	
22.11.1893	*Dryad*	Torpedo Gunboat	1070	
9.12.1893	*Forte*	Cruiser	4360	
19.12.1894	*Magnificent*	Battleship	14900	
23. 9.1895	*Minerva*	Cruiser	5600	
19.10.1895	*Victorious*	Battleship	14900	
17. 9.1896	*Illustrious*	Battleship	14900	
9.12.1897	*Vindictive*	Cruiser	5750	
23. 3.1898	*Goliath*	Battleship	12950	
15.12.1898	*Irresistible*	Battleship	15000	
28. 6.1899	*Pioneer*	Cruiser	2200	
2.11.1899	*Venerable*	Battleship	15000	
5. 3.1901	*Albemarle*	Battleship	14000	
25. 3.1902	*Prince of Wales*	Battleship	15000	
27. 5.1902	*Challenger*	Cruiser	5880	
30. 4.1904	*Devonshire*	Armoured Cruiser	10850	
20. 5.1905	*Africa*	Battleship	16350	(last and largest battleship built at Chatham and first launching from No. 8 slip)
20. 9.1906	*Shannon*	Armoured Cruiser	14600	
8.1907	*Iphigenia*	Minelayer	3600	(conversion from cruiser)
13. 8.1908	*C.17*	Submarine	280	(first submarine built in a royal dockyard)
4. 9.1908	*Grappler*	DY Tug (paddle)	690	
10.10.1908	*C.18*	Submarine	280	
12.10.1908	*Rover*	DY Tug	620	
20. 3.1909	*C.19*	Submarine	280	
4. 8.1909	*Apollo*	Minelayer	3400	(conversion from cruiser)
2. 9.1909	*Atlas*	DY Tug	620	
2. 9.1909	*Pilot*	DY Tug	620	
13. 9.1909	*Andromache*	Minelayer	3400	(conversion from cruiser)
10.1909	*YC.62*	DY Lighter	185	
3.11.1909	*YC.92*	DY Lighter	110	
3.11.1909	*YC.93*	DY Lighter	110	

HMS *Venerable* (1899)   (Courtesy of MoD)

HMS *Kent* (1926)   (Courtesy of MoD)

Date	Name	Type	Tonnage
27.11.1909	*C.20*	Submarine	280
10. 5.1910	*C.33*	Submarine	280
8. 6.1910	*C.34*	Submarine	280
23. 8.1910	*Firm*	DY Paddle Tug	690
23. 8.1910	*Alliance*	DY Tug	620
23. 8.1910	*Naiad*	Minelayer	3400 (conversion from cruiser)
27. 9.1910	*Intrepid*	Minelayer	3600 (conversion from cruiser)
14. 1.1911	*D.7*	Submarine	550
23. 9.1911	*D.8*	Submarine	550
19.11.1911	*Chatham*	Cruiser	5400
9.11.1912	*E.1*	Submarine	660
23.11.1912	*E.2*	Submarine	660
1913	*YC.94*	DY Salvage Vessel	790
23. 4.1913	*Lowestoft*	Cruiser	5400
5. 7.1913	*Attendant*	RFA Oiler	1935
2.10.1913	*E.7*	Submarine	662
25.10.1913	*Arethusa*	Cruiser	3500
30.10.1913	*E.8*	Submarine	662
26. 5.1914	*Servitor*	RFA Oiler	1935
5. 9.1914	*E.12*	Submarine	662
22. 9.1913	*E.13*	Submarine	662
17.12.1914	*Calliope*	Cruiser	3750
20. 1.1915	*Conquest*	Cruiser	3750
31. 3.1915	*F.1*	Submarine	353
14. 8.1915	*G.1*	Submarine	700
23.10.1915	*G.4*	Submarine	700
23.11.1915	*G.5*	Submarine	700
23.12.1915	*G.2*	Submarine	700
22. 1.1916	*G.3*	Submarine	700
1.10.1917	*Hawkins*	Cruiser	9750
25. 4.1918	*R.1*	Submarine	420
25. 4.1918	*R.2*	Submarine	420
8. 6.1918	*R.3*	Submarine	420
8. 6.1918	*R.4*	Submarine	420
	Warren	Destroyer	1325 (ordered 26.11.18, cancelled 8.19 — only destroyer ordered at Chatham)
16. 6.1923	*X.1*	Submarine	2780 (largest Chatham-built submarine)
16. 3.1926	*Kent*	Cruiser	9850 (largest Chatham-built cruiser)
24. 9.1926	*Oberon*	Submarine	1311
8.1927	*Centurion*	Target Ship	25000 (conversion from battleship — last battleship to enter Chatham)
5. 5.1928	*Odin*	Submarine	1475
22. 6.1928	*Parthian*	Submarine	1475
	Maidstone	Depot Ship	(ordered 22.3.29, cancelled 1.30)
14. 5.1930	*Rainbow*	Submarine	1475
22.11.1930	*Shoreham*	Sloop	1105
1. 6.1931	*Challenger*	Survey Ship	1140
16. 7.1931	*Rochester*	Sloop	1105

HMS *Modeste* (1944)   (Courtesy of MoD)

XI, the largest Chatham built submarine.   (RN Submarine Museum, Gosport)

10.11.1931	*Swordfish*	Submarine	640
8. 1.1932	*Sturgeon*	Submarine	640
1. 9.1932	*Guardian*	Netlayer	2860
20. 9.1932	*Dundee*	Sloop	1060
15.11.1932	*Seahorse*	Submarine	640
14. 3.1933	*Starfish*	Submarine	640
6. 3.1934	*Arethusa*	Cruiser	5220
31. 5.1934	*Shark*	Submarine	670
25.10.1934	*Snapper*	Submarine	670
5. 2.1935	*Deptford*	Sloop	990
25. 2.1936	*Grampus*	Submarine	1520
30. 9.1936	*Sunfish*	Submarine	670
22. 9.1937	*Sterlet*	Submarine	670
27. 9.1938	*Seal*	Submarine	1520
6. 6.1939	*Euryalus*	Cruiser	5450 (last cruiser built at Chatham)
31.10.1939	*Tigris*	Submarine	1090
9. 4.1940	*Torbay*	Submarine	1090
30.12.1940	*Umpire*	Submarine	540
10. 6.1941	*Una*	Submarine	540
19. 1.1942	*Splendid*	Submarine	715 (originally P.228)
17. 4.1942	*Sportsman*	Submarine	715 (originally launched as P.229)
1. 6.1942	*AFD.XIX*	Floating Dock	
7.12.1942	*AFD.XXII*	Floating Dock	
11.12.1942	*Tradewind*	Submarine	1090
24. 3.1943	*Trenchant*	Submarine	1090
22. 4.1943	*Shalimar*	Submarine	715
29. 1.1944	*Modeste*	Sloop	1350
29. 1.1944	*Nereide*	Sloop	1350 (the last sloop built at Chatham)
24. 7.1944	*Moorpout*	Mooring Vessel	1000
24. 7.1944	*Moorsman*	Mooring Vessel	1000
5. 8.1944	*Turpin*	Submarine	1090
27. 6.1945	*Thermopylae*	Submarine	1090
	Adept	Submarine	1120 (ordered 28.5.43, cancelled 23.10.45)
	Nonsuch	Sloop	1350 (laid down 26.2.45, cancelled 23.10.45)
	Nymphe	Sloop	1350 (laid down 26.2.45, cancelled 23.10.45)
25. 3.1947	*Acheron*	Submarine	1120
31. 7.1951	*Vidal*	Survey Vessel	1940
	Wharton	Survey Vessel	1940 (ordered 20.6.49, cancelled 1950)
18. 7.1959	*Oberon*	Submarine	1610
17. 9.1960	*Onslaught*	Submarine	1610
5. 5.1962	*Ocelot*	Submarine	1610
29. 2.1964	*Ojibwa*	Submarine	1610 (for Canada)
25. 9.1965	*Onondaga*	Submarine	1610 (for Canada)
17. 9.1966	*Okanagan*	Submarine	1610 (for Canada)
10. 2.1971	*M.A.C. 1012*	Dockyard craft	

Appendix Three

THE SITE OF THE TUDOR DOCKYARD AND ITS LATER HISTORY AS A GUNWHARF

Reference in the text has been made to an original Tudor dockyard that was established immediately below St Mary's church. As also noted, a massive re-building programme was undertaken during the seventeenth century, with an entirely new dockyard established on land that is currently administered by the Chatham Historic Dockyard Trust. Such an expansion programme resulted in the eventual abandonment of the Tudor dockyard, the site subsequently used by the Board of Ordnance as a store for naval guns. At some point the original dry dock was filled in, whilst the Ordnance Board made use of some existing buildings. At first, of course, the area continued to be referred to as the 'old dock', but gradually the term 'wharf' was introduced. Likewise, the Ordnance Board began to plan out the area, making it more suitable for their particular needs. The older, and more tumbled down, buildings were replaced, whilst in 1708 a new storehouse was erected. In later years a series of carriage sheds, cranes and Master Gunner's House were to be added.

As regards essential usage, the gunwharf changed little over the next hundred and fifty years. A description written by Edward Hasted in the 1790s, could both apply to a much later as well as a much earlier period:

> The guns belonging to the royal shipping in this river are deposited on this wharf in long tiers, and large pyramids of cannon-balls are laid on it, ready for service; there is likewise a continued range of storehouses, in which are deposited the carriages of the guns, and every other kind of store, usually under the care of this office; in one of them is a small armoury of muskets, pistols, cutlasses, pikes, pole-axes, and other hostile weapons arranged in proper order. This department of the ordnance is under the management of a storekeeper, who has a good house here to reside in, a clerk of the survey, and clerk of the cheque . . .

To this can be added Brayley's description, taken from *The Beauties of England and Wales* (1808):

> The Ordnance Wharf which is not unfrequently called the Old Dock occupies a narrow slip of land below the chalk cliff, between the Church and the river. Here great quantities of naval ordnance are deposited in regular tiers, and abundance of cannon-balls piled up in large pyramids. Great numbers of gun carriages are also laid up under cover; and in the Store houses, and small Armoury, are vast quantities of offensive weapons, as pistols, cutlasses, pikes, pole-axes etc.

Eventually changes came to the Gunwharf, especially when the smooth bored cannon, unrivalled for numerous decades, gave way to the more sophisticated weapons of the nineteenth and twentieth centuries. Changes which, incidentally, were accelerated by the adoption of steam power and the removal of rigging from the deck of warships. Guns became much bigger, ceasing to be mounted broadside, and promoted, instead, to deck top turrets. As such, guns could no longer be simply removed and left for several years in storage. Instead, the emphasis was placed upon maintenance, with the Chatham Gunwharf building up a team of experts. Heavy lifting gear was soon introduced to the wharf side as gun-less destroyers, frequently anchored close by, had their quick firing 4.7 inch guns carefully inspected before immediate replacement.

Today, of course, the gunwharf no longer exists, with part of the site being acquired by Lloyds and the eventual construction of their purpose built office block. Specialising in maritime insurance, their occupation of the original dock-yard site is far from inappropriate.

BIBLIOGRAPHY

Primary Manuscript Sources

Because Chatham dockyard is a national institution, much of the relevant source material is held either in the National Maritime Museum or the Public Record Office, although additional material can be found within the British Library. Undoubtedly, of all these, I found the Maritime Museum to possess the most comprehensive set of records. Apart from manuscripts, the museum also holds numerous paintings, maps and a contemporary dockyard model. Within the library there are several hundred volumes of letters, contracts, orders, warrants and minutes. Naturally, I was not in a position to use all these, and tended to centre upon certain known events or periods of interest. As a result, letters addressed to the commissioner (CHA/E), together with any replies made to the Navy Board (CHA/L) were the most extensively used. Additionally, relevant Admiralty records (ADM/B) held at the same museum were also of use.

As regards the Public Record Office, I found the numerous visitation reports (especially ADM 7/659 and 660) particularly useful in assessing progress within the dockyard during the eighteenth century. Additionally, manuscripts relating to the Naval Works Department provided comprehensive details on construction work carried out within the yard.

Within the British Library, Kings 43 and 44 proved of particular value. Kings 43 provides a complete record of the dockyard for the period 1688 to 1698. All buildings, dry docks and slipways are described together with expenses incurred. Kings 44 is rather similar, providing a description of the dockyard for the year 1774. A very handsome book, it was produced as a birthday present for the reigning monarch. This latter should be used in conjunction with the 1774 dockyard model held at the National Maritime Museum.

Locally, there were two archive sources providing material used in the book. At Maidstone, the County Archive Office has numerous deeds, leases and conveyances relating to property within Chatham. Such information allows an assessment to be made of that town's particular growth as affected by the dockyard. Also useful were the parish registers and minute books. From the former it is possible to gauge population growth rates. The second local archive source is that of Rochester Museum holding, as it does, a number of borough rate books for the eighteenth century.

Other Primary Sources

First, and foremost in this area, were the interviews I conducted with former employees of the yard. A number had memories which pre-dated the first world war, whilst most could recall the interwar period. A full list of names appears under acknowledgements. The newspaper file at Rochester library proved of immense value, with the 'Chatham News' providing a detailed record of all building works and launchings which took place during its period of publication.

Articles

Coad, J.G., 'The Chatham Mould Loft and Mast House' in 'Mariner's Mirror' (1975).

Coad, J.G., 'Chatham Ropeyard' in 'Post Medieval Archaeology' (1969).

Cull, F., 'Chatham Dockyard; Early Leases and Conveyances' in 'Archaeologia Cantiana' Vol. LXXIII (1959).

Cull, F., 'Chatham — The Hill House' in 'Archaeologia Cantiana' Vol. LXXVII (1963).

Haas, J.M., 'The Introduction of Task Work in the Royal Dockyards, 1775' in 'The Journal of British Studies' Vol. VIII:2 (1969).

Johns, A.W., 'Phineas Pett' in 'Mariner's Mirror' Vol. XII.

Knight, R.J.B., 'Pilfering and Theft from the Dockyards' in 'Mariner's Mirror' Vol. LXI:3.

McGurk, J.N., 'Armada Preparations in Kent and Arrangements Made After the Defeat' in 'Archaeologia Cantiana'.

Macleod, N., 'The Shipwrights of the Royal Dockyards' in 'Mariner's Mirror' Vol. XI.

Macleod, N., 'The Shipwright Officers of the Royal Dockyards' in 'Mariner's Mirror' Vol. XI.

Morriss, R.A., 'Labour Relations in the Royal Dockyards, 1801-1895' in 'Mariner's Mirror' Vol. LXII:4.

Ranft, B. McL., 'Labour Relations in the Royal dockyards 1739' in 'Mariner's Mirror' Vol. XLVII.

Richardson, H.E., 'Wages of Shipwrights in HM Dockyards, 1496-1788' in 'Mariner's Mirror' Vol. XXXIII.

Secondary Sources

For the most part, it is probably of greatest value just to list secondary sources referred to. Perhaps though, before doing this it might be worth pointing out those articles or books which were most extensively used. In this category, therefore, falls 'Some Notes on the History of Chatham Dockyard' by J.G. Grace, which provides, in chronological form, a detailed history of the yard. Also extensively used were the two highly researched articles by Jonathan Coad who is, it should be pointed out, a Department of the Environment Inspector whose particular province is that of historic buildings within the various Royal Dockyards. Publications of the Navy Record Society and Edwin Harris' 'Eastgate Series' also fall into this category. James Presnail's 'The Story of Chatham' was useful, but must be handled with care owing to inaccuracies.

Unpublished

Crawshaw, J.D., 'History of Chatham Dockyard School' (1955).

Knight, R.J.B., 'Royal Dockyards in England at the time of the American War of Independence' (1972) London University Ph.D.

Morris, R.A., 'The Administration of the Royal Dockyards in England' (1978) London University Ph.D.

Printed Books

Anderson, R.C. (ed), 'Journals and Narratives of the Third Dutch War' (Navy Records Society) 1943.

Barnes, G.R. and Owen, J.H. (ed), 'The Private Papers of John, Earl of Sandwich' (Navy Records Society) 1938.

Baugh, D., 'British Naval Administration in the Age of Walpole' (Princeton) 1965.

Baugh, D., 'Naval Administration' (Navy Records Society) 1977.

Brown, D.G., 'The Floating Bulwark' London 1963.

Buglar, A., 'HMS Victory: Building, Restoration and Repair' (London) 1966.

Chalklin, C.W., 'Seventeenth Century Kent' (Rochester) 1978.

Cowburn, P., 'The Warship in History' (London) 1963.

Ehrman, 'The Navy in the War of William III' (Cambridge) 1953.

Fenwick, K., 'HMS Victory', (London) 1959.

Gardiner, L., 'The British Admiralty' (London) 1968.

Gill, C., 'Plymouth: A New History', (Newton Abbott) 1979.

Grace, J.G., 'Some Notes on the History of Chatham Dockyard' (Chatham) 1946.

Gulvin, K.R., 'Kent Home Guard' (Rainham) 1980.

Harris, E., 'Description of Chatham in the Year 1838' (Eastgate series)
        'History of Chatham Dockyard' (Rochester) 1911.
        'History of Chatham' (Rochester) 1912.
        'History of St Mary's Church' (Rochester) 1913.
        'History of the Chatham Chest' (Rochester) 1915.

Hasted, E., 'The History and Topographical Survey of the County of Kent' Vol. IV (Reprinted 1972).

Horsley, J.E., 'Tools of the Maritime Trades' (Newton Abbot) 1978.

Howarth, D., 'Sovereign of the Seas'. (London) 1974.

Jeffereys, W., 'An Account of the Fire which Happened at Chatham, 1880' (Chatham) 1801.

Knight, C., 'Shipbuilding at Gillingham' (Chatham) 1938.

Lambarde, 'A Perambulation of Kent' 1970 reprint.

Landstrom, B., 'Sailing Ships' (London) 1978.

Longridge, C.N., 'The Anatomy of Nelson's Ships' (London) 1961.

Marcus, G.J., 'Heart of Oak' (London) 1975.

Merriman, R.D. (ed), 'Queen Anne's Navy' (Navy Record Society) 1961.

Morris, C. (ed), 'The Journey of Celia Fiennes' (London) 1947.

Oppenheim, M., 'A History of the Administration of the Royal Navy' (London) 1896.

Perrin, W.G. (ed), 'Phineas Pett' (Navy Record Society) reprinted 1980.

Presnail, J., 'The Story of Chatham' (Chatham) 1952.

Preston, J.M., 'Industrial Medway' (Rochester) 1977.

Smith, P.C., 'Hit Hard, Hit Fast' (London) 1979.

INDEX

INDEX OF SHIPS

SUBMARINES